Adventures in
Egypt and Nubia

Adventures in Egypt and Nubia

The Travels of William John Bankes (1786–1855)

Patricia Usick

THE BRITISH MUSEUM PRESS

First published in 2002 by The British Museum Press
A division of The British Museum Company Ltd
46 Bloomsbury Street, London WC1B 3QQ

A catalogue record for this book is available from the British Library

ISBN 0 7141 1803 6

Designed and typeset in Baskerville
by Harry Green

Printed and bound in Hong Kong
by C&C Offset

Contents

ACKNOWLEDGEMENTS

My greatest thanks are due to Vivian Davies, Keeper of the Department of Ancient Egypt and Sudan at the British Museum. Without his suggestion in 1993 that I might work on the archaeological significance of the Nubian drawings in the portfolio of William John Bankes, neither my thesis nor this book would exist. He has most generously allowed me to carry out my research within his department, where every member of staff, past and present, has been unfailingly kind and helpful, from answering my continual queries, to lifting the heavy boxes containing the drawings. I owe a special debt of thanks to Richard Parkinson for his constant encouragement, and to Claire Thorne and Audrey Hutchison who took infinite pains to produce the map of Greece and Asia Minor.

The National Trust, who took over Kingston Lacy and its estates in 1981, kindly permitted the Egyptian drawings and manuscripts to come on temporary loan to the British Museum to enable me to work on them. Both Anthony Mitchell and James Grasby, of the Wessex Regional Office, lent their enthusiasm and support to the project. As did the staff at the house, in particular Howard Webber, former administrator of Kingston Lacy, and Kate Warren, collections manager.

I have greatly benefited from conversations with Harry James, who also read the manuscript and offered many useful comments with his usual wisdom and kindness. Many colleagues have helped to fill in the missing pieces of my research, in particular Marcel Kurz and Pascale Linant de Bellefonds for Linant's manuscripts in Paris, and Deborah Manley and Peta Rée, who have continually proffered nuggets of information and sensible advice. Norman N. Lewis most generously provided me with the fruits of his own research, without which I would have been unable to write of Bankes's travels in Syria and the Near East. Sarah Bridges and her subsequent colleagues at Dorset Record Office were indispensable in helping to make my rushed days in Dorchester as productive as possible. So many members of the Association for the Study of Travel in Egypt and the Near East have generously contributed important details, gleaned from their own research, that it would be impossible to thank them all by name.

The efficient numbering and identification of the drawings in Bankes's Egyptian portfolio comprised only a fraction of the work accomplished by the indomitable Dr Rosalind Moss, who died in 1990. I was not fortunate enough to meet her or thank her for her groundbreaking investigations into the drawings. Without her contribution, my task would have been almost impossible, unless I had followed her example in living for a hundred years.

I have to thank Teresa Francis and Rebecca Russel Ponte at the British Museum Press for their help, encouragement, and painstaking editing.

Roger Rosswick, despite having instituted a time limit on my burbling about Bankes, accomplished some vital esoteric library research for me, and read through the manuscript. His advice and support have been invaluable.

This book is for my father, Ben Lane.

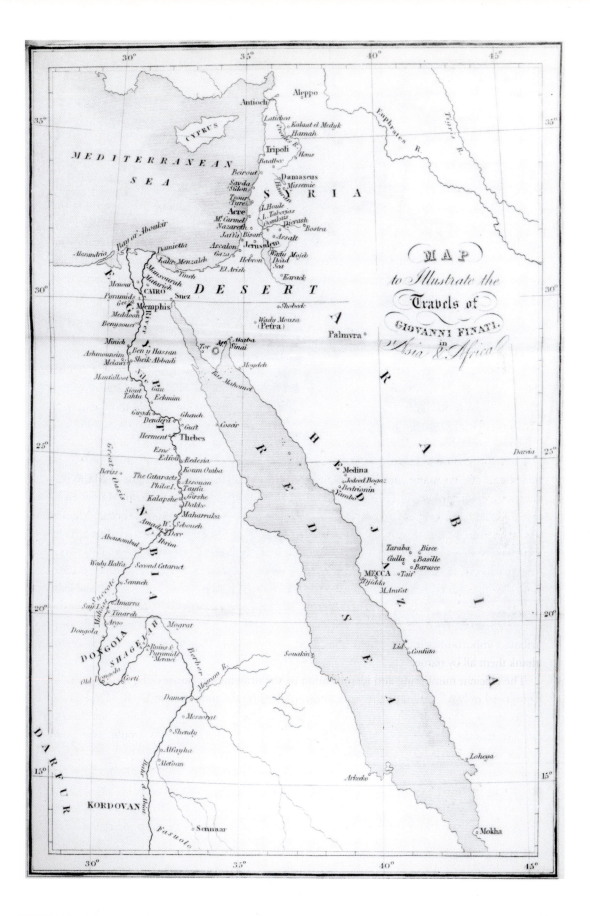

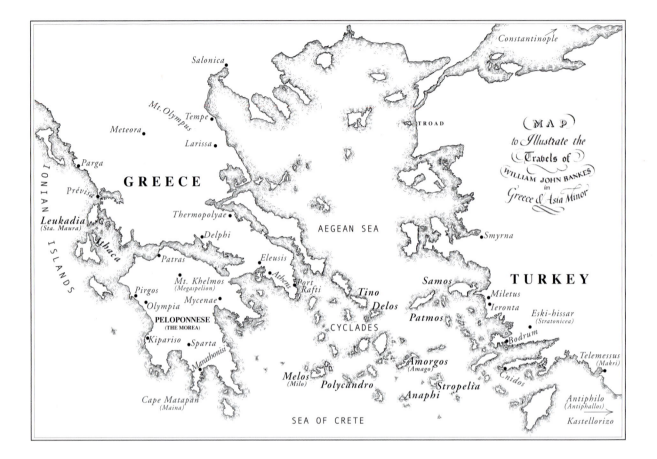

Constantinople

Salonica

Mt. Olympus
Tempe
Meteora
Larissa

Parga

GREECE

Prévisa
Leukadia
(Sta. Maura)

Ithaca

Thermopolyae

Delphi

Patras

Mt. Khelmos
(Megaspelion)

Pirgos
Olympia

Mycenae

PELOPONNESE
(THE MOREA)

Kipariso
Sparta

Marathonisi

Cape Matapan
(Maina)

IONIAN
ISLANDS

TROAD

AEGEAN SEA

MAP
to Illustrate the
Travels of
WILLIAM JOHN BANKES
in
Greece & Asia Minor

Smyrna

TURKEY

Samos
Miletus
Ieronta
Eski-hissar
(Stratonicea)

Bodrum

Patmos

Telemessus
(Makri)

Cnidos

Antiphilo
(Antiphallos)

Kastellorizo

Eleusis
Athens
Port
Rafti

Tino
Delos

CYCLADES

Amorgos
(Amago)

Stropelia

Anaphi

Melos
(Milo)
Polycandro

SEA OF CRETE

[8]

PROLOGUE

THE PLAY ANNOUNCED AT ONE OF THE THEATRES TONIGHT IS CALLED EMILIA DA
LIVERPOOL<u>T</u> [*sic*]… THE AUTHOR PROBABLY SAW THE EMILY OF LIVERPOOL UPON
LLOYD'S LIST & MISTOOK HER FOR A LADY – I WONDER WHETHER WE MAKE SUCH
MISTAKES WHEN WE WRITE ABOUT PROPER PLANS & PROPER PEOPLE! LET US HOPE NOT –
William Bankes's letter to Lord Byron, from Bologna, 20 January 1820

FROM THE WINDOWS OF THE ATTIC ROOM at
Kingston Lacy which once served as the family nursery, the vista across the lawn focuses on a
garden ornament, remarkable even for a house as grand as this (pl. 6). It is an original
ancient Egyptian obelisk, plucked from the debris of the temple of Philae at the border of
Egypt and Nubia. For many years it may have been the sole visible reminder of a former
owner's obsession with exploration and discovery, and his passion for ancient Egypt. Within
a specially designed cabinet in the same attic room lay a record very different to that collected by the average gentleman-traveller of the early nineteenth century. Amongst the
watercolour views of spectacular temple and tomb remains were hundreds of working drawings: site plans and ground plans, descriptions, measured sections, elevations, architectural
details, and fine copies of relief scenes and inscriptions in Greek, hieroglyphic, and even
more mysterious scripts.

William John Bankes (1786–1855) was a brilliant and unusual man whose friends feared
he would dissipate his talents and very considerable scholarship by the breadth of his interests and his volatile personality. Handsome, rich, and confident, his conscious adoption of
immense style, his wit, and his pretentious grandeur while still an undergraduate at Trinity
College, Cambridge, may have outshone even his fellow student Lord Byron, who was to
remain a close and lifelong friend. As the heir to a distinguished family, mixing in high government circles, there seemed little to stop him making a name for himself, not just among
his contemporaries but for future generations. He was to be a pioneer Egyptologist and
archaeologist before these sciences were founded, and he made extraordinary discoveries
among the ancient ruins of Egypt and the Near East. Byron declared that 'William Bankes
hath made a stupendous traveller'[1] and he brought to his investigations an acute eye, a fine
memory, and great powers of common sense and logic. Yet his contemporaries' fears were
well grounded, and, although he was lionized as 'the Nubian Explorer' by his own generation, the work he accomplished was never published and the dust settled on his portfolio,
which was gradually forgotten. Scandal clouded his achievements and his obituary in *The
Gentleman's Magazine*[2] barely mentions his travels.

By all accounts he had made rather more of an impression in society than in Parliament
when in 1813 at the age of twenty-six he began his journey. First following in the footsteps of
Byron and William Beckford to Portugal and Spain, he chose to pursue a Bohemian lifestyle
among the gypsies at Granada. James Stanhope wrote: 'I met at Oporto [Porto] the other

day a very extraordinary young man – Mr. Bankes who is a great friend of Lord Byron ... I never saw so singular a compound of eccentricity and judgements, of trifling & study, of sound opinions about others and wild speculations about himself, good talents applied to no future object and a most wonderful memory prostituted to old songs and tales of Mother Goose ... I like the man much for he appears to have an excellent temper, a good heart and independence in opinions which I do not think the travellers who come to this country generally possess.'[3] It was to prove a very fair assessment of Bankes's strengths and weaknesses – although Stanhope was mistaken about the 'excellent temper'. In Spain in the aftermath of the Duke of Wellington's victories in the Peninsular War, and in Italy following Napoleon's defeat, Bankes responded with alacrity to the unique opportunity in the art market by acquiring an important collection of paintings.

During the years 1815–19 Bankes criss-crossed Egypt and the Near East, where he accumulated a vast portfolio of notes, manuscripts, and drawings, his passion for exploration surpassed only by his energy in investigating and recording. Since he was a fine amateur architect and a careful epigrapher, skilled in copying ancient inscriptions, Bankes's extremely high degree of accuracy reveals valuable lost information about many ancient monuments, now moved, damaged, or entirely lost. An impressive Greek scholar and familiar with both classical and contemporary works on ancient Egypt, he hoped to make historical discoveries through his collection of ancient Greek, hieroglyphic, and little-known inscriptions such as Meroitic and Nabatean. His own discovery of the name 'Cleopatra' on the obelisk he brought back from Philae and placed in his garden was to be instrumental in the race to decipher Egyptian hieroglyphics. Other explorers, skilled artists, and draughtsmen, were engaged to add to his Nubian portfolio.

Bankes returned home to indulge another passion: architecture. The family house, Kingston Lacy in Dorset, was extensively redesigned, rebuilt, and refurbished to form a splendid backdrop befitting the paintings of a connoisseur of Old Masters. Charles Barry,[4] met while travelling in Egypt, was nominally his architect but his own taste and designs prevailed. Meanwhile, unexpected events, stemming from his personality, were to conspire to disrupt the work on the house, his parliamentary life, and his plans for publication. Dangerously, a near-addiction to risk fuelled both his travels and his life, forcing him to flee England for exile abroad. Already embroiled in an affair with a married woman, he had further scandalized society with two arrests for homosexual offences. Despite bringing the full weight of the British Establishment to his support, Bankes ended his life a legal outlaw, unable to return to England or to see the house and collections he so loved. Although he continued to embellish them from abroad, they could be enjoyed only on fleeting clandestine visits.

Circumstances and the flaws in his own character combined to dash the hopes and dim the constant expectations of his friends that he would publish his discoveries. Though Bankes was seldom mentioned by his colleagues without reference to his outstanding abilities and surely destined to produce a book to surpass all others, his ultimate failure to publish has led to his travels and his achievements being clouded by a veil of errors. The foremost of these is the much-quoted and still continuing reference to the publication of his journeys as *Travels in the East*.[5] No such book exists, Bankes simply never got round to writing it. This account is an attempt to remedy that loss.

CHAPTER ONE

THE UNEXPECTED HEIR

TRIFLING AND STUDY

WILLIAM JOHN BANKES was born on 11 December 1786, the second son of Henry Bankes of Kingston Hall (later to be known as Kingston Lacy), Dorset, and the former Frances Woodley (pls 2 and 3). She doted on her son, being a caring and responsible mother to all her brood; all their childhood ailments and remedies were carefully recorded, from the wet-nurse for Master William in 1787 to the shared outbreaks of measles and mumps.[1] There were five other children. Henry, the eldest, and George, a year younger, were followed two years later by Anne, to whom William became greatly attached. Another daughter, Maria, was born in 1791 and a son, Edward, in 1794.

William was educated at Westminster School from the age of nine, and was followed there by his brothers.[2] He went up to Trinity College, Cambridge, on 22 June 1803 at the age of sixteen, obtaining his BA in 1808 and his MA in 1811. When his elder brother Henry was lost at sea in a shipwreck in 1806 at the age of twenty-one, William, at twenty, unexpectedly found himself heir to the house and its estates.[3] It was said that 'At his desire, his father had purchased young Henry a commission in the army and he was on his way to join his regiment in Sicily when the ship hit a rock. He was entreated to come into the boat but refused saying, He had considered it, & thought it most safe to remain in the ship – the boat got safe to shore.'[4] Whether this epitomized the family obstinacy (as family legend had it), poor judgement, or simply bad luck, is not known. 'Mr. Bankes was extremely affected by the loss of his Son; it appeared to make a stronger impression on him than on Mrs. Bankes.'[5] William himself was desolate at having obtained his social and financial position at the price of a much-loved brother. To Byron, who also inherited his title by chance circumstance, he wrote: 'I have been deprived of a *dear & affectionate* Brother, with all the aggravations of unnecessary risk, & a violent Death. – If you imagine that I have no feelings, I do not ask your pity, look upon me with the eyes of the world, consider rather the *Aggrandizement* of my inheritance than my loss of Comfort – & think me happy.' And congratulating Byron on the success of a lawsuit to recover his property: 'I am inclined to draw a melancholy comparison: *Your* wealth is not purchased by affliction, nor made a mockery of grief by pretending compensation – You have no brother to mourn for, & to succeed.'[6] He wrote from Trinity, then moved to London to comfort his unhappy family.

Although not aristocratic, the Bankes family were leading gentry. Educated, travelled, and cultured, they had traditionally represented the family seat in Parliament, and mixed easily with the highest in the land. Since Sir John Bankes had purchased the estates of Corfe Castle in 1635, followed by those of Kingston Lacy, they had been prominent and wealthy landowners in Dorset. After the devastations of the Civil War, in which Corfe Castle was destroyed, Cromwell restored the family fortunes. Ralph Bankes, who was knighted in the Restoration, married well and built a new family seat, Kingston Hall,[7] designed by Sir Roger Pratt. Although his expenditure left him in debt, his will shows his concern for the education and travel of his sons, and the protection of his collections of books, pictures, and objects.

Subsequent generations increased the estates, altered and improved the house and grounds, and added to the family treasures. Their fortune was augmented by the substantial income from their control of a graphite mine in Cumberland, thanks to the political manipulations and astute business sense of William's grandfather Henry, who also consolidated his position by marriage to an heiress. William's acquisition of major paintings while abroad, his commissioning of bronzes, and his redesign and embellishment of Kingston Lacy merely continued a long family tradition of accumulating splendid paintings, objects, and furniture. His father Henry made the Grand Tour, married well, and remodelled and redecorated the house. Henry was a Member of Parliament and represented the British Museum there as a Trustee. He added works on history and classics to his library and himself wrote *A Civil and Constitutional History of Rome* in 1818. William's great-grandfather, Bishop Wynne, had also published: an *Abridgement of Locke's Essay on the Human Understanding* in 1696. Henry, a personal friend of Wilberforce, Pitt, and Wellington, held a seat in Parliament for over fifty years, was a conservative in politics and took an active if not a leading part in nearly every debate of his time. 'Mr. Bankes, father of the Egyptian traveller, was one of the trustees of the British Museum. In that capacity he was chiefly remarkable for the obstinacy with which, on all occasions, he opposed grants of money, whence he was generally called Saving Banks.'[8]

Henry, although generally supportive, was occasionally baffled by his son's interests: 'Hunting for lost cities in the region of Decapolis would not excite in my mind so violent a spirit of enterprise, but he would laugh at me with as much reason for fatiguing myself in the pursuit of partridges or woodcocks.'[9] Watching the foundations for his son's obelisk being prepared in 1829, he declared: 'I submit to it as a disorder in the Bankes family, which sometimes passes over one generation, like madness or gout, or the king's evil, and breaks out again in the next: my uncle … could not help erecting two Obelisks.'[10] But there was still *carte blanche* during his father's lifetime for William's acquisitions for the house and his plans for its reconstruction. In any case, even before his father's death William was enjoying an income of £8000 per annum.[11]

At Cambridge, Bankes's wealth, self-confidence, and style made him a leading member of a fast set of outstanding young men which included Byron (pl. 4), John Cam Hobhouse,[12] and Charles Skinner Matthews.[13] Byron, two years Bankes's junior, had arrived at Trinity in 1805, miserable at leaving Harrow 'to which I had become attached during the last two years of my stay there; wretched at going to Cambridge instead of Oxford (there were no rooms vacant at Christchurch); wretched from some private domestic circumstance of different kinds, and consequently about as unsocial as a wolf taken from the troop'. Bankes, already established at Trinity for two years, was to be his 'collegiate pastor, and master and patron' and this established their initial relationship.[14] Bankes's later reputation for witty and biting repartee was developed at Cambridge where Byron said that 'while he stayed, he ruled the roast – or rather the *roasting* – and was father of all mischiefs'. ('Roasting' denoted the merciless ridicule which they deployed in their conversations.) As to the nature of the mischiefs, the later behaviour of both men indicates that they were unlikely to have been particularly innocent.

Bankes's acerbic critical faculties were already well developed. Byron shrank from showing him his early poetry because 'I know his *Talents* as a *Critic*, to be so far superior to mine as a *Rhymer*, that I would have rather passed the *Ordeal* of an Edinburgh *Review*, than offered my unfortunate "*Juvenalia*" to his inspection. – He has too much of the *Man*, ever to approve of the *flights* of a *Boy*, & I await in trembling suspense my *Cruxifiction* from his Decree.'[15] It was a mutual friend, Edward Noel Long, who showed the poems to Bankes (who held heretical views about Shakespeare[16] and was himself the author of poetry, plays, and a nuptial masque). The tone of his first review of some poetry in 1807 shows Bankes at his most detached and formal; being 'exceedingly pleased' with them although 'there appeared to me a considerable inequality … the love-poems appeared to me the least valuable'.[17] Despite his fearsome reputation, Bankes's verdict on the works was favourable (although not of course lacking suggestions for their improvement). He wrote in 1808 of finding stanzas on the death of Cromwell 'vigorous & sublime' *but* 'Might I venture to propose one alteration?' It is offered sensitively and with a light touch: 'What will you not expect? What mangling, what amputation, what cruel & distorting operations on your works!' He suggested replacing the line 'By that remember'd, or for e'er forgot' with 'By that remember'd, *or with that* forgot', and followed with cogent argument for the change. Byron, tellingly, chose to adopt this alteration in the following edition of the poems.[18] It requires, at the very least, an overdose of confidence in one's own superior judgement to suggest improvements of any kind to any poet. The young Byron was perhaps encouraged by the frank advice of his clever and sophisticated senior who recognized the value of his early work, and this was undoubtedly an important element in their relationship. Byron wrote: 'Your critique is valuable for many Reasons … It was the only one in which flattery was not a motive … I was more anxious to hear your critique however severe, than the praises of the Million.'[19] Byron was to say, 'He is very clever, very original and has a fund of information; he is also very good natured, but he is not much of a flatterer …'[20]

Above all, Byron valued their friendship. 'I need not repeat to you, that your conversation for half an hour would have been much more agreeable to me than gambling or drinking, or any other fashionable mode of passing an evening … Believe me, with that deference which I have always from my childhood paid to your *Talents*, and with somewhat of a better opinion of your heart than I have hitherto entertained …'[21] Byron later admitted that his only intimate friends at Cambridge had been Edward Long 'and William Bankes, who was good-naturedly tolerant of my ferocities'.[22] It was in Bankes's rooms that Byron first read the poetry of Sir Walter Scott. In 1809 Byron arranged for George Sandars to paint a series of portrait miniatures of his friends and it is possible that the 1812 portrait at Kingston Lacy belongs to this group (pl. 1). Bankes is every inch the image of a young Romantic with his curled light auburn locks, soulful expression, and cupid's lips. He wears the fur-collared robes of an academic gown while a stone column in the background hints at classical architecture. Perhaps his hair was less ginger in colour than it appears, since Byron once asked him whether red hair was to his liking. The portrait is hardly recognizable as the same man pictured in Sir George Hayter's vivid oil sketch (pl. 104), where his dark colouring and aquiline nose suggest a stronger and more vigorous character. This was a study for a huge group portrait showing 375 members of the Reformed House of Commons (the first Parliament to meet after the passing of the Reform Bill of 1832).

In 1809 Bankes toured Wales with his future brother-in-law, Lord Falmouth, encouraged by his great-uncle William who would leave him the land and property in Flint, Canarvon, and Merioneth which he himself had inherited on his brother John's death in 1804. (Bankes was already using Soughton Hall in Wales as a residence by 1811.) The young men visited the notorious Ladies of Llangollen: Lady Eleanor Butler and Miss Ponsonby. Celebrated virgins who had resolved to live together in isolation from society, they were invariably dressed in a semi-masculine costume. All tourists in Wales sought an introduction to them and many made the journey to Llangollen specially.

Until Byron's fame and adulation on the publication of *Childe Harold* in 1812, Bankes may have been the more dominant figure in the friendship, but this was fleeting and their relationship subtly reversed. Virtually all of Bankes's entertaining letters are soon full of entreaties for Byron to reply, to visit, to join him abroad, claims of 'a studied change of manner' towards him, and denials that he was jealous of Byron's success. Their attachment was almost broken by a row in 1812: 'there were no pains spared to break that intimacy that subsisted between us'.[23] Another letter claims 'I did begin to suspect that you had exchanged your friends as Aladdin did his Lamp – the old for the new'.[24] By 1822 Bankes, sending him proofs of his obelisk engravings, was to accuse Byron gently of having forgotten him. 'I suspect that I am one of the very few that are left to you, who, much as I admire your writings, do not, when I think of you, associate you exclusively with them, nor with your fame, who continue to feel towards you just as I did before you ever published, & to think of you, as, had I the fame that you have, I could wish that you should think of me.'[25] Bankes's attachment did not wane but, to his confidante, the society diarist Mrs Arbuthnot, he was to speak scathingly of Byron's excesses.

If Bankes was the leader of this Cambridge elite, he was also considered to be its most conceited and pretentious member. Hobhouse comments in a letter to Byron in 1808 that 'William Bankes is here at the Master's lodge, Trinity hall, living in state so he tells me' and, on Bankes explaining his need to hunt in Dorsetshire 'for popularity's sake', complains: 'Is this not complete Corfe Castle all over?'[26] Byron too, ridiculed Bankes's grand manner, writing to Scrope Berdmore Davies in 1811, 'I am invited by you, & (now for an Omega) I am invited by *Wm. Bankes* to One of my places in Wales!!! but which of all these places this Deponent knoweth not, do you think Lewellyn ever invited anybody to one of *his* places in such a manner? One would think Corfe Castle had perched itself upon Penmanmaur – I have heard of purse-pride and birth-pride & now we have Place-pride.'[27] To Hobhouse, he referred to this as an invitation 'of the patronizing kind'.[28] That year his scathing reaction to hearing that Bankes had spoken of him was: 'I know the Mr Bankes you mention though not to that "*extreme*" you seem to think, but I am flattered by his "boasting" on such a subject (as you say) for I never thought him likely to "boast" of anything which was not his own.'[29] Nor was Bankes popular with fellow students Lord Palmerston and Michael Bruce, who ridiculed his spying on a meeting of the exclusive debating club known as the 'Speculative'.[30]

The hothouse atmosphere of Cambridge was not all style and surface. Bankes's great-uncle Sir William Wynne, Master of Trinity Hall, bombarded him with letters packed with advice on his studies, in particular of the classics. Cicero was high on the recommended reading lists, and he should read Locke and spend time on the ancient and modern historians. Encouragement was in order since, having attained a high standard of knowledge prior to his arrival, the student was finding the classical lectures uninspiring. Wynne presciently reminded the future traveller that 'Chronology and Geography must accompany History to make it at all intelligible' and suggested practical systems for improving his memory and his mode of expression. 'Scarce any book should be read without taking notes of it' and these should be read again the following week. When encountering a particularly striking passage he should 'lay aside the Book, and endeavour to express the substance of it aloud, in as correct Language as you can'. Much of this advice was absorbed, in particular the suggestion that 'Notes should be taken of all books read'. Wynne was pleased to hear that Bankes would be called upon to give a declamation as his 'very good voice and pronunciation' would make him appear to advantage. He also supplied the prints of English cathedrals which the young man requested to ornament his rooms in Great Court, which were decorated in the Gothick taste in emulation of William Beckford's Fonthill. Astonishingly, despite later violently anti-Papist views, he was half-suspected of being a Papist; having almost frightened the Trinity Fellow Dr Ramsden to death by building in his rooms an altar 'at which he daily burned incense, and frequently had the singing-boys dressed in their surplices to chant services'.[31] Was this related to what Bankes referred to as, 'a feebler & earlier architectural folly of mine … the construction of that little chapel which must recall to both our minds some singular, some pleasant, some bitter associations. I have not seen it since I returned to England'?[32]

At Cambridge Bankes displayed many of the facets of character which would remain throughout his life. He was proving a good friend if a harsh critic; he was proud, arrogant and patronizing; he became easily bored, and loathed the bother of writing. This aversion was well known to Byron, who excused his own failure to reply on the grounds that 'my silence … merely proceeded from a notion founded on your own declaration of *old* that you hated writing & receiving letters'; adding teasingly, 'Besides how was I to find out a man of many residences?'[33]

Bankes's taste was already elegant, fastidious, and esoteric, he fancied himself an architect and designer, and had refurbished his room in great style. At the same time he was extremely well-read, seriously intent on 'reading history methodically', a fine classicist, and fluent in Italian. Were there already signs of a dangerous temper, a penchant for risk, and a lack of self-restraint?

More serious matters called for which his studies had prepared him. His father had a steady, if not illustrious, reputation in Parliament, and his son joined him there in 1810 at the age of twenty-four, representing Truro, a seat in the gift of his sister Anne's prospective husband Edward, Earl of Falmouth. Except for the period of his travels and a single three-year gap Bankes remained in Parliament until 1834, when his career was abruptly ended by the circumstances of his arrest the previous year. He represented Truro 1810–12, Cambridge University 1822–26, Marlborough 1829–32, and Dorset 1832–34. With a reputation as a high Tory, he voted in support of his father's efforts to abolish sinecures but was otherwise 'as decided a friend as any in the House' to administration, and voted with the Tories on the regency issue, 1 January 1811. He attended a ministerial dinner on 20 June 1811. *The History of Parliament*[34] presents his parliamentary career as comic novella and his maiden speech (incorrectly) as his last. It is described as 'a singularly paradoxical one damning Catholic Relief with faint praise, 23 Apr. 1812. He doubted whether the time was ripe and regarded the pro-Catholic party as a group dangerous to political stability, doubting whether emancipation would bring strength and unity as its advocates supposed.'[35] (In fact Bankes spoke in the House several times on various aspects of this issue in the 1820s, always from a staunchly anti-popery stance and reiterating his belief that the people did not wish to see Catholic Emancipation.) Wellesley Pole was astonished by its delivery: 'like a ranting whining bad actor in a barn speaking a full tragedy part, and mix'd up with the drawls and twangs of a Methodist preacher'.[36] (Perhaps Bankes's debut had been less ridiculous than suggested for five months later Byron was encouraging him to speak in Parliament more frequently.)[37] Much later, a rival candidate dismissed him as having 'floundered whilst deep in a rhetorical allusion to the lake of Geneva' and sarcastically suggested that his subsequent absence abroad on antiquarian research, 'passing his time, as his talented mother informed me, in scratching the back of the sphinx', was due to his having drowned in the waters of the lake. Although the draft for the speech certainly rambles – 'the channel for this body to pass in amongst us ... as the Rhone through the lake of Geneva ... it may deepen its shallows but will it introduce no cross current ... slumber in the calm still bosom of the lake & forget its homage and tribute to the Ocean'[38] – this last stab can be attributed to a bad attack of sour grapes. Bankes went on to beat eight candidates (including the writer Lord Teignmouth) to obtain the Cambridge University seat in 1822, by means of his 'colloquial facility' and by having cunningly insisted on the payment of non-resident voters' travelling expenses, thereby forcing Teignmouth to stand down because of the expense.[39] When the Speaker of the House became a candidate Bankes retired from the running, although none of the other candidates did, and it was not until the Speaker withdrew that 'Bankes proceeded with a *bona fide* canvass' to his victory.[40] Bankes's printed canvass letter of 5 November 1822 solicits support by explaining why he stood down for the Speaker, adding: 'more especially as my political sentiments in general coincide with his. Upon that great question [Catholic Emancipation], respecting which the feeling of this University has been so repeatedly declared, I may refer, not to professions only, but to the line of conduct which I thought it my duty to adopt, whenever it was brought forward, during the short time that I sat in Parliament. This conduct is the pledge, which I now have to offer, of the most steady and decided opposition to any measures tending to undermine or alter the established Church.'[41] The traveller's wit and charm made his personal canvass irresistible. 'What could I do, Sir? He got me into the centre of the great pyramid, and then turned around and asked me for my vote', was an unwilling supporter's description of the way in which a promise had been extorted from him.[42]

Social life was definitely to Bankes's taste, and the glittering London Season a chance to shine on its stage. In the winter of 1812, just a month before leaving England, Bankes had made overtures to Annabella Milbanke (pl. 5), a blue-stocking and an heiress, who declared: 'One of my smiles would encourage him, but I am niggardly of my glances.'[43] It was one of several proposals that she was to rebuff, her other suitors being Byron, Augustus Foster, son of the second Duchess of Devonshire, and Frederick North Douglas.[44] Bankes's over-confidence in his chances is reflected in her comment: 'Indeed I was tormented by that impudent

Bankes, who seems really to consider me as his property and will not understand any rebuffs.'[45] He left so many visiting cards that she contemplated returning them for the sake of economy.[46] Although Holland House was the centre of the moderate Whig camp, which suited Byron's politics, Byron was also a visitor to Melbourne House, where he had met Annabella. She was twenty, lovely if not strictly beautiful, and the only daughter of Sir Ralph Milbanke, Lady Melbourne's brother. This was her second London season. She had been brought up quietly in a house on the bleak coast of Durham, and was something of a *savante*, with an interest in mathematics, classical literature, and philosophy. A perfect choice then for Bankes but perhaps less so for Byron, who was simultaneously engaged in liaisons with various other women including his half-sister Augusta Leigh, and the wife of William Lamb, Lord and Lady Melbourne's second son, the infamous Lady Caroline Lamb. Her reckless and passionate behaviour, obsessive and indiscreet, perfectly matched that of Byron himself (they were perhaps both 'mad, bad, and dangerous to know'). In any case Byron did not consider himself at that time in love with Annabella despite his proposal. She had first read *Childe Harold* when Bankes lent her his copy and, like half the women in London society, was immediately intrigued by the poem and its author. It was published in March 1811 and was an immediate sensation, so that Byron 'awoke to find himself famous'. In August 1813, with Bankes abroad, Byron was still writing to Annabella and told her of Bankes's crestfallen appearance on her refusing him: 'the following circumstance will convince you – and may at least afford you a moment's amusement. – My equally unlucky friend W. Bankes – whom I have known many years – paid me a visit one evening last Winter with an aspect so utterly disconsolate that I could not resist enquiring into the cause – After much hesitation on his part – & a little guessing on mine – out it came – with tears in his eyes almost – that he had added another name to our unfortunate list. – The coincidence appeared to me so ludicrous that not to laugh was impossible – when I told him that a few weeks before a similar proposal had left me in the same situation. – In short we were the Heraclitus & Democritus of your Suitors – with this exception – that our crying and laughing was excited not by the folly of others but our own – or at least mine – for I had not even the common place excuse of a shadow of encouragement to console me.–'[47] Assuring her there would be no revival of his own proposal, he wrote: 'I was rather sorry (though probably *they* would not believe me) for Bankes and Douglas – who are both very clever and excellent men – & attached to you.' As the author of his own misfortune he would have been glad to have seen one of them 'in a fair way for happiness'. Byron eventually persuaded Annabella to accept him in September 1814. Had he been refused again, he had already decided to return to the Mediterranean with Hobhouse, and Bankes left England in the expectation that they should meet up again abroad that summer and that Byron might join him in Egypt. Instead, the marriage, with its disastrous results, took place in 1815, the year that Bankes made his first journey to Nubia.

In November 1812, 'instead of becoming an Orator & a Statesman & I do not know what (perhaps a Baronet) [Hobhouse had just been elevated] here I am out of Parliament. It is all my own doing & I am perfectly satisfied.'[48] He had begun to dream of travelling. The Grand Tour was a family tradition and well suited Bankes's genuine inclination to the arts of painting and architecture. Italy, however, was still impossible because of the Napoleonic Wars but Spain and Portugal, in the process of the last offensives of the liberation from Napoleon by Lord Arthur Wellesley, soon to become the Duke of Wellington, could be visited meanwhile.

Bankes contemplated the Alhambra, and perhaps Sicily and Malta, but nothing was yet fixed. Plans were made quickly for he left England on 20 January 1813, intending to visit Egypt and the Near East although not perhaps to occupy almost eight years with continuous travel. 'I have a servant, a Bed, a Canteen, some maps, a pair of Breeches, & a stick of sealing wax, what else should I have?'[49] Byron, who had journeyed in Greece and the Near East in 1810 with Hobhouse, replied to several lively playful letters and questions by furnishing him with letters of introduction to important contacts in Gibraltar, Albania, and Thebes, although most of the people met there had now returned and Bankes would soon discover that 'a man of any Consequence has very little occasion for any letters but to Ministers & Bankers … Be particular about Firmans [permits] – never allow yourself to be bullied – for you are better protected in Turkey than any where – trust not the Greeks – & take some "*knicknackeries*" for presents – watches pistols &c. &c. to the Beys and Pachas.' 'Mind you visit Ephesus & the Troad [Troas].'[50] 'I hope to join you however – but you will find swarms of English now in the Levant.'[51] William Wynne helped to finance his travels and was pleased to hear that Bankes was not setting off casually just to 'tourify', as Byron put it, but with a serious intent and properly prepared.

'The last lines that I shall write on British ground', penned hurriedly as the ship was about to set sail from Portsmouth for Portugal, were to Byron, begging him to write often, send him 'Childe Harolde the very instant it comes out … join me in the Summer in Albania & come & buffoon with me in Palestine & Egypt'.

⤬⟁⤬

Byron, of course, failed to write. 'I doubt the dead letter office somewhere will be quite choked with their accumulation'[52] came Bankes' sardonic response from Lisbon in March 1813 to the lack of mail. The climate though was delicious and, having arrived on 2 February, he was sufficiently hardened against dirt and stench. He had completed a tour of Portugal following many of Byron's suggestions, and discovered copies of *Childe Harold* in three private libraries: 'I have been loaded here with sweetmeats & civilities, & am to travel upon mules & Letters of Recommendation.'[53] He found Arrabida wild and solemn, even more so than Sintra, and delighted in the profusion of its flora. He was heading for Porto but there his excursions would depend upon the movement of the army who were expected to set forward early in April, and spoke confidently of being soon possessed of Madrid. Scribbled on the back of his passport for Portugal is one of his own Latin poems.

With as great a taste for art and architecture as travel, Bankes began serious collecting in Spain in 1813 at the age of twenty-six. He began keeping notes, sketched and painted, frequently recording the architecture and drawing views of 'almost every remarkable building in the Peninsula';[54] although he used scrap pieces of paper rather than a proper drawing-book. His architectural draughtsmanship is extremely skilled; he had learned perspective drawing although there is no evidence he had received any more formal training. The comparatively inferior quality of the watercolours led an art historian to suggest that they might be by a different hand.[55]

If Bankes was a skilled draughtsman and familiar with the terms and techniques of architecture, it was perhaps more of an acceptable skill for a gentleman interested in architecture by the early nineteenth century than it had been for Lord Burlington, who had been criticized a century earlier for exploiting his skills to become virtually a professional rather than remaining just an accomplished dilettante. Jean Nicolas Huyot, the French architect whose name is associated with the Arc du Triomphe, who travelled with Bankes in Nubia in 1819, is said to have joked sarcastically among the travellers that Bankes practised architecture in the same way that the architect and traveller Franz Christian Gau copied classical inscriptions; that is, without any real understanding.[56] Bankes's architectural pretensions were well known and his knowledge and interest perhaps derided amongst the professionals. While an interest in the Moorish architecture of the Alhambra at Granada was a frequent starting point for a Near Eastern tour in the nineteenth century,[57] Bankes also clearly enjoyed there a certain frisson or even *nostalgie de la boue* in the freedom of a lifestyle among the gypsies at their encampment at Granada. Annabella Milbanke reports hearing that 'he is living there in a beggarly, eccentric fashion'.[58]

With Bankes already taking an active part in the embellishment of the family house and grounds, and his father's trust in his taste and judgement, he could exploit the unique opportunities to purchase works of art offered by the postwar chaos of Spain, and later Italy. After the battle of Salamanca, Bankes visited Wellington's headquarters in an unofficial capacity, apparently using it as a base for collecting fine Spanish paintings for Kingston Lacy. The circumstances were propitious for the easy acquisition of valuable objects on terms that must have appealed to father and son, both later to be accused of being, at best, careful with their fortune. When Wellington instructed his troops to refrain from looting, he is said to have added: 'and remember, Bankes, this applies to you also'.[59] This story may even originate from Bankes himself, who was to entertain the London salons on his return with embroidered tales of his adventures. Madame de Lieven recalled one such occasion which had the company in fits of laughter when they dined with the Duke of Wellington on 21 February 1822.

'A certain Mr Bankes was at dinner, a great traveller… He was in Spain during the last war & he had been living in disguise at Pampeluna while the English laid siege to the city. He went to dinner with the commanding officer, who regaled him with a meal of rats washed down with strong drink, & after dinner obliged him to buy a Raphael, which he had stolen from the Escorial, & a donkey, which I don't think he had stolen from anybody. Bankes had spent all his money in purchasing the Raphael; and a few days later, he had only just what he needed to pay his passage on the boat which was to bring him back to England, together with his donkey, to which he was particularly attached. When he presented himself on board with the animal the captain declared that "*the jackass should pay, like a gentleman*". At this, there was a burst of laughter; and from that moment, the poor man could not open his mouth or move his arms (he makes the quaintest gestures) without my exploding. I laughed for two hours, and spent nine hours of sleeplessness in bed; I had become almost hysterical with laughing.'[60]

In addition to obtaining the Raphael masterpiece *Holy Family* (originally in Charles I's collection), he was one of the first Englishmen to show an interest in Spanish painting, purchasing works by Velasquez and Murillo, Ribalta and Zubaran (fine works but many now reassessed as 'school of'). A Murillo fragment was said to have been removed on a Spanish battlefield from the body of a dead soldier who had cut it out and used it to cover his knapsack. All his works of art were chosen with the decorative scheme of the house foremost in his mind, particularly for the creation of a Spanish dining room with gilded leather wall-coverings (pl. 108). His taste was formed early; he had no interest in Dutch realism, French eigh-teenth-century work, landscape, or still-life, and disliked purely historical paintings. Although he was accused of extravagance, the bulk of the Spanish and Italian purchases of 1813 and 1819–20 were acts of shrewd opportunism, taking advantage of a buyer's market in a climate of political and military upheaval, as was a later purchase in Venice, during the Siege of 1849 when 'It was the accident of my being here during all the Siege that enabled me to pick up all these fine things, since nobody had a farthing, anything might be had for money.'[61]

The end of the Napoleonic Wars was to reopen the Grand Tour of Europe to wealthy young men, and Bankes appears to have travelled through Italy and seen Naples and Rome. With or without Byron, he was now set on visiting Greece, Constantinople, and Syria-Palestine. From Malta, he wrote to his sister Maria that a short stay in Egypt would suffice to see the pyramids. But as Bankes's great-uncle and mentor Sir William Wynne wrote to him prophetically early in his travels, 'You do not I suppose begin to think as yet of a return to England as all the World is now open to the Curiosity of the Traveller.'[62]

CHAPTER TWO

The Pyramids in Sight

Alexandria, Cairo, and Sinai

'THE VERY EVENING OF MY ARRIVAL at Alexandria, we were made to change our anchorage that it might be proved how the new town wall would bear the discharge of cannon... the wall stood it to the surprise of those who made it & the ablest Turkish engineers.'[1] Of contemptible strength (part of it fell before it was finished), militarily vulnerable and built at vast cost, the wall summed up all William Bankes's preconceived ideas about the ineptitude of the despotic Ottoman regime of Egypt in August 1815. Only faint traces of the cultivated style of the Alhambra in Spain could be discerned in the town, whose walls enclosed 'bare desert full of holes & heaps & barking dogs & dead camels'. The new barracks had been designed with a whimsical sort of perverse symmetry, and the tyranny of the Albanian troops was by all accounts intolerable. On the quay hundreds of ragged pilgrims on their way to Mecca lay huddled together. It was an inauspicious introduction to a country which was to provide some of the most memorable experiences of almost eight years of constant travel. Fortunately he arrived not as an adventurer seeking employment from the Pasha but as a twenty-eight-year-old gentleman-traveller, in search of the remains of the once-great civilization of ancient Egypt.

Napoleon's defeat in Egypt in 1801 by combined British and Turkish forces had led to the Rosetta Stone, the key to the decipherment of hieroglyphs, being brought to England as the spoils of war, but the French continued to publish the researches of their savants who accompanied Napoleon's expedition. In 1809 the first of the twenty-four unwieldy elephant-folio volumes of the *Description de l'Égypte* was published, stimulating a scientific approach to the study of all aspects of ancient and modern Egypt throughout Europe, largely ignored since classical times. Together with the accessibility of more popular (and happily for travellers, more portable) books such as Vivant Denon's *Travels*[2] (immediately translated into English) and the scholarly *Aegyptiaca* of William Hamilton[3] (a book much consulted by Bankes containing a transcript and translation of the Rosetta Stone), they awakened travellers' interest in Egypt. The narrow Nile route, common to all travellers, became a focus for visitors. The result was an influx of those referred to by Henry Salt as 'the rest of the travelling authors, who, as the Indian expresses it, "take walk – make book"'.[4] If mass tourism had yet to be invented, travel snobbery was already rife and the Count de Forbin, travelling into Nubia in search of antiquities, was entirely put off by the apparent ease with which even family parties with children might now travel to areas formerly the preserve of intrepid explorers.[5]

From 1805 to 1848 Egypt was ruled by the Pasha Mohammed Ali, an Albanian-born soldier, first as Viceroy of Egypt, an impoverished dependency of the Turkish Ottoman Empire, later independently. Having defeated the Mameluke administration, he brought stability to the political disruptions in Egypt, and it became a magnet for adventurous travellers and travelling adventurers. Wishing to adapt Western technology to industry, agriculture, and irrigation in Egypt, Mohammed Ali welcomed Europeans, assisting and protecting their travels. From his patronage flowed permissions to travel, and the provision of *firmans* (permits or licences), which allocated areas for excavation and authorized the removal and ownership of antiquities. Impoverished explorers and early Egyptologists were drawn to Egypt by the lure of employment: Giovanni Belzoni had arrived in Egypt just weeks before Bankes with a speculative project for a new irrigation device, Frédéric Cailliaud was to be employed as a mineralogist, and Louis Maurice Adolphe Linant de Bellefonds (pl. 78), finding himself in Egypt by chance, settled there and made his career in Mohammed Ali's service.[6] All were giants of early investigative archaeology (at a reputed near-seven-foot tall, literally in the case of Belzoni).

Having arrived in Alexandria in the summer of 1815, Bankes began much as any modern tourist, travelling for pleasure and new experiences, but he too was soon overwhelmed by the antiquity of Egypt and the splendour of its monuments, although his admiration was always tempered by criticism when they frequently failed to reach the demanding standards of a classically educated nineteenth-century aesthete. His first impressions begin what was to be the single largest section of his journal; a work which only ever existed as a muddle of undated fragmentary notes, inconsistently scribbled down on scraps of paper. Like the outstanding drawings in his portfolio which were never to be published, his journals and notes were to become lost among his piles of papers.

Bankes began to keep an orderly journal with the best of intentions. It lasted for just twenty-five legible pages of a large bound notebook. It resembles a letter he might have sent home for his siblings; to enlighten his brothers and amuse his sisters with his first impressions of the exotic, if seedy, Orient, as epitomized by Ottoman Egypt. Letters were actually a well-established format for publication used by many travellers including his later companions, Charles Irby and James Mangles. There is no lost manuscript of *Travels in the East*, but it would never have contained these intimate impressions, so revealing of his lively personality and interests, which were continued only in family correspondence. This delightfully relaxed account, displaying his knowledge of architecture, his love of gardens, and many of his own foibles, would not have survived in print. The endless reams of paper to be filled with Greek and hieroglyphic inscriptions and plans of temples still lay in the future.

The danger of the plague had moved on to Rosetta, so Bankes was safely lodged in Alexandria with Colonel Missett, the British consul, who kindly provided him with every information and assistance and, on 7 August 1815, a safe passage for a journey into Upper Egypt.[7] Armed with their letters of introduction, travellers looked for lodging, social life, and travel advice to the consuls at Alexandria and Cairo, having perhaps consulted other travellers earlier at Rome or Constantinople. With little in the way of official duties, with British political interests concentrated on Napoleon in Europe, and with few permanent European residents, the consuls had plenty of time for their antiquarian interests and collections and to entertain travellers with a round of receptions, concerts, and dances. Apartments in the

Residency contained 'every domestic convenience, indeed luxury' since Colonel Missett, although extremely disabled, was a '*bon-vivant*'.[8] He provided sumptuous breakfasts, gourmet dinners, and morning rides on Arab steeds to different parts of the city.

Bankes was shown the field of battle, still strewn with skulls and bones, where the Anglo-Turkish forces had defeated the French in 1801. The broken pottery smothering its surface hinted at the existence of a vast city of which the present Alexandria was but a shrunken remnant. With typical perception he noticed that one of the battle's hotly contested strongholds was of Roman construction and not Saracen, as was generally believed, and closer examination proved the unusual semicircular buttresses to be original. He found the scenery about Alexandria glaring and unpleasant and regretted that the British army had missed the opportunity of removing Cleopatra's Needle to grace a London square. Antique fragments embedded in later buildings and some wrought basalt lying on the shore were among the few reminders of former greatness. The catacombs were not worth visiting after those of Syracuse, and Cleopatra's Baths 'may have been baths, but not Cleopatra's'. (He thought them to be tombs encroached on by the sea.) Further off he could make out the outlines of an ancient circus.

To engage in contradicting previous accounts was a popular pursuit for all travellers; but few did so with more relish than Bankes. On reading Sir Robert Wilson, Bankes found it extraordinary that Wilson had not noticed how the poor workmanship of the pedestal and capital of Pompey's Pillar deformed the fine shaft. It was 'so obviously contrary to the fact' that the *errata* of the book were consulted.[9] Delighting in a further discovery of his own, he could make out signs of something having been attached to the original shaft: possibly some bronze ornament.

The consul owned a pet chameleon, a sluggish harmless creature, and Bankes himself rather soft-heartedly purchased a jerboa in the street. A small nocturnal rodent with sandy fur and long hind legs, it was destined for the cooking-pot. Instead it was installed in a cane cage and fed with bread and grain. Its comical appearance and speed brought to his mind the vision of a woman in silk stockings running across London streets with her gown tucked up very high and one garter draggling behind her. It struck him as rather stupid ('I have seen it go to sleep upright & fall down'), like another novel species, ostriches, but he was impressed by some genuine ibises, collected up to be sent to the King of Naples, the colonel's friend and patron.

Ramadan had begun, and at sunset the minarets were illuminated and guns were set off over the city which disturbed him throughout the night. It required some firmness of resolution to persist in his planned voyage to Cairo, as a boat had just sunk with all lives lost in the turbulent waters at the mouth of the river (the fate of his own elder brother), and the accounts of the plague at Rosetta were becoming worse and worse. To avoid the risk of infection he engaged a large vessel at a cost of 250 piastres to take him all the way to Cairo. Pelicans and what he thought flamingos were dotted over the sandbars, enlivening the otherwise featureless coast, as he passed through to the richness and fertility of the Nile. Rosetta was in the sweetest situation imaginable with its minarets bosomed in palms and fruit trees, and the taste of the tawny-coloured water of the Nile was surprisingly pure. He was met by the British agent, who advised against entering the town; eight people had died in the course of the day and the Europeans were shut up and in the greatest consternation. The Turks themselves seemed oblivious to the danger, continuing with their daily occupations. He was sent peaches, grapes, melons, and bananas; the latter were new to him. He ventured on shore to inspect a very fine alabaster urn inscribed with hieroglyphs but purchased instead a bronze seated scribal figure. Rosetta was alive with rumours that the Pasha's attempts to modernize his army had produced a mutiny at Cairo and he had retreated into the castle.

Much as any tourist today, Bankes was enchanted by the life of the riverbank, thronged with people and cattle. The villagers were darker-complexioned than he had expected and displayed no sense of shame at their nudity; the women covering their faces before covering their bodies. The minarets of the villages reminded him of the recently seen Moorish towers of Valencia and old Castile, and he wandered through a bazaar where the overhanging wooden lattice-work of the upper storeys almost met across the narrow streets and mat awnings kept out the scorching sun. At night the heavy dew rusted steel, even when kept in his pocket. The abundance and variety of the foodstuffs astonished him, reminding him of a Snyders still-life. The river teemed with boats loaded with grain and passengers, and children of four and five rode on buffaloes down into the river as he had seen pictured on 'Indian' screens. On the bank sat men carrying hooded hawks.

When a whirlwind blew up (he had already experienced one at La Mancha with Wellington's youngest brother, Sir Henry Wellesley), a monotonous cry of alarm arose from the crew. Going ashore at a wretched village, he found a manufactory of gunpowder, a project of the Pasha's. It was supervised by a Christian with a delightfully luxuriant garden filled with dates and pomegranates, vines, and orange and lemon trees, and butterflies which seemed almost tame. Mercifully there were few mosquitoes, but the troublesome crawling and obstinate flies represented a true plague of Egypt.

At last he had the pyramids in sight, but not yet Cairo. Then at night, in a whirlwind of sand, Cairo lay before them, almost invisible against the sandy desert hills, the lanterns of its houses twinkling. Over the city, bristling with minarets, loomed the citadel. The city was not safe; all the shops were shut and guards were needed night and day. The Pasha had banished the unruly Alexandrian soldiery to Cairo, where they had pillaged and sacked almost all the town. The gates dividing the city quarters had been closed to protect the citizens and their property, and the Pasha, after indemnifying his citizens against any loss, had sought refuge in the citadel. There were four thousand troops on the rampage; the Pasha had two thousand with him but was unsure of their loyalty. There was a scene of dreadful confusion and violence, with looting but little bloodshed. Undeterred, Bankes entered the narrow streets, reminiscent of the alleys off the Strand and St Martin's Lane, to assess the architecture of the city gates and view the main square with its capricious, graceful minarets, the coarse exteriors of the houses revealing delicate woodwork and marble floors within. He found much that was elegant and pleasing in the Moorish style of architecture, admired the tombs, and peered into the mosques, where as a Christian he was forbidden entry (a situation which he would later remedy by disguise). What he saw convinced him to formulate a first theory of his own and lay out his proofs: that the European Gothic style was of Eastern origin.

The Latin convent[10] where he lodged was unremarkable but he slept in an open gallery at the very top and enjoyed the rich tones of its organ on high days. From there all the main sights of the city could be explored and described, every detail scrutinized to gauge whether it was recent or ancient, and declared fine or coarse.

When he was to be presented to the Pasha, a richly caparisoned horse was sent down to fetch him with a train of attendants. Passing through several gates he found himself in the court of the citadel surrounded by a mêlée of horses and soldiers. The audience hall dating from the time of the Beys was plain, not overly large, and possessed a tawdry ceiling, out of tune with the rest. The Pasha's suite had been recently decorated in the taste that prevailed at Constantinople. Wood had been used lavishly although it was scarce at Cairo – 'a more trumpery building or in worse taste it is difficult to conceive'. The hall that he now entered commanded the finest views imaginable of the city and the pyramids of Giza, Dahshur, and Saqqara. There was time to enjoy this at his leisure for, since it was Ramadan, nothing could be done until after sunset, and the silver dishes of food waited at the door of the great saloon for the signal-gun. 'There was a crowd of servants & persons richly dressed passing backward & forward & some of the raggedest beggars I ever saw within the threshold (for there was no guard to keep them out).' While the Pasha ate, Bankes persuaded the interpreter to show him the other apartments (no doors were ever closed to Bankes that he could not persuade or prise open). The two little gardens were 'full of the gaudiest & sweetest flowers', and the octagonal kiosk with its fountain and wonderful prospect from its windows, delightful. 'The beauty of the situation & of the form is so great that I was quite angry with the heavy clumsy sashes & the abominable painting of the roof & walls.' Here he illustrated his journal with a floor-plan to make his descriptions intelligible; our first example of his fortunate realization that, however fine the description, plans and diagrams were essential to the full understanding of a structure. While English architecture was conceived for the 'Damp & Cold & Dullness' of the climate, here the heat encouraged cool breezes and open prospects, fountains, and open galleries and terraces. (Mindful of this and hating winter cold, he was later to design a model for a comfortable draught-free English country house, although he was to be seduced by the Italianate style into giving his own house a long open terrace.) It was this practical difference which he felt made Homer's description of Ulysses' house and the structure of Pliny the Younger's villa almost impossible to follow, despite the detail. 'The pasha passes a great part of his mornings in his kiosk & so should I too; it is delicious.' He was received in the Saloon: 'a room of fine size & very rich decoration but without taste. The Pasha was sitting in one corner of the divan upon some raised cushions with five candlesticks as large as the largest that are set upon an altar burning before him on the floor & a little nearer to him was the glass vessel to which the pipe which he held in his hand was attached in the manner of an Indian Hooker, the handle was studded or rather covered over with very large diamonds: on one side of him was a tall nosegay, like a wand, of tuberoses. His dress was a plain full crimson with a little gold about it, he desired me to sit down by him & coffee which had a sort of perfumed taste given to it was brought in little golden cups.' His slaves knelt as they changed his pipe. 'He is a middle aged man, & I should think rather little, there is a great deal of vivacity & intelligence in his eyes & his conversation is ready & sprightly.' Bankes offered some flattering remarks on the Pasha's military successes against the Wahabees and the recovery of Mecca and Medina. 'I carried my army, he told me, an hundred & thirty leagues into the Desert where there were no water or provisions. He did not tell me what multitudes he had sacrificed there & between ten & twenty thousand camels. He had never expected, he said, that Bonaparte's last project would succeed & seemed to wonder that we did not cut off his head. He was glad when Europeans came to travel in the country.' Bankes was accompanied out by the light of burning torches, having received the promise of the protection of Mohammed Ali's son in Upper Egypt.

Early one morning he climbed the Mokattam hills to see the bird's-eye city view that Henry Salt had painted for a Panorama in London, but he found something unpleasant in the monotonous colours of the desert landscape and city. It was the first day of the festival of Bairam, a day of feasting, and the city below bustled with gaudy cavaliers making their way to the court of the citadel 'crowded with fine drapes & rich harness like a bed of tulips'. Troops of women with herbs and palm branches were decking out the tombs where families would picnic. Booths had been set up to sell cakes and sweetmeats, with toys and trinkets for the children. If Christians passing through the narrow streets could be caught by the sharp spurs worn by the gaily dressed cavalcades, so much the merrier.

The unrest at Cairo was exacerbated by the Pasha's remaining within the citadel. He was not a timid man, and people reasoned that he must know something that others did not. Meanwhile Bankes visited the egg-hatcheries, poor shabby-looking places full of stench and stifling hot, where chickens were brought out of the ovens by the basketful. Along the river the vista 'which no landscape gardener would alter or could improve' formed a backdrop for the mosque of the Dervishes. Since it was not the proper season for observing their 'extravagances' he continued past the nitre warehouses to visit the Patriarch to obtain a recommendation to Mount Sinai. The church was certainly of architectural interest but he noted in his journal that he was 'disgusted beyond measure by the slovenly mode of interment among the Christians; the smell of the bodies as I passed along was intolerable & after the plague of last year not a pleasant circumstance'. The grotto where the Holy Family was said to have rested was a 'sad sorry hole'. The ancient Nilometer used to measure the levels of the annual inundation, was in poor condition but the height of the Nile was still called in the streets each morning. The dusty decaying fabric of the city was redeemed only by the charm of its gardens opulently scented with mimosa and shaded by noble sycamores, a species unlike our own. A morning was devoted to taking a Turkish bath. Having remained too long in the hottest part, he found himself faint and languid, 'but the sensation of having the limbs so pulled & scraped & stretched is pleasant & refreshing'. The floors however were 'disagreeable & dangerous' and as slippery as ice, and he could not keep the coarse wooden sandals on his feet. Wishing to experience everything, he sent for a juggler and a conjuror with scorpions and snakes. The slave market provided another diversion, but slaves were disappointingly scarce and expensive since the plague. They were sold naked, and their mouths and tongues particularly examined to judge their health. They were purchased on approval for two days and returned if they snored. An acquaintance had refused to purchase a female slave as she came with an infant: 'What a cruel situation for a human being to be reduced to.' He met a Greek who brought news from the capital of Abyssinia, where the city was no more than thatched hovels. Two Englishmen (one being Nathaniel Pearce, whom Bankes was later to meet) were settled there with their wives and were suspected as being secret agents of the British government.

⁕⁑⁕

Bankes had no intention of travelling beyond the pyramids nor of remaining any time in Egypt until his encounter with the experienced Swiss explorer Johann Ludwig Burckhardt, which was to have a profound effect on his future, inspiring him with a deep desire to explore and record Nubia in a serious fashion. Burckhardt, travelling for the African Society under the name of Sheikh Ibrahim, spotted the potential in guiding this fearless and promising young man towards travelling to some positive purpose. Bankes saw in him the ideal traveller: full of energy and enterprise, 'with a great exactness of memory, perfect master of Arabic & of all the customs of the peoples of the East; rather a man of general knowledge than a learned man, but observing & retaining everything. He is one of the few people I should have liked to travel with had our routes lain the same way. I expect that he will do great things in the interior of Africa, he already knows Syria & Palestine & great part of Yemen better than anybody & has given me invaluable information & advice as to my route … [he] has penetrated higher than anybody else into Nubia having reached within a days journey of Dongola… It is chiefly his persuasion that has induced me to resolve on going beyond the first Cataracts.' Burckhardt in turn found him 'a very superior man, who bears his faculties, & rank, & fortune most meekly, and is both indefatigable & accurate in his researches.'[11] Burckhardt advised him to adopt Oriental dress (Bankes had prudently purchased such dress in Malta to avoid the risk of infection) and made out a list of sites to be seen on both banks of the Nile, beginning at Philae and going up to Wadi Omki, just beyond Wadi Halfa. Having travelled through Nubia in 1813, Burckhardt was the first European to discover the Great Temple at Abu Simbel, and, in Syria, the first to enter Petra, although his account was published only posthumously.[12] On his way to Abu Simbel he had encountered Thomas Legh (a traveller who would later infuriate Bankes by pre-empting him in publishing), who was then travelling with the Reverend Charles Smelt and their guide, François Barthow, who was now to be employed by Bankes.

Although the areas of Thebes and the Giza pyramids were now being explored, few European travellers had passed far beyond the First Cataract at Aswan, the gateway to Nubia.[13] The rocky barrier of the Second Cataract was seldom negotiated, and the Kushite sites further up the Nile remained unexplored. The town of Sennar, on the Blue Nile south of modern Khartoum, was virtually unvisited. Of the early explorers, James Bruce had been the first to identify correctly the site of the lost city of ancient Meroe, but in Britain many of his exploits were greeted with disbelief. After a long stay in Abyssinia he returned via Aswan in 1772, travelling through Sennar and Berber.[14] But between 1772 and 1821, when Linant de Bellefonds travelled there on Bankes's behalf, no European was to reach Sennar.

The Reverend George Waddington and Barnard Hanbury were among the few other contemporary travellers in this southernmost area of Nubia. Later, in 1828–9, the joint expedition of Jean-François Champollion and Ippolito Rosellini would reach the Second Cataract, but it was not until the 1830s that both George Hoskins and Giuseppe Ferlini explored and documented the areas further south.[15]

Bankes's own record of the ancient sites of Nubia and the Sudan is particularly important. Until recently, the study of the history and archaeology of the ancient Kushite sites of the northern Sudan was somewhat neglected, Kushite cultures tending to be regarded as subordinate to Egyptian civilization or as a degenerate mixture of Egyptian and indigenous cultures. Today it is recognized as a significant civilisation in its own right. This renewed African perspective, the establishment of the Sudan Archaeological Research Society in London, and the increase in archaeological work in the Sudan parallel the awakening of early nineteenth-century interest in the exploration of Africa. The African Association had been founded in London in 1788 for 'Promoting the Discovery of the Inland Parts of that quarter of the World', and sponsored both Burckhardt and, later, Linant. On his return, Bankes was to join the committee of the Association. It was to William Hamilton, Secretary of the Association from 1811, that Henry Salt, the British consul-general, sent back some of his own work on Egypt, and Bankes's father was a colleague of the eminent natural scientist Sir Joseph Banks, a founder member and also President of the Royal Society. The drama and mystery of the disappearance of the African explorer Mungo Park was well known to the public, and Bankes's correspondence contains copies of reports on Park's possible where-abouts, collected by the British resident at Mocha, and forwarded to the Association in London.[16] Bankes himself had hoped to reach Dongola and Meroe on his second journey, and subsequently talked of returning to Egypt to investigate the sources of the Nile.[17]

The fabled Meroe, known to Bankes from the classical authors, had replaced Napata as the centre of the kingdom of Kush from c.300 BC until the end of the kingdom in AD 350. The sites of Napata and Meroe were neither securely identified in Bankes's time, and knowl-edge and accurate mapping of the passage of the Nile through and beyond those regions was sketchy. Bankes's draughtsman Alessandro Ricci seems to have imagined he had found Meroe at Sai island, while Linant wrote to Bankes expressing his surprise at the length and nature of the Nile's Dongola bend, avoided by both ancient and modern travellers. Earlier exploration had done little more than follow the centuries-old and well-travelled land-cara-van trade routes, cutting across the desert between the great curves of the course of the river.

Other than Burckhardt, who obviously made an enormous impression on him, Bankes is reticent about mentioning other travellers he met (the presence of others detracted from tales of exploration). He is careless about dates but had reached Cairo by 16 August 1815, for on this day the traveller William Turner, who had just arrived back after a fatiguing visit to Sinai, records meeting him there and simultaneously receiving the latest news from Europe.[18] Visiting Peter Lee, Turner found Youssef Boghos the Pasha's secretary and Bankes, 'who was just arrived, and preparing for the journey from which I was now returned.[19] After learning the details of the victory of Waterloo, I returned to the convent, unpacked, and went immediately to the bath.'[20]

Turner adds in a footnote to his journal: 'since this time Mr. Bankes has twice visited Upper Egypt, where he penetrated higher than any of his predecessors; has travelled all over Syria, including the East Coast of the Dead Sea, which no one else, except Sheikh Ibrahim [Burckhardt], had seen, and to Palmyra. His publication will teach us more respecting the East than that of any traveller who has yet described it; for he goes everywhere, fearing nei-ther danger nor fatigue, collecting more information than any other man could obtain, and never forgetting what he collects. I freely own my own anxiety, that my humble journal, if printed at all, should appear before his return, for I should not expect any one would read it after the publication of his.'

The following day, Turner 'dined with Mr. Cocchini, the "British Canceliere", at whose table I met Mr. Bankes … In the evening I made a donkey excursion with Mr. Bankes, who is quite of my opinion as to the folly of guiding one's self by information obtained from the Franks; the traveller who did so, would never move from his room.'[21] These were uncertain times in Cairo but, despite the warnings not to venture outside the Frank quarter because of the danger of being insulted, if not fired at, by the troops, they sallied forth into the streets.

There were armed soldiers about but no incidents occurred. Fruit stalls remained open but the bazaars were all shut and the streets deserted. They rode to the tombs of the Caliphs and Beys, south-east of the city, but there were no means of getting up the almost perpendicular rock to investigate the caves in the burying-ground. On their return to the convent, Mr Aziz, the consul's Egyptian interpreter, called on them bringing the news of Bonaparte's surrender.[22] At the same time they learned that the Ottoman Empire had confirmed the Pasha, Mohammed Ali, as ruler of Egypt.

Bankes set off the next day for the journey from Cairo to Mount Sinai and back, accompanied by an Alexandrian Arab interpreter, Haleel, whom he had engaged on first landing in Egypt.[23] The Sinai journal is just a single torn scrap of paper crammed with minute notes. Beyond Suez the journey was not a very comfortable one. 'A camel's pace is very unpleasant going down hill & not very safe going up.' The water was nauseous and there were sand-flies and a monstrous scaly lizard about a yard long. Heavy dews and cold nights necessitated three blankets instead of the usual sheet for indoors. He got on sociably enough with the Arab men, but the women kept out of his way. The novelty of the natural features – palm oases, monolithic rocks, grasshoppers, birds, and plants – delighted him. His first sight of Mount Sinai was romantic and fine, and at St Catherine's Monastery, the focus for all travellers, he was drawn up by a rope over the garden wall, then entered the building through a subterranean passage and iron door. Some idea of the practicalities of travel can be had from a glance at the expenses which Turner had just incurred on his own journey.[24] Turner reckoned Sinai to be a twenty-five-day trip (although Bankes accomplished it in a bare sixteen days).[25] The greatest expense was the 45 piastres to the monastery at Sinai for their lodgings. The hire of camels and donkeys for the journey is the next largest item, with additional costs for drivers and porters. The provisions included meat and birds, two geese, vegetables, coffee, sugar, lemons, tamarinds, butter, biscuit, eggs, watermelons, cheese and milk. Rice, coffee, honey, flour, and butter for the Arabs are listed separately. A kid, at 5 piastres is noted as very dear, and there is an item for 'Bagshish to Arab for catching Lizard at foot of Sinai'.

Turner also provides us with some information on Bankes's activities at St Catherine's Monastery.[26] Turner, on enquiring after manuscripts and a library, had been told by the priests that they possessed only three bibles. He took their word for this as 'Pococke states that they had no rare manuscripts. But Mr. Bankes, by persevering and rummaging, found out a library of 2,000 volumes, of which three-quarters were MSS, and of these, nine-tenths were Greek … Mr. Bankes brought away, 1 – a thick M.S., containing Hephaestis on the Greek Metres, an Oration of Isocrates, the Letters of Phalaris, (which were the subject of much controversy some years ago): 2d., Another containing the three first Books of the Iliad, and part of the fourth; two Tragedies of Aeschylus, and much Greek poetry; 3d., Another thin one, containing the Medea of Euripides, and the beginning of his Hyppolitus; 4th., An historical Work of Cedrenus (a Byzantine historian, quoted in Gibbon): 5th., A very fair one, containing, it appears, all the Physics of Aristotle, probably of no remote antiquity, as it is written with contractions, which were not used in the early ages.' Bankes found that the books in many places 'stand three deep, are full of dust and haunted by hideous spiders'.[27]

How Bankes was allowed to leave with these volumes, whether legally or improperly, is not made clear. Only one of them is to be found in the library at Kingston Lacy: a 1503 copy of

Euripides annotated on the flyleaf as having been 'Brought from the convent of St. Catherine upon Mount Sinai in August 1815 by Wm. John Bankes'. The others were not amongst the books which Bankes presented to Cambridge University Library, which are listed in the Library's accessions book, and appear to have been returned to the Library at St Catherine's, suggesting contrition at what may have been their unorthodox removal.[28]

The portfolio drawings from Sinai, views and copies of various inscriptions (pl. 7), were made later by Linant and Ricci in 1820.[29] Bankes was already searching out and examining inscriptions in Sinai and was particularly interested in the unknown script of some he found at the base of Mount Sinai, but he drew views only of St Catherine's Monastery. He discussed the inscriptions with Burckhardt, who visited Sinai later, and Turner tells us that at that time Bankes thought them to be Phoenician. Turner also comments on Bankes's opinion of some inscriptions 'in the mountains of El Chuttel' near the Red Sea, but the location of these is unclear.

The journey to Sinai had filled in the time while he was waiting for his hired boat to be equipped. Now he was to undertake his first voyage into Nubia.

CHAPTER THREE

Calm, Heat, and Crocodiles

The first Nubian Voyage

Having left Cairo for Sinai on 18 August 1815, Bankes was back by 3 September, warning his father that there would be no letters for the next two months as he was about to set off for Nubia. Arrangements for money supplies were proving inconvenient and expensive so he requested his father to make some arrangements through London bankers. He joked that he was 'obliged to travel with a vast apparatus *en grand seigneur*'. Like the French army, he too had his brigades in case 'I choose to remove a Pyramid or the statue of Memnon [pl. 8].'[1]

Travellers on the Nile invariably began in the north and sailed up river, taking advantage of any north winds and stopping only when these were absent. Without the requisite north wind the boat would need to be rowed or else numbers of local men employed to tow it by rope from the riverbank. Returning downstream they could rely on the current and plan their stops; therefore most investigation and recording was done then. The party that left Cairo by boat on 16 September 1815 for his first voyage into Nubia consisted of Bankes, François Barthow (a French subject born in St Domingo employed by Bankes as his main guide and interpreter), Giovanni Finati (a former soldier known to travellers by his adopted Muslim name Mahomet), Antonio da Costa (the Portuguese servant who followed Bankes's travels), and Haleel his Alexandrian interpreter.[2] All were employed for the practicalities of travel, not as artists or draughtsmen. Finati had been engaged by Barthow on Bankes's behalf as their dragoman and janissary and was to remain in Bankes's service as his general factotum, interpreter, and guide.[3]

From this point, the meeting of master and servant, the story of Bankes's travels opens in the *Narrative of the Life and Adventures of Giovanni Finati*, dictated by Finati and translated from the Italian and edited by Bankes. This provides an outline of the journeys, supposedly written by Finati, but actually padded with material from Bankes's own journals. Bankes reserved his own voice for the erudite footnotes. From a compilation of this story with random fragments of manuscript, correspondence, and contemporary journals, a fuller account emerges of Bankes's itinerary, his activities, and his opinions.

In Bankes's own journal, the first voyage to Nubia tumbles out over four loose pages of disjointed prose with little punctuation. The tone is spontaneous and personal as he dashes down whatever catches his eye; yet it was still read through and corrected.[4] He hired a large 'Mash' boat at 600 piastres per month, boasting two masts and two small cabins. He incorrectly dated their departure to the night of 15 August – it was actually 15 September.[5] The island of Roda, scattered with water-fowl and pelicans, and the scenery were as delightful as at first sight. Unfortunately a mast broke that evening forcing them to stop for repairs at a village in front of the pyramid of Meidum. There he saw indigo fields and Christian houses distinguished by white crosses on their doors. He was amused by the music and extraordinary suppleness of the 'indecent motions & attitudes' of the dancers on a boat moored nearby. 'Some of the villagers had been useful to us, so I gave them some dinner: and was rewarded for it … by the loss of one of my dishes'. (A small boy was seen speedily swimming away with it.) The local magistrate offered him a saucepan lid by way of amends and they sailed on by moonlight. Landing at Beni Suef, he went through the bazaar. When the boat became stuck on a mudbank he noted that the sailors threw salt in the fire to avert the evil eye. The interesting subject matter of the wall paintings took second place to his extensive description of the architecture of the 'grottoes' (rock-cut tombs) of Beni Hasan. He was surprised that Hamilton's *Aegyptiaca*[6] had failed to notice what seemed to him their most remarkable aspect: their resemblance to early Greek architecture: 'either the link betwixt the parent Egyptian & the Greek architecture, or we have a sort of bastard Greek grafted on the Egyptian in the time of the Ptolemies'. This brief section of his journal ends at Antinoe.

Twelve days' journey from Cairo brought them to Thebes but an attack of ophthalmia deprived Bankes totally of his sight during his ten-day stay. (He was to be afflicted by this infection on several occasions in Egypt, and it remained a hazard for travellers. Baedeker's guidebook of 1914 was still warning that 'it is inadvisable to allow one's field-glass to be used by strangers, especially natives, for fear of infection'.)

⁂

A further three pages of fragmentary journal picks up many miles further south, covering the first cataract at Aswan to Qasr Ibrim. Their boat being too large to pass through the first cataract, they were obliged to hire a roughly built and poorly equipped second vessel which they boarded at Philae beyond the rocky outcrops. There was no cabin, and room for only Bankes to sleep on board. Travelling south, Bankes and Barthow, still in European dress, excited much local interest. In turn, Bankes's own curiosity was aroused by the myriad novelties on view: 'A ship of baby black slaves at Assouan [evidence of the active African slave-trade] … a present of live locusts tied by their legs on a palm branch shredded into filaments – great swarm of locusts passing over glittering like a snow [They also alighted like a snowfall, covering clothes, boats, and crops, the peasants attempting to beat them off with sticks and loud cries] – almost all the men at Assouan carry long stout poles as well as other arms.' He examined the 'Apple of Sodom', learning that the woody substance within was good for timber, and the milky stalk was in some places burned with charcoal to make gunpowder.

He was struck by the beauty of the temple complex on the island of Philae, where, among the remains, he found a fallen inscribed obelisk.[7] He also investigated the beautiful ruins of Biga, the island opposite. An ugly incident prevented him from making drawings in the temple when a Nubian put his hand across the paper and menaced him with a knife, 'demanding a present'. Finati was about to draw his pistol when the fortunate arrival of the Casheff of Aswan with a retinue of soldiers sent 'every inhabitant precipitately from the island'. (Bankes himself briefly and coolly described his naked aggressor who carried a short crooked knife in a sheath buckled on his left arm.) Apart from this occurrence, and some minor incivility at Akhmim, they generally felt safe under the protection afforded to strangers by Mohammed Ali.

1 Miniature of William John Bankes (1786–1855), by George Sandars, 1812.

2 Henry Bankes
(1757–1834), painted
in Rome by Pompeo
Batoni, 1779.

3 Frances Woodley
(1760–1823), who
married Henry Bankes
in 1784. Portrait by
George Romney,
1780–81.

4 Lord Byron in Greek dress,
by Thomas Phillips, 1813.

5 Annabella Milbanke,
by Sir George Hayter, 1812.

6 The south front of Kingston Lacy with the Philae obelisk on the lawn.

7 A view of the inscribed stelae at Serabit el-Khadim, Sinai, by Linant.

8 The bust of Rameses II,
known as the 'Younger Memnon',
recovered by Belzoni and donated
to the British Museum by Salt
and Burckhardt in 1818.

9 A Coptic fresco of the fiery furnace, covering reliefs in the hypostyle hall of Kalabsha temple. Painting by Bankes.

Ground plan of the Ruins   at Kalapshe

11 ABOVE The buried façade of the Great Temple of Abu Simbel in 1815. Drawing by Bankes.

12 RIGHT Are the colossi standing? Bankes's speculative sketch of the Great Temple of Abu Simbel, 1815.

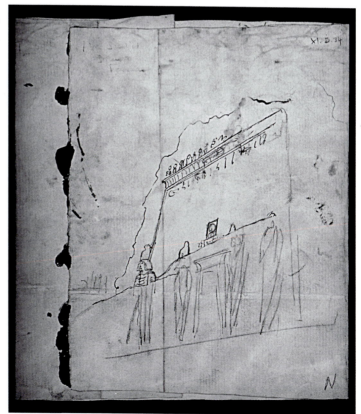

10 OPPOSITE Bankes's plan and description of Kalabsha temple, 1815. The plan shows Christian alterations, later destroyed, and, south of the pylon, what may be the lost *mammisi*.

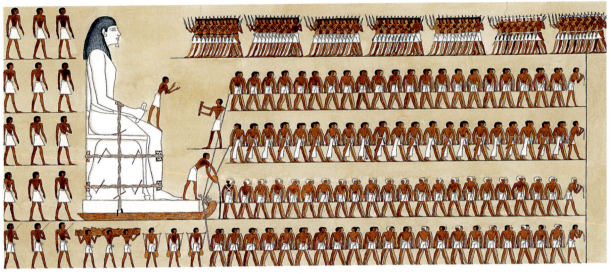

13 A scene showing the transportation of the colossal statue of Djehutyhotep, from the tomb of Djehutyhotep at Deir el-Bersha. Painting by Ricci.

14 A painted fragment showing musicians and dancers from the lost Theban tomb of Nebamun. Painting by Linant.

15 A scene showing fowling in the marshes from the lost Theban tomb of Nebamun. Painting by Linant.

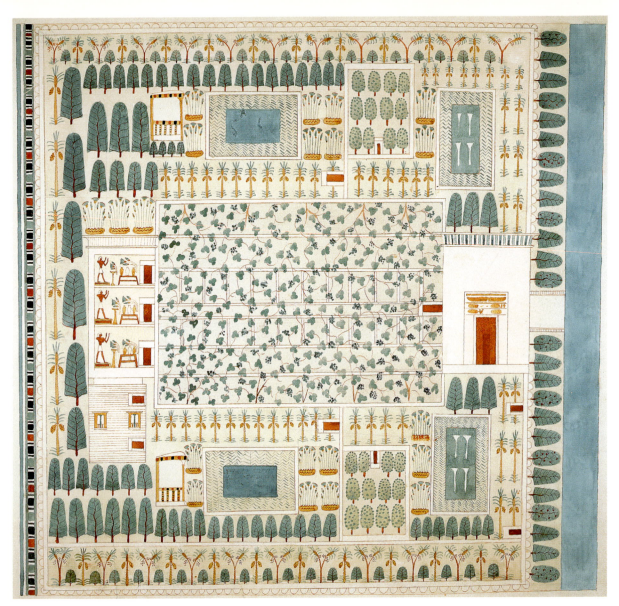

16 A garden scene from the tomb of Sennefer at Thebes. Painting by Ricci.

17 ABOVE Linant's view of the lost temple of Amenhotep III at Elephantine.   18 BELOW The gate of Alexander II at Elephantine, by Linant.

21 ABOVE The lost portico inscription
from Dabod temple, copied by Beechey.

22 RIGHT Ricci's drawing of the lost
inscribed shrine from Dabod temple.

19 OPPOSITE ABOVE A view
of Philae temple, by Linant.

20 OPPOSITE BELOW Belzoni's distress
as the Philae obelisk sinks into the
Nile, before being successfully
refloated. An illustration from
a moral tale for children, entitled
Fruits of Enterprize, by Sarah Atkins.

23 ABOVE A panoramic view of Dabod
temple, by Beechey. His notes, written
upside down, can be seen on the right.

24 RIGHT A view through a
doorway into the sanctuary of
Dabod temple. Copied from a
drawing by Salt.

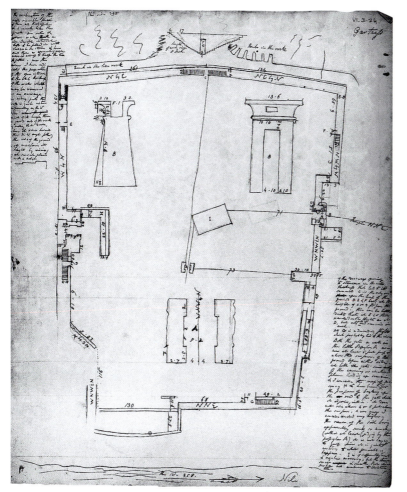

25 ABOVE
The kiosk-temple
at Qertassi,
by Beechey.

26 LEFT Bankes's
ground plan of the
fortress at Qertassi.

27 A view of Wadi Hedid temple, by Bankes. The outline of the ruins of Gamli temple can just be seen on the left, on the far bank of the river.

At 'Debode [Dabod] temple – women bring in a coarse cake – sour milk with onion – village in the desert… Moonlight, pass Gartassy [Qertassi], column… a Boy's back burned just below the shoulder with a red hot iron as a strengthener to the lungs & preventative against headache & loss of appetite… Kalabshe – violent storm of thunder & lightning & rain during the night. Calm, heat, crocodiles – Fish leaps on board.' The villagers understood Arabic although their own language was totally different. This factor, and the scarcity of visitors beyond the cataract, led to him being mistaken for the tax collector. At Kalabsha he heard the first of many stories of buried treasure, recently discovered, according to the villagers, but taken by the Beys. 'Dendura [Dendur] looks well from the river… Coban [Quban] – could it not have been a Roman walled camp of Tiberius's time? it is square & the wall from 20 to 26ft. high & very thick – a row of columns towards the river – here the natives suppose is a treasure concealed.'

His impressions of the local population and temple of Dakka are followed by comments on the strange food: 'Eat a crane with dark plumage – like hare – Eat locusts roasted pulling off the wings – I used to observe the roasted wings lying very thick sometimes on the ground – a sign such repasts were very common with the natives – the flavour is like a shrimp.' There were also wild ducks, partridges, and crocodiles. Derr, which had been the capital only since the destruction of Ibrim by the Mamelukes four years earlier, had houses but no bazaar.[8] 'One of the Cashiefs received me sitting on a raised platform near the mosque upon a carpet – I was served to coffee & dates with bread – he afterwards made me a present of a sheep & some fowls [and a sack of dates] – I presented him with some soap & candles [these, and gunpowder, were preferred to the European-manufacture articles which Bankes had brought for use as gifts] – he pays a sort of tribute to the Pasha of Egypt.' Bankes was informed that the fine horses at Dongola cost the equivalent of eight slaves; a slave being worth 300 or 500 piastres, 'a prodigious sum'.

Except for the effects of the light, the grotto of Derr was not beautiful. Above it lay the remains of an old monastery. Grain was plentiful although he had been warned that it might be scarce. Soaked and baked it was palatable. Sour milk was refreshing and at Derr brandy was distilled from the dates, but a doctor had warned him that it caused dropsies. As they approached Qasr Ibrim, a vast ruin spread over the summit of an imposing cliff in a strong defensive position on the river, his first view of its situation was very impressive.[9]

After explaining the local practice of levying taxes, Bankes goes on to describe the natural pyramids of rock and artificial features on the way to Ibrim. 'On the surface of a rock on the river side there is traced out the mouth of an arched Grott, & the excavation has been just begun.' Another, higher up, was completed but inaccessible. He was struck by the noble aspect of Ibrim. 'I took a path across a corner of the desert through a multitude of tombs, none of which are inscribed. As it is only four years ago that the town was pillaged & dismantled… rather a place abandoned than a place destroyed… All the signs of everyday life remain in place… it is a sort of Nubian Pompeii.' He described the church, surprised to find such a large Christian establishment so high up the Nile. He was bewildered by an inscription in Greek script built into the wall of a house, and copied the letters but could make no sense of them, perhaps because the language was Coptic. Descending into the plain upon the opposite side he found more tombs and, creeping round under the face of Ibrim's great cliff, discovered the entrances of 'four grottoes enriched with Hieroglyphics. Two were at a great height & seemed quite inaccessible, but one of my boat's crew contrived to climb up & fasten a rope by which I drew myself up, it surprised me to find the signs of (at least occasional) habitation within, the stones upon which a fire had been lighted & ashes about it; I could not learn what sort of people can haunt such a place, but it was evident that our contrivance of the rope had been often resorted to, the pole to which it was fastened retaining the marks. The painting in these grottoes is wonderfully well preserved. I made drawings of them.'

While the master of his boat regaled him with a wondrous tale of a moving statue at Ibrim, he now first noticed the high rock-cut hieroglyphic inscription which he was later to have carefully copied by Henry Beechey. 'A little above Ibrim a part of the face of a rock is smoothed into a sort of Tablet & inscribed with hieroglyphic figures; almost contiguous is the representation of a long line of camels.' He assumed the camels to be of the same period from their proximity, but Bankes was wrong since the camel was unknown in ancient Egypt. Another fish leapt on to their boat as they passed the district of 'Phareg', where the wailing voices of women wafted across the water. There were no antiquities to be found when he went on shore, although he had been informed otherwise. The inhabitants of the village were not surprised at seeing Europeans, as two of them, whom Barthow recognized, had gone down to Cairo and worked as servants; a common practice. Bankes recounts at length the hospitality shown by the village, where he 'learned the first tidings of the Hippopotamus' – one had been shot near the village three years earlier. He also heard there were some five to six hundred Mamelukes gathered at Dongola.

At Abu Simbel the façade of the Great Temple, discovered when Burckhardt had stumbled across it only two years earlier, was partially visible above the level of the sand, its entrance buried, and the interior undiscovered (pl. 11). Bankes later regretted not attempting to excavate the entrance at that time and be the first person to enter. As a rough sketch jotted on the back of an envelope shows (pl. 12), he was still speculating on the possibility that the colossi were standing figures, since except for their heads and shoulders their shrouded form remained unknown below the huge sand-drift.

At daybreak he was shown 'the great grotto'. He passed by 'a small one … & after looking at the colossuses of Ipsambol at a distance we crossed over a part of the desert & so made our way round a Mountain betwixt which & the river there is no direct passage at this season. On the Western side of which opening directly upon the Nile is the door of the great grotto of Addé. Our boat still not appearing I strolled on to a hill that is near, covered with Ruins, called … [Bankes frequently omitted the names] where I found the remains of a Xtian Church & an interesting Fragment in the Egyptian style. It is singular that this morsel perhaps the most remote of any that exists, is unique in some respects & has a nearer resemblance to the architecture of Greece & Rome in detail than any that is found lower down.' Cries drifted across from the village opposite, which was being pillaged by desert Arabs. Barthow killed several wild geese of a similar species to those kept once at Kingston Hall, and there were more stories of the hippopotamus, but he saw only basking crocodiles, several ruins that appeared to have been churches or monasteries, gazelles, and some large lizards. The wife of the Casheff of Derr sent them a present of bad watermelons, and another of the three local Casheffs, who had 'always taken more part with the Mameluks than his brother', offered them hospitality with horses and camels to take them on to the Second Cataract in case there was no wind. The end of this informal journal contains notes, added later, from the relevant sections of Gibbon, Strabo, and others on the history of the area.

Wadi Halfa was the furthest point south reached by boat, although they ventured a little further on by camel to Wadi Omki, where Bankes painted a panorama of the view. The puzzling ruins at Wadi Halfa remained much buried in the sand and it was not until his next journey that he excavated them. On their return journey they were 'landing almost continually, wherever there were tidings or expectation of any vestiges of antiquity'.

Finati tells us that the ruins of Derr, Amada, Sebua, Maharraka, Qertassi, Gerf Husein, Dakka, Dendur, Tafa, Kalabsha, and Dabod were examined for antiquities and inscriptions. Bankes spent some days at Philae and discovered by the light of his candles at night a previously unknown inscription: 'Interesting as mentioning the two Cleopatras (successively wives of Ptolemy Lathurus), the same who are addressed on the pedestal of the obelisk.'[10] He had made a first attempt, unsuccessful 'for want of proper tackle', to remove the obelisk, but managed to uncover its hitherto buried pedestal.

The islands of Biga and Elephantine were explored and the ancient granite quarries at Aswan investigated. At Aswan on their return, they were rejoined by da Costa, who had been left in charge of their original boat, and they had acquired a Nubian interpreter while they were in the upper country.

They sampled the local 'booza', a type of beer, and visited the two temples of Kom Ombo, the quarries of Silsila, Edfu and Esna temples, and Armant, before arriving back at Thebes, where some time was spent examining the astonishing remains. A dawn visit to the colossi of Memnon statues failed to provide their legendary musical sound. This did not surprise the sceptical Finati, although Bankes had noticed that temperature changes in the stones did produce strange sounds from the portico at Philae, similar to the ancients' description of a harp-string note. An attempt to remove the colossal stone bust known as the head of Memnon from the Ramesseum had reluctantly to be abandoned despite his having 'brought with him a proper rope with pullies and machinery, for the purpose' after hearing Burckhardt's description of it. To compensate, he removed two of the large Sekhmet statues from the temple of Mut at Karnak (which were shipped home but which subsequently disappeared from his collection) and purchased a papyrus. At Gurna, Bankes and Finati amused themselves by agreeing to be bitten and stung by snakes and scorpions carried by an itinerant juggler who promised them immunity as a result. They assumed this would be ineffectual since the venom must have been removed previously. On to Dendera and Akhmim. At 'Gau' [Qau el-Kebir] nine columns of the temple still remained standing, but by their next visit only one remained and that fell soon after. Bankes expressed his disapproval to Mohammed Ali's son, Ibrahim, who had himself pulled down an ancient structure to build his new palace at 'Siout' [Asyut]. They explored tombs during the day, and at night were entertained by dancing-girls at the house of Ibrahim's European physician.

Stopping at 'Radamone',[11] Ashmunein, Beni Hasan, el-Minya, and Beni Suef, they were soon back at the pyramid fields of Meidum, Dahshur, Saqqara, and Giza, where after viewing them externally, and mounting to the summit, Bankes fainted in the sarcophagus chamber of the Great Pyramid while exploring the interior by torchlight, and had to be carried out into the air to be revived. The pyramids at 'Illahoun' in the Fayoum, the large fertile depression south-west of Cairo, were less explored so consequently of more interest. He considered that the ruined site was connected with the much-sought-after building known to the ancients as the labyrinth. The footnotes to Finati's *Narrative* show that he remained perplexed that there were no pyramids to be found at Thebes, 'nor at all in Upper Egypt, nor till they are found again in quantities in the heart of Ethiopia', not realizing that pyramids as royal burial structures, although adapted and revived much later in the Kushite kingdoms, had been replaced in the New Kingdom at Thebes by rock-cut tombs. Burial practices had altered during different periods of Egyptian history.

⁂

Bankes's descriptions and drawings from this first solo voyage in 1815 were eventually to be subsumed into the great mass of papers; disappearing into anonymous folders arranged by site regardless of date or authorship. The separate records of 1815 and 1818, as well as the unsigned and undated work of Linant, Ricci, and Beechey, have had to be retrieved and reconstructed. What distinguishes Bankes's 1815 presence is not only his handwriting and drawing style but his tone. Unlike that in the rough journals, a self-conscious and didactic prose style embodies portentous opinions on subjects such as the antiquity of the ruins or their relationship to classical examples. These would give way to the more fluent and descriptive archaeological notes of the second voyage; less pedantic and florid, and, although often corrected, never contrived as they would undoubtedly have been for publication. Comments and comparisons from classical sources would be added later at his leisure.

This noticeable metamorphosis in style is owed to the time lapse between the two Nubian journeys: almost three years gaining experience and maturity while exploring and documenting around the Near East. It also reflects the fact that Bankes stands on the cusp of the change from eighteenth-century beliefs and ideas about the nature of ancient Egypt to those of the new century. His first journey is both a personal encounter with the Orient and redolent of the old antiquarian concerns; the second represents a leap towards a scientific approach to ancient Egypt and archaeology. His early references to ancient standing stones spring from eighteenth-century ideas of the connection between Egyptian civilization and that of the Druids and the construction of British sites such as Stonehenge and Avebury. He was also preoccupied with the evidently remote, but still unmeasured, antiquity of Egypt and in the relative chronology of Egypt, the classical age, and the Bible. At this stage, by assembling a corpus of architectural elements such as column capitals he hoped to understand what he perceived as stylistic evolution from ancient Egyptian to Greek forms.

On 16 December 1815, just three months after their departure, they returned to Cairo. Bankes had 'done' Nubia. He had carried out some interesting investigations and completed a formal series of watercolour plans and views of the temples and ancient sites, with descriptions written in an elaborate calligraphic script (pl. 10), along with a clutter of useful notes. He had jotted down an informal travel journal and, alone, roughly paced out the longer measurements for his plans. His obsessions had been gratifyingly well exercised; most other authors could be proved to be inaccurate, and he had formed an opinion on the relationship of ancient Egypt to the culture of ancient Greece and Rome. Fearless and adventurous exploration had resulted in several new discoveries. He need only use common sense and close observation to make certain deductions about the dating of monuments as the layers of construction and the inscriptions could be unravelled to produce a comparative chronology. And all this achieved even before cracking the hieroglyphic 'code' which still concealed the history of Egypt.

CHAPTER FOUR

RUINS, INSCRIPTIONS, AND SEMIRAMIS

SYRIA, GREECE, AND ASIA MINOR

AFTER A VERY BRIEF REST Bankes began his first journey to Syria around 22 December 1815, taking with him Finati and da Costa.[1] Burckhardt was among a crowd of friends and former servants who saw them off at the great gate of Cairo. On Burckhardt's advice Bankes had now grown a beard and donned the turban: Turkish dress was a disguise which he maintained for more than two years.[2] The first benefit had been to enable him to explore the mosques of Cairo.

Thus began nearly three years of almost constant travel in Syria and around the eastern Mediterranean with little rest; a journey as arduous and dangerous as his Nubian travels, and equally occupied with scholarly discoveries and recording. He took advice from John Barker, the British consul at Aleppo, and more importantly Burckhardt, now an intimate friend as well as mentor, had supplied him with maps, notes, and lists of sites to visit, as he had done for Nubia. Although Bankes travelled more freely than Burckhardt had done and expense was no problem, attempts to reach the sites were to be hampered by dissension among their Arab guides and escorts.

Bankes's Syrian journeys were made in two parts, with an intermission in Greece, Constantinople and Asia Minor (the Turkish coast). They took him through what are now Israel, Jordan, Syria, and Lebanon. The opportunity to examine the little-known Roman remains and record the many Greek inscriptions in the Decapolis and the Hauran regions attracted him to visit and revisit those areas.

As usual we must have recourse to his companions to piece together his journeys but in Syria there was no lack of these – although, unfortunately for Bankes, they were all all eager to publish their accounts. Until recently Bankes's own achievements in Syria remained unknown, and his papers on Greece and Asia Minor still await study. As a Near-East specialist has put it, his portfolio 'confirms the position of William John Bankes as one of the great oriental travellers of the nineteenth century'.[3]

⤷◉◐

Bankes set out for Jerusalem on camels provided by the Pasha, who also sent the son of the Sheikh of el-Arish for their safe conduct. Two impoverished young Hanoverians, 'who had scrambled their way to Cairo' purely through restlessness and curiosity, attached themselves to the party. The other members, including Bankes, obligingly dismounted to allow them the occasional ride. To their amusement, one, a cabinet-maker by profession, would remove his stockings to wade across the frequent water inlets running parallel to the Nile, while the other, a veterinary surgeon, climbed up on his back to be carried across. The first night out they all slept in the open street on buffalo-hides which had been spread on the ground to dry before tanning; the following night they were housed by the local sheikh. The travellers shortly found themselves in the desert and glad of their tent and fires. Reaching the seashore, they stopped to examine the long mound and ruined fort of Pelusium at the eastern mouth of the Nile Delta, walking barefoot across the mudflats. A small European gun-carriage lay stranded there; a nostalgic remnant of Napoleon's expedition. In a small reed hut lay a sick young man who pleaded with them for medicines to relieve a wound received as a result of circumcision. Bankes was less suspicious of his story than the others, having heard that adult circumcision was sometimes practised.

The camels picked their way across a snowy desert of salt as they rode along the coastline. At el-Arish Bankes discovered a monolithic Egyptian granite shrine being used as a drinking trough. He later attempted to have it sent home to England but it proved too difficult to move. While they were being lavishly entertained by the local sheikh with lamb, rice, and butter, the young Germans, their European hats having already endangered the party by attracting the attentions of a hostile tribe of Arabs, disgraced themselves by becoming very drunk on a case of spirits which Bankes had with him. A cellar was not an unusual addition to the baggage of travelling gentlemen in Egypt, but from then on Bankes travelled without one.

At Gaza, alerted to their imminent arrival by Lady Hester Stanhope, the governor was at their service. Lady Hester, having heard that Bankes was heading for Syria, had invited him to stay with her there. Unlike guests such as James Silk Buckingham who were most entertaining but *knew* no one, Bankes, who moved in the highest circles, could provide her with news of friends at home. According to Dr Charles Meryon they were already well acquainted. Lady Hester was the niece of the Prime Minister William Pitt, a close friend of Henry Bankes, and from 1803 until 1806 acted as his hostess in Pitt's London home. When her beloved Sir John Moore died at Coruña in 1808, and having only a small pension from her uncle, she moved abroad with her physician Meryon and Miss Williams her maid for company. Intending to travel and then return to Europe, she soon fell in love with Syria and the Arab way of life, and settled into a convent building at Mar Elias on Mount Lebanon. As the years passed she grew increasingly influential in the area, but more eccentric. She became known to visiting travellers as Queen Zenobia, 'a heroine who marches at the head of Arab tribes through the Syrian desert', reigning over what Meryon described as 'her ladyship's somewhat visionary empire in the East'.

Ten days after Bankes's departure from Cairo they reached Jaffa, passing by the ancient ruins of Ascalon, where the previous year Lady Hester had hazarded her sole attempt at excavation. Although she was quite uninterested in ruins or antiquities, an Italian letter had come into her hands with instructions for finding hidden treasure, supposed to be a buried hoard of money. The experience proved both costly and pointless, adding debts to her already rather shaky financial affairs. The only treasure discovered was in the form of ancient remains. They unearthed foundations, terracotta sherds, and a magnificent six-foot antique statue clad in tunic and armour which Lady Hester, to Meryon's horror, promptly ordered to be broken into a thousand pieces lest the Porte (the Ottoman court in Constantinople), imagine that she too, like other European travellers, was hunting for antiquities. Bankes, in contrast, was fascinated by the deep rose-coloured stone of the column remains at the site, wondering where they, and pieces of similar stone found as far inland as Palmyra, might have been quarried.

At Jaffa resided the improbably dressed consul Damiani, the butt of many travellers' derision in his grotesque combination of 'powdered hair and a gold-laced cocked hat, with the flowing oriental habit'. Charles Irby and James Mangles describe him as an ill-kempt man of sixty with an old, greasy, cocked hat, and a week's growth of beard. The flea-ridden consular building was so full of rat-holes that Finati was unable to find a secure footing for the bedstead and was forced to place Bankes's mattress on the floor. He reports that Bankes complained that 'the delivery of the consul's son's wife, which happened that night in the room underneath, might just as well have taken place in his apartment'.[4] Despite the amusingly anecdotal tone of Finati's narrative, Bankes was stopping to examine with care every ancient ruin and early church on their route, and encountering considerable Arab hostility in so doing.

In Jerusalem they lodged in the Roman Catholic convent. After further scrapes, including disappearing for a night and finding themselves locked out of the city gate, the Hanoverians unwillingly departed; Bankes, probably with some relief, had paid for mules to take them on to Acre.

After viewing all the well-known sights of Jerusalem, Bankes determined on visiting Bethlehem to observe the Greek Christmas ceremonies. In the crowded underground sanctuary they were jostled by the unruly throng of pilgrims, witnessed the sparse fasting meal of olives and snails, and on the morning of 17 January 1816 attended a mass baptism in the river Jordan. After taking a Bedouin escort for an excursion of two uneasy nights around the lawless area of ancient Jericho, they were glad to return to the comparative safety of Bethlehem. Here Bankes was to do a good deed for which he was to be amply rewarded. He arranged for the son of one of his Bedouin guides to be released from prison, and in return arrangements were made for a safe-conduct to cross the Jordan and, after four days' further journey, to visit the magnificent ruins of Jerash (ancient Gerasa). These elegant remains exceeded their expectations, and were duly recorded in drawings and plans (pl. 74). Because of local hostility, a second visit to Jerash was won only by the sacrifice of a scarlet pair of boots to their reluctant guide, before they moved on to the site of Oomkais (ancient Gadara).

Only at this point in his narrative does Finati reveal that they had not been alone from Jerusalem to Jerash. 'This is the journey in which Mr Buckingham was in our company, bearing, however, no part in it either with his purse or with his pencil: yet this did not prevent all that inconvenience which resulted from it afterwards, both to myself and to my master, who had certainly every reason to have looked for a very different return.'[5] This 'inconvenience' was to be a dramatic libel trial in 1826.

Finati fails to add the details surrounding this momentous encounter for both men. They had met up at Jerusalem, where they had shared a room in the convent. Bankes had shown him his portfolio, already some two hundred drawings made in Egypt, Nubia, and Syria, and they had agreed to travel to Jerash together.

James Silk Buckingham (pl. 75) was born and would die in the same year as Bankes. Both were stubborn and reluctant to give way, both were convivial in society, both became Members of Parliament, but their backgrounds were very different and shaped their personalities. Bankes had the idleness, impatience, and arrogance that came with social position and financial security. Buckingham, needing to establish himself by his own wits, was a hyperactive opportunist and adventurer. He was *en route* for Bombay on behalf of the trading house of Lee and Briggs, and carried a trading treaty from the Pasha of Egypt. But instead of proceeding directly to India he was said to be using their funds to travel about Syria and collecting material for a book. An anecdote recounted by Buckingham shows how the differences in their status and their respective mode of travel must have rankled. Soaked in a downpour on their ill-fated visit to Jerash, the two bedraggled travellers, Bankes dressed as a Turkish soldier, Buckingham as a Syrian Arab, returned to their inn. But while Buckingham stripped off and huddled shivering between two straw mats, Bankes's servant provided his master with dry clothes and hung his fine-quality calico shirt and drawers to dry off by the fire, thereby raising the suspicion of the natives as to his true identity and endangering both their lives.

Jerash, the site at the heart of their dispute, was a particularly important one for Bankes, who was anxious to identify its ancient name, and he was the first traveller to make drawings there, revisiting with Irby and Mangles in the spring of 1818 and again in June of that year. With their help he accumulated more material on this site than on any other in the Decapolis region. He carried with him Burckhardt's copies of some four or five of the inscriptions, which he was able to improve on, and discovered others which were previously unknown. One of these, from Nebi Hud near Jerash, is an important addition to the corpus, giving us a date for the introduction of a new civic official whose name was previously unknown.[6]

Both Burckhardt and the German explorer Ulrich Jasper Seetzen (who visited the area in 1806) had identified Jerash as ancient Gerasa; Bankes would have been aware of their opinions and had no doubt seen Seetzen's 1810 publication.[7] The Decapolis had been a group of ten cities in the eastern half of the Roman Empire, situated, with the exception of Scythopolis (Bankes's 'Bisan'), to the east of the upper Jordan and Lake Tiberias. The cities' association took place soon after Pompey's campaign of 64–63 BC. Subject to the Governor of Syria, they maintained communications with the Mediterranean ports and with Greece. Although the precise nature or date of their league is still not fully understood, it represented a geographical enclave of Hellenistic culture.[8] Having used the Antonine Itinerary as a tool to identify the Roman cities of Nubia, Bankes now looked to the ancient sources which described the Decapolis, in particular to Pliny and to Josephus' *Jewish War*, to try to match the sites to the cities.[9]

And yet at first, despite the resemblance of the names, Jerash seemed too magnificent, too varied and vast, to be identified as the ancient city of Gerasa, which historians such as Pliny and Josephus had not considered particularly important. Bankes had found nothing in the inscriptions at Jerash to declare it Gerasa, and the historians had not offered any clues to its geographical position. Nor did it appear to fit the descriptions of ancient Pella. Irby and Mangles were also, as we shall see, ambivalent about the identification. Nevertheless by 1822, in his review of Buckingham's *Travels*, Bankes had changed his mind and concluded that it was in fact Gerasa.

The portfolio of Jerash contains Bankes's own watercolour views and pencil sketches as well as plans, architectural details and notes. He later added to it several plans and sketches made by Charles Barry in 1819, including a large sheet composed expressly to compare his own plan, the plan published by Buckingham, and 'Mr Barry's plan drawn from the observations and measurements of Messrs. Bankes, Mangles & Irby made in 1818 collated with his own measurements & memorandums taken on the spot in 1819'.[10] These had been painstakingly redrawn to the same scale and pasted up side by side to prove that Buckingham's published plan of the site was none other than Bankes's own, conflated with some fictitious additions. Together with similarly contrasting plans of the theatre and temples (one of the few signs of actual arrangement in the entire portfolio), these were created to be used as evidence for the libel trial.

Bankes eventually recognized 'Oomkais' as Gadara although his original sketches and notes are titled 'Gamala'. He made a fairly accurate plan of the site and drew the landscape. The actual site of Gamala was identified only in 1968. Many of the tombs recorded by Bankes did not survive, and other monuments he described are now known only from later excavations.[11] He attempted to fit the story of the Gadarene swine into the topographical context he had observed and concluded that our translation of the New Testament presented 'a most serious difficulty in saying that they ran violently down steep places & perished in the lake' in that there were no steep places on the side bordering the lake. The original version of the New Testament, he noted, was probably correct 'as it says not a word about steep places'.

Once Bankes had parted company with Buckingham, the next excursion was to 'Bisan' (Scythopolis, now Beth Shan), Tiberias, Caesaria and Acre, and they were vexed by fleas, drought, and the threat of smallpox. Tyre led them to Sidon on 23 February 1816 and to Mar Elias, Lady Hester's lonely residence on the slopes of Mount Lebanon. Here the simple stone convent building surrounding a courtyard had been repaired and furnished for her use, including the installation of a vapour-bath. Bankes was lodged in the house, but the accommodation was quite small and her physician, Meryon, lived in the nearby village. The villagers grew tobacco and cultivated mulberries, figs, and olives. Lady Hester, now aged forty, 'wore the male attire of that country, but very seldom left the house', where Meryon would read to her in the evenings. Inclement weather during his stay kept Bankes within the vicinity, attracted by an underground tomb of the Roman period which had been discovered only by accident two years earlier when a camel's hoof had slipped into it. The funeral chapel was decorated with delightfully painted frescos and inscriptions which he copied in watercolour by candlelight, adding notes and a plan. Nine figures, male and female, were represented bearing platters of funeral meats (pl. 73). Bankes compared the frescos with those of Pompeii and Herculaneum although Lady Hester perversely thought them much inferior. Many similarly painted tombs were later to be discovered in the area. To Meryon's chagrin, Bankes, having seen frescos removed from Pompeii, decided to hack out pieces from the tomb to send back to England. After Bankes's departure Meryon packed the watercolours and papers into a tin case and the frescos into a wooden crate which Bankes, believing that Meryon planned a return to England, asked him to bring back personally. Unfortunately Meryon himself later destroyed part of a figure while trying to detach the plaster, and other figures were later both vandalized and accidentally damaged in an attempt to revive the colours by rubbing them with oil.

Impressed by Meryon's abilities and having heard that he was about to leave her service,

Bankes wrote to Lady Hester in June requesting her permission to invite Meryon to be his secretary during a leisurely return voyage through Italy, since he badly needed an 'amanuensis' to write up his many notes. He enclosed a letter for Meryon but begged Lady Hester to burn both letters and say nothing if she disapproved of the scheme. Bankes's letter to Meryon offered to pay all his expenses but did not mention any salary or remuneration. This was the final straw for Lady Hester, who had already written of Bankes to her lover Michael Bruce: 'He … has been very civil to me but he does not suit me, he bores me, tho' thought vastly agreeable by Europeans & equally unpopular here. After all his talk he is naturally very mean, he wishes to see every thing & wishes it to cost him nothing.'[12] But even Bankes's volubility could have its uses: 'He is a great talker, & just the person I wanted to out talk those, who as he says spread about in England that you left me in a state of delirium. I simply explained the truth'.[13] Since Bankes had a later reputation for monopolizing the entire conversation at a soirée and the lady herself was renowned for forcing her visitors to stand while haranguing them – 'sometimes talking for an hour or more without stopping, and prolonging her remarks until two or three in the morning.'[14] – it seems hardly surprising that they failed to enjoy each other's company. To Buckingham, now in Damascus, she wrote that Bankes had annoyed her by changing his itinerary without warning her (going off to Damascus instead of heading for Baalbec), and that she considered his approach to Meryon both impertinent and parsimonious. (Buckingham was to repeat this accusation of meanness in his libel trial.) She told Meryon he could do whatever he wished but made her feelings clear, telling him she would not keep Bankes's drawings, packing-cases, or baggage under her roof a moment longer. Meryon duly had it all packed on to mules and sent off, together with a letter to Bankes explaining that he was not leaving Lady Hester and so could not accept his proposition. The baggage did not reach Bankes in time for his departure for Cyprus in June and was sent back later.

The Sidon tomb, whose unique form and decoration survives only through Bankes's plan, description, and watercolours, is now totally lost. It was believed that the two frescos he cut out had met the same fate, but the portraits are safely at Kingston Lacy and now recognized as the ones from Sidon. Bankes's work has enabled modern scholars to read and interpret the names of the tributary figures represented and assess the significance of the imagery and decoration of the tomb.[15]

After three weeks spent with Lady Hester, Bankes's party crossed the snow-covered mountain pass to Damascus, stopping to visit the palace of the Prince of the Druses. Buckingham was at Damascus and the two men exchanged information and discussed the possibility of a joint publication. Both of them were to invite Burckhardt to join them in this project. Burckhardt's response to Bankes refused him in the politest terms, citing his obligation to the African Society as an excuse, but privately adding that he had no wish to be associated with Buckingham.

Provided with a military escort and with directions from Burckhardt, Bankes now began a tour of the Hauran province, where the ancient sites and Greek inscriptions attracted his interest, but after five weeks the hard weather forced him to quit the region. Later in his Syrian travels he was able to return, eventually covering virtually every important site in the region and visiting some fifty-eight villages. He managed to copy almost three hundred Greek and Latin inscriptions, many of which have never been seen since. (Some of these can be seen on thirteen of the lithographic stones at Kingston Lacy.) The opportunity to inspect domestic buildings of the Roman period, let alone those still in habitation, was rare, and Bankes left some beautiful as well as scholarly watercolours of the towers, which particularly intrigued him (pl. 72).[16] Where else other than Pompeii, he wrote, would one find Roman houses? Here, many were still inhabited, with doors and roofs intact and horses eating in the same mangers as they had done sixteen hundred years earlier. Much of what he recorded is now lost, making his fine records of the temples, public buildings, and tombs very important. For example the Nymphaeum at Suweida, a public water fountain imprecisely described by other travellers, now has a concrete reality thanks to Bankes's detailed architectural drawings and epigraphy, which date it to the reign of Trajan.[17] His detailed drawings and measured plans of the temple façade at Hebran and the temple of Sleim show that reconstructions suggested a century later were incorrect. Both structures were later severely damaged, and in 1867 many of the blocks of Sleim were incorporated into the local 'House of the Sheikh'.[18]

Bankes moved on to Baalbec, where the vast temples were examined, but to reach Palmyra necessitated a dangerous desert crossing for which escorts and permissions had to be procured from the local powers. Palmyra caused another rift in his relationship with Lady Hester, who was in the habit of using her influence with certain Bedouin sheikhs to procure a safe-passage to the city. She would furnish her guests with letters of introduction which bore her seal. There were two classes of visitor: a single seal denoted an ordinary person, but a double seal requested special treatment for a visitor of high rank and importance. Knowing this, Bankes had opened the letters and, finding a single seal, was so angry and offended that he refused to use the letters of introduction. As a result he was forced to open negotiations with the sheikhs himself. Dealing with them proved costly and complicated, although he did eventually manage to reach the site. Burckhardt informed him later: 'Queen Zenobia, or Semiramis as you like to call her, is dreadfully angry with you for having slighted her advice, & is making very free with your name – almost as free as she did with mine, alleging as ostensible reason your little liberality to Bedouins.'[19]

When his first negotiations for a safe passage to Palmyra broke down, Bankes moved on on 17 May to Aleppo, where he was hospitably received by the British consul, John Barker. (Barker was later to seek Bankes's support for the procurement of Salt's office of consul-general in Egypt when the latter died unexpectedly in 1827.) With new Ottoman Pashas installed at Aleppo and Damascus, further talks with the Bedouin ensued over Palmyra. A payment of 1,200 piastres was demanded, but Bankes prudently also took a Bedouin sheikh hostage against their safe return. They finally reached Palmyra four days later only to be held hostage themselves, imprisoned in one of the temples by the sheikh's brother until a further 200 piastres had been extracted. None of this impeded Bankes's assiduous recording, and his observations included both a 'singular' Hebrew inscription and descriptions of the unusual stone doors on the tombs. On 9 June they returned to Hamah, where Finati had to be concealed for his own safety after wounding a Turkish soldier in a gambling brawl. From Tripoli, Bankes went up to visit the famous cedars of Lebanon at Eden. The magnificent and now fully mature cedars gracing the grounds at Kingston Lacy were grown from seed which he collected up (the result of 'two days plundering for a log and twenty cones') and which was brought back to England and carefully propagated. By 1821 the seedlings were large enough to plant out. With his usual painstaking attention to detail, a letter to his father adds the postscript: 'I hope that my mother will not forget that I have yet 18 Cedars for which proper places to be found, but if not planted this season they should be shifted into larger pots.'[20] In 1827, when the Duke of Wellington came to Kingston Lacy to formally lay the foundations of the obelisk, he also planted two or three of the cedars, and by 1837 Bankes could admire a whole avenue of cedars from the approach to his house.

Avoiding the mountains, where the French traveller Boutin had recently been murdered, they then turned towards Antioch, where Finati and Bankes were to part at the nearby port of Seleucia. Finati sold off the horses, and Bankes and da Costa set sail alone for Cyprus on 26 June 1816.

⚬⚭⚬

Bankes did not intend to return to the Near East. He had received news of the death of his great-uncle and benefactor, Sir William Wynne, and planned to return home, albeit by a leisurely route. 'The intelligence of my poor old Uncle's death … has made it very necessary that I should be expeditious in my journey homewards.'[21] 'Expedition', however, still entailed an itinerary through the islands by Smyrna and the Troad to Constantinople, and then through Greece and the Ionian islands to Italy. He planned to winter there, not revisiting Naples, but 'making my way to Venice & Milan & Bologna then to Florence & perhaps a third time to Rome'.[22]

Without the account of a companion it becomes difficult to trace Bankes's exact movements through the eastern Mediterranean. The evidence however confirms that he did visit 'all Asia Minor, and the islands of the Archipelago and Adriatic, Constantinople and all Greece, with Albania and Roumelia, and even Maina', but in what order and at which dates we do not know.[23] More confusingly, although the place-names of most of the drawings are carefully marked, some terms, such as 'the Morea' and 'Maina', although commonly used by travellers at that time, are no longer in common use today. 'Roumelia' lay adjacent to Macedonia across the river Struma.

Gentlemen-travellers such as Bankes were usually attracted to Greece by its ancient history – modern Greece then being held to be 'no more that the thinly populated province of a semi-barbarous empire, presenting the usual results of Ottoman bigotry and despotism'.[24] Bankes was particularly anxious that the political and economic facts which he had observed under the Ottoman Empire should be brought to the attention of the government at home. Regarding the disastrous cession of Parga (of which he sketched a view), the port of Prévisa in the Ionian sea, to the 'despotism and oppression' of the Turkish government, he asked for his strongly critical views to be made known to Lord Castlereagh.[25] In 1814 the city had accepted British protection but in 1819 England invoked the Russo-Turkish Convention of 1800 under which Parga reverted to Turkey, provided no mosque were built or Muslims settled there. Fearful of Turkish rule, about four thousand inhabitants migrated to the Ionian islands.[26]

As was his practice, Bankes visited but made no attempt to record the best-known sites, but instead sought out anything unusual and undiscovered. 'The Morea' was the medieval name for the Peloponnese, which at that time had been very little explored, leaving the real topography of the interior unknown. 'Maina' was the barren and mountainous highland region which forms a spine along the southern peninsula of the Peloponnese ending at Cape Matapan. It was renowned for the independence of its inhabitants, who had never co-operated with their neighbours. The Turks, unable to subdue them, recognized their principal chieftain as the 'Bey of the Maina', who owed only a nominal allegiance to the Porte. Bankes had conversed with the Bey and obtained information on the population of the area and its political situation. He asked that this information be passed on to Sir Thomas Maitland in the hope of encouraging commerce. While in that area he visited Sparta and Marathonisi.

As to the dates of his visit, there are few clues on either the drawings or notes. A letter of 1 July 1816, written from Aleppo, is addressed to Bankes in Constantinople,[27] and he had arrived there by 20 September 1816,[28] where he was to collect some of his drawings, including those of Palmyra which had been worked up by M. Vincent, an artist.[29] He was in Athens on 23 April 1817, where he gave a ball at the house of the pro-consul.[30] On 14 June he was at 'Sta. Maura' (Leukadia, an island south of Corfu). There are only very fragmentary journal sections on scraps of paper. He noted plants and wildlife and the landscape he passed through, adding occasional comment on the habits of the natives. He endured 'Two dreadful days and nights of storm' in the Aegean to reach 'Amago'[31] … where I am told there are inscriptions & sculpture', and at Delos he found 'mosaic pavements washed by the sea'. A pair of gold earrings in his collection at Old Palace Yard in 1844 was 'dug up at Delos', and he purchased many other items in Greece and on his travels which are not recorded in his journals, such as Greek vases from Delos and Athens. There were four antique medals 'from the East' for which Richard Payne Knight, another connoisseur, had offered him 100 guineas. At Milo (Melos), he drew the theatre. One of the smallest islands of the Cyclades, Polycandro, held many interesting ruins and intriguing inscriptions. At the beautiful bay of Port Rafti, east of Athens, he painted a curious watercolour of the huge headless statue of Oikoumene, thought to have been an ancient light beacon, with a top-hatted young man on her shoulders, presumably to indicate the scale. He drew inscribed stones, classical friezes, 'whimsical pigeon houses', and the collection of ancient helmets owned by Mr Cartwright at Patras, the largest and most important commercial town in the Peloponnese. There are some rough plans of ruins, fine copies of inscriptions and several dramatic and striking views of the perched monasteries.

Bankes had collected various handwritten itineraries as a guide; one suggested that at Thermopolyae he must measure the whole pass as this had never been done. He himself noted down which ancient remains warranted investigation. Among the places he visited were Mount Olympus, Eleusis near Athens, and Tempe, said to be one of the most beautiful valleys in the world, between Larissa and Salonica. He was most fascinated by the 'convents in the air': monasteries perched inaccessibly atop steep rocky heights. He drew the monastery of Megaspelion at Mount Khelmos, later described as the wealthiest monastery in the kingdom, where 'Travellers must bring their own provision, as the convent supplies nothing beyond bread and wine, with olives in Lent, and cheese at other times. A cup of coffee is served on arrival.' Arrangements were more complicated at Meteora, where Bankes sketched the spectacular group of monasteries perched on almost vertical rocks, on detached pinnacles separated by deep chasms. The guide shouted up to attract attention 'while the traveller gazes up in wonder'. A series of vertical ladders which are pulled up at night for security are to be undertaken only by a sailor or one with an exceptionally firm grip and steady hand. 'A monk mounting by one of them looks from below like a large black fly crawling on the face of the precipice.' The alternative was to be winched up in a net in which the traveller is 'gently shaken into a ball, and, except for a strange sensation of absolute helpless-ness, the ascent is not otherwise than agreeable'. He is given a cup of coffee, shown round, leaves a tip, gets back into the net and is 'gently pushed over the precipice'.[32]

In Asia Minor Bankes visited Cnidos and Miletus. At the latter, the theatre (unusually free-standing) and a tomb were the only visible remains of the most powerful maritime and com-mercial city of Ionia. Nearby at Ieronta he found the stately Ionic columns of the temple and the site of the most celebrated oracle of Apollo in Asia. At 'Makri' (Telemessus near Bodrum), one of the most ancient towns of Caria, were rock-hewn houses and tombs. He made a very fine plan of the remains of Halicarnassus (Bodrum) the site of the Mausoleum, one of the seven wonders of the world. He was at Tarsus, and attracted to the Lycian tomb at Kastellorizo on the island of Megista in the Dodecanese, seventy-two miles east of Rhodes. Opposite, on the coast of Turkey, were more Lycian tombs and ancient remains at 'Antiphallos' (Antiphilo). But his most exciting discovery was made at Stratonicea (Eski-hissar), where on the cella wall of the temple he uncovered a long inscription in both Latin and Greek recording an Edict of Diocletian. It consisted of a long list of items from food-stuffs to labourers' wages for which the maximum price was fixed throughout the Roman Empire in AD 303.[33] Bankes had no idea that it had in fact been discovered and recorded (although less entirely or accurately) many years earlier by Sherard, and set about making a very careful and accurate copy, preserving the palaeography. Waddington, the famous nine-teenth-century epigrapher, was to praise Bankes's copy as an almost perfect facsimile. Also unknown to Bankes (until he was informed by William Martin Leake, the eminent scholar-traveller and later a colleague of Bankes in the African Association) was the subsequent dis-covery in the Levant of a fragment of the same Edict which preserved the names and titles of the ruling sovereigns, missing from Bankes's version, thereby enabling it to be dated. Its Italian discoverer, L. Vescovali of Rome, had seen a copy of Bankes's lithographic print, which had been given to the libraries of the British Museum and the University of Cambridge, and proposed to publish (without, it would appear, consulting Bankes).

Despite having made up his mind to return home that autumn, now, on a sudden whim which he said would have surprised him six months earlier, the 'dread of the approach of winter' and the desire to return to Egypt made Bankes decide to make a second journey through Syria, where much remained to be seen.[34]

CHAPTER FIVE

The Traveller who Leaves
Nothing Unexplored

Jerusalem, Petra and the Dead Sea

There were changes in Egypt during Bankes's absence. In March 1816, just two months after Bankes had left Cairo for Jerusalem, Henry Salt arrived to replace Colonel Missett as the British consul-general. At the age of thirty-five Salt was already an established scholar-traveller, having accompanied Lord Valentia on a tour of the East and made the drawings for the plates of Valentia's *Voyages and Travels* (1809). His own adventurous solo diplomatic mission, *Voyage to Abyssinia*, was published in 1814. He arrived accompanied by the twenty-seven-year-old Henry William Beechey, the eldest of fifteen children of the portrait painter Sir William Beechey. It was hoped that a spell abroad 'would be singularly useful as at present he is losing his time in England and hanging a heavy burthen on his Father [a phrase diplomatically edited out by Salt's biographer] – He draws well, & understands both French and Italian.'[1] An unpaid secretary would be useful and pleasant for Salt even though he must foot all the expenses from his meagre salary.

Having left Bankes at Antioch in June 1816, Finati had returned to Egypt and rejoined the army, since the newly arrived Salt, busy with excavations at the pyramids, could find him no work with other travellers. Eventually Salt sent him up to Thebes, ostensibly with supplies, but actually as a janissary providing additional security for his excavations there. Finati took part in Belzoni's Nubian expedition which succeeded in opening the Great Temple of Abu Simbel, and after this he accompanied the travellers Colonel Stratton, Captain Bennett, and Mr Fuller into Nubia. Their return to Thebes coincided with the arrival of Lord Belmore's family. Lord Belmore was travelling in his own yacht with a vast ménage of family and staff which included his wife and young children, nursemaids, and other domestic paraphernalia, all 'anxiously talking of Elephantina'. It was Belmore's family whom Forbin was to meet in Thebes, causing him to abandon his projected exploration of Nubia. The perilous journey was now rendered mundane: 'the illusion vanished; the fascination … had now become commonplace'. Encountering a lady's maid with a rose-coloured spencer and parasol in the dead and deep silence of the venerable ruins of Luxor, he fled.[2]

Bankes now sent for Finati to rejoin him at Acre. Finati travelled with Mrs Belzoni and her young servant James Curtin, arriving at Jaffa on 9 March 1818 only to find that Bankes was again on the move.[3] Having arrived back in Syria in November 1817 and tired of waiting for Finati's arrival, he had taken on another janissary and set off through the Bekaa valley to the source of the Jordan, then travelled around the lakes of Houlie and Tiberias. From

Damascus he had again toured the Hauran, and reached Jerusalem after being obliged to escape Assalt hurriedly and swim the river on horseback in fear of an Arab attack.

Bankes had met up with the two naval captains, Charles Irby and James Mangles, in Aleppo on 25 November 1817. They were all about the same age and, finding the captains agreeable and scholarly (that is to say willing to defer to his opinions and put themselves at his service), he had invited them to travel with him 'as he heard that we were the only travellers he had met that go after his method'.[4] Since Bankes had lost Buckingham's services and the prospect of Meryon's help, the newcomers were immediately of use in assisting him to trace some drawings of the local 'Persian' architecture. In the comfort of the consul's house they discussed travelling plans. Bankes spoke of revisiting Nubia, 'having some idea of penetrating from the second cataract into Abyssinia'. They all wished to visit Baghdad to see the ruins of Babylon but were informed that there was absolutely nothing to be seen there. Irby and Mangles left Aleppo determined to see Palmyra. With Bankes's experiences in mind they bargained hard over the going rate, and after further prevarication but lavish hospitality from their Bedouin guides (camel's hump being among the delicacies served) arrived at Palmyra. This striking plain filled with columns impressed them more by the quantity rather than the quality of its remains. The coarse sculpture and inferior marble did not resemble the fine work to be seen in the plates of Wood and Dawkins's celebrated publication.[5] The captains agreed with Bankes's opinion that Wood and Dawkins's supposed enclosed temples were merely the open courts of private houses which enclosed fountains like the ones at Pompeii. Irby and Mangles are careful to state that the Hebrew inscription 'was a discovery of, and information we received from Mr. Bankes'. Despite the sordid bargaining, Irby and Mangles were impressed with the dignity of the Arabs they met and their code of hospitality, but the comforts of a return to Damascus were welcome, after thirty-eight days camping in freezing conditions. A note informed them that Bankes had left Damascus on 10 January 1818 for his second tour of the Hauran. He had left them some information about the site of ancient Abila and some inscriptions he had found which identified the site (one of the few discoveries for which Bankes received the credit). Their letters constantly defer to Bankes's superior erudition (which contributed to the harmony of their relationship, all being of one mind on the subject). What they thought to be sepulchres near Safed, Bankes, 'who leaves nothing unexplored', declared to be natural caves. Through their comments, which constantly quote Bankes's opinions, we can follow Bankes's 'researches'.

After Bankes's tour of the Hauran they rejoined him at Tiberias on 2 March, and Bankes proposed a joint expedition, following Burckhardt's route, beyond the Jordan and round the Dead Sea to Petra ('Wadi Mousa') and Jerusalem. According to Irby and Mangles, Bankes 'has the merit of being the first person travelling as a European, who ever thought of extending his researches in that direction: and from his profound knowledge of ancient history, as well as his skill in drawing, he was by far the best calculated to go on such an expedition'.[6] Now that Burckhardt was dead, no living European had seen the magnificent rock-cut ruins of Petra, the capital of ancient 'Arabia Petraea'. In addition, Burckhardt had been considerably hampered in making his description of Petra by the fact that he travelled disguised as a Muslim pilgrim and was forced to conceal his note-taking lest he be discovered as an explorer writing a report. As W. M. Leake remarked: 'as a great part of the country visited by Burckhardt has since his time been explored by a gentleman better qualified to illustrate its antiquities by his learning; who travelled under more favourable circumstances, and who was particularly diligent in collecting those most faithful of all geographic evidences, ancient inscriptions, it may be left to Mr. W. Bankes, to illustrate more fully the ancient geography of the Decapolis and adjoining districts, and to remove some of the difficulties arising from the ambiguity of the ancient authorities'.[7]

Before leaving Tiberias, Bankes made a short visit alone to Safed, and then with the captains investigated the nearby Roman baths and measured a fortification which Bankes thought pre-Roman. They moved on to the rich remains of 'Bisan' (Beth Shan), which Bankes correctly identified as Scythopolis, the largest city of the Decapolis. A fine pen-and-ink plan was made of its well-preserved theatre. Bankes was excited to discover oval recesses which he thought were the cells for holding 'sounding vessels', corresponding to those Vitruvius had referred to in discussing theatres. Vitruvius stated that these devices, which were spaced out around the theatre to amplify the sound, were not found in the ancient theatres of Italy. Bankes wrote on the plan: 'I hardly know anything that was more to be desired & less to be expected than the discovery of a theatre in which these appendages may be distinctly traced ... It is a point of high interest to the antiquary and the architect.'[8] There is still debate as to the purpose and function of these cells despite the excavations there since the 1960s, but it is considered today that Vitruvius' explanation was probably correct. The theatre was one of the few monuments visible at the site at that time. Bankes's notes describe what he calls the Acropolis of the city, but he failed to recognize that it was in fact an archaeological *tell*, a huge mound containing the earlier levels of the site.

Local flora, ancient caves, tombs, or Islamic architecture: nothing escaped their scrutiny. Together they made what was Bankes's second visit to Jerash, which was carefully surveyed over several days, the captains measuring and 'Mr Bankes drawing, copying inscriptions &c.'. Even this visit was marred by problems with their Bedouin guides and the theft of Bankes's telescopes by a trusted servant. Irby and Mangles' journal shows that they were still unsure whether to identify Jerash as Pella or Gerasa; therefore we may assume that Bankes, whose opinions they cite, had not yet committed himself on this point.

A payment of 1,000 piastres was paid in advance (very unwisely as Irby and Mangles point out) to the 'Benesuckher' Arabs who were prepared to escort them as far as Kerek, three days north of Petra, where another Christian tribe controlled the area. Unfortunately, after much wrangling with the Arabs, the journey to Petra had to be abandoned. Instead, following Burckhardt's route, they skirted the south end of the Dead Sea and made their way to Jerusalem.

At Jerusalem the spring of 1818 found a large group of British travellers assembled. Finati rejoined Bankes in the company of Irby and Mangles, Lord Belmore, and his 'family and suite', also Mrs Belzoni and James Curtin, her young servant, and Thomas Legh of Lyme Park, an experienced traveller and author of *Narrative of a Journey in Egypt and the Country beyond the Cataracts* (1816). Using Maundrell[9] as their guidebook, Irby and Mangles enthusiastically visited the sites. With Bankes they followed the thousands who made the Easter pilgrimage to the river Jordan. They took the opportunity of experiencing a dip in the unexpectedly unpleasant, greasy salt waters of the Dead Sea: 'those of our party who could not swim [which included Bankes], floated on its surface like corks'. Bankes had tried, but failed, to obtain a *firman* at Constantinople to excavate a vault in the Jerusalem tomb-complex known as the Tombs of the Kings in search of additional chambers and entrances. Undeterred by this refusal, they procured pickaxes and, leaving the city in the evening by separate gates to avoid suspicion, a clandestine digging party consisting of the captains, Bankes, Legh and Captain Corry (Lord Belmore's illegitimate brother) with five servants worked through the night. A large stone was found to be blocking the vault entrance, so the following night they heated it with burning charcoal and then poured on cold vinegar to break it up. Unfortunately they were quickly reported to the authorities, which put an end to their efforts.

One of Bankes's main objects in returning to Syria was to enter Petra. But when in Constantinople, Bankes, although supported by Bartholomew Frere, the British minister, had experienced great difficulty in getting Petra written into the Porte's *firman*. He also hoped to discover the palace of the Jewish prince Hircanus, a fortified temple called Carnaim, and the tomb and town of King Herod. Heading for Petra, a party of eleven persons consisting of Irby and Mangles, Bankes, Legh, and their servants set out on 6 May 1818, dressed as Arabs of the desert, for a three-week tour of the Dead Sea region.[10] They donned 'Bedouin Arab dress of the most ordinary description' and took Eastern names: Legh as 'Osman', Irby as 'Abdallah', and Mangles 'Hassan'. Bankes, who took the name of 'Halleel', added the title 'el Beg' (the prince). Their dress consisted of coarse linen drawers and frock with a broad red girdle and a red, green, and yellow striped silk and cotton headcloth secured with a circlet of brown rope. Over this was worn a woollen cloak. They sent their baggage and valuables on to Acre, keeping only essentials with them, but were well-armed, having six muskets, one blunderbuss, five brace of pistols, and two sabres. Their money was concealed in leather belts under their clothing. They still had no promise of an official safe-conduct, being passed from one authority to another to no effect. Even Bankes's gift of a handsome spyglass to the Governor of Jerusalem had failed to obtain the desired object, but they were resolved to continue. They were a large well-armed party and depended on negotiating with the individual local sheikhs as they passed from camp to camp.

At Hebron they were entertained by the sheikh with a novel drink of warm rice-milk with sugar, taken before small cups of coffee. Bankes was particularly interested in the architecture of the building that housed the tomb of Abraham, but as Christians, apart from Finati (who, as he was to explain at the libel trial, was a Muslim in the Near East but a Christian in Europe), they were forbidden to enter it. There was a Jewish community of one hundred houses in Hebron; they were received by the 'priest', visited the synagogue, and were offered letters of introduction for the journey ahead. Much haggling now ensued with the authorities over arrangements for guides; the first of many such bargains which had to be made before they could reach Petra. In the end the travellers simply gave up, exhausted by the effort and lack of progress, and set off with the aid of their own compass. The journey was arduous but through varied and fascinating terrain. Camping by the Dead Sea, they found the driftwood too impregnated with salt to kindle a fire. That night, unable to bake bread or brew coffee, they drank down a raw mixture of flour and water to stave off hunger, and their sleep was disturbed by the distant barking of dogs. The morning brought them to a sparse farming settlement where they were liberally fed but annoyed by swarms of horseflies. As they travelled, the strangeness of their environment served to take their minds off their discomfort. There were fallen stalactites of rock-salt on their path and many unusual varieties of local flora and fauna, all to be noted. Their track was strewn with beautifully coloured fragments of granite, porphyry, serpentine, basalt, and breccia, which Bankes collected up as specimens. The scenery was impressive, and Bankes sketched the beautiful ravine, shaded and perfumed by abundant and vividly flowering shrubs and trees. When they stopped he drew a view of the Dead Sea. As they ascended the rugged mountain road which ran alongside a steep ravine, Bankes made a further sketch of the distant sea from a high vantage point. At last they emerged into a fertile valley with cornfields, cattle, and purple oleander in full bloom. They were now in sight of the ruined castle of Kerek, territory where they would need to deal with a different group of Arabs.

The local Arabs proved no easier to persuade, but finally, on 14 May, they were able to set off south towards Petra, passing from camp to camp among the warring clans who impeded their progress by putting every difficulty in their way. The cause of the conflict between them was control over a disputed water source at Wadi Mousa itself. As usual the travellers' protestations of having no interest in such matters but wishing only to survey the ancient sites were greeted with incomprehension and disbelief. Having finally talked themselves into being led within sight of Wadi Mousa, they were refused further passage, just as Moses, they recalled, had been prevented from entering the land of Edom in that same region. Tantalizingly, with a spyglass, they could just make out in the distance the ruins of Petra: its 'palace', the theatre, and several tombs. Only after four days of laborious negotiation between the quarrelsome tribes was agreement reached for them to set out. Legh wrote: 'We remounted our horses and rode into a most sombre and terrific pass, varying from eight to fifteen feet in width; the sides of which were formed by completely perpendicular precipices…' Bankes's field-notes, minutely and often illegibly scrawled on scraps of paper, record that they collected up 'some specimens of an opaque milky spar different from that pellucid glittering sort which we found above'. The gloomy winding passage led into Wadi Mousa itself and the outskirts of the vast necropolis of Petra, with its remarkable tombs cut into the rock. Typically, Bankes was not so awed by the sight as to lose his critical and aesthetic judgement in questions of architecture. He felt it to be in bad taste and the assemblage of classical elements unsatisfactory. Irby and Mangles quote his opinion of one structure: 'It has more the air of a fantastical scene in a theatre then an architectural work in stone; and for unmeaning richness and littleness of conception, Mr. Bankes seemed to think, might have been the work of Boromini himself, whose style it exactly resembles, and carries to the extreme. What is observed of this front is applicable, more or less, to every specimen of Roman design at Petra.'[11] He did however admit that certain elements were not just poor imitations of Roman architecture but represented 'a peculiar and indigenous style'. Those structures bearing an unknown script (Nabatean) 'afford an additional presumption that these peculiar mausoleums are indigenous and previous to the Roman conquest'. No telling detail escaped him, from the metal stains denoting former bronze studs for fastening inscriptions, to the rough chiselled surfaces which 'were certainly stuccoed over'. Although a fine description of the architectural detail is to be found in Irby and Mangles (taken from Bankes's notes), Finati's version (no doubt also written by Bankes) is limited to a brief comparison with Egyptian tombs and general impressions of the strange effect 'especially from the strong orange and purple tints of the sandstone itself'.

The natural features of the defile grew more and more imposing until it presented a continuous street of tombs. 'It is impossible to conceive any thing more awful or sublime than such an approach.' The sides were almost perpendicular and up to seven hundred feet high. They overhung the narrow path in which barely two horsemen could ride abreast, almost blotting out the sky and daylight. They were unsurprised to learn that this winding passage through the rock had been the scene of a massacre of pilgrims returning from Mecca the previous year: 'Salvator Rosa never conceived so savage and suitable a quarter for banditti.' Overhead, eagles, hawks, and owls soared and screamed and their passage was often choked with the luxuriant tamarisk, wild figs, and oleander. Not far from its beginning, the pass was spanned by a great arch linking the cliffs, which Bankes surmised to be, if not natural an aqueduct. After nearly two miles confined by the narrow cliffs they suddenly saw ahead that 'Where they are at the highest, a beam of stronger light breaks in at the close of the dark perspective, and opens to view, half seen at first through the tall narrow opening, columns, statues, and cornices, of a light and finished taste, as if fresh from the chisel, without the tints or weather stains of age, and executed in a stone of a pale rose colour, which was warmed at the moment we came in sight of them with the full light of the morning sun [pl. 77] ... We knew not with what to compare this scene; perhaps there is nothing in the world that resembles it.'[12] Before them, framed by savage scenery, stood an almost perfectly preserved great temple, cut from the live rock. Its dome was surmounted by an urn which the Arabs declared to be 'the deposit of a vast treasure', giving the edifice its name: 'Treasure-house of Pharaoh'. Despite attempts by the Arabs to bring the urn down by musket-shot, it had remained beyond reach. Finati tells us that Bankes's ink-and-wash drawing of the façade (pl. 76) was the work of many hours while the others waited patiently in a tuft of oleander. This drawing, the first image to be made of the Khasneh, now synonymous with Petra, was nearly lost when it was stolen from Bankes by his Arab escort and had to be negotiated over before finally being returned. (Pilfering of this kind was not unusual; Bankes was to lose two paint boxes and Mr Legh his bible on this journey.) Further on, yet more tombs filled a second rock passage which led to the theatre 'and here the ruins of the city burst on the view in their full grandeur'. With much labour Bankes endeavoured to copy the unknown characters of a long Nabatean inscription high up on one of the façades. His rough journal noted that he recognised the script: 'the character is (to me at least) unknown but it is the same which is found in such profusion on the rocks of Wady Makuttub in the road to Mt. Sinai & which I copied from a Rock at Coban in Nubia'.[13] Had he published, as he intended, the inscriptions which he so painstakingly and accurately copied but which remained unknown for nearly a century, the study of the Nabatean script and its decipherment might have been brought forward by many years.

A bare two days was all that Sheikh Abu Rashid, the young guide who had led the final part of their journey, would allow them to remain in Petra, fearful of the hostility of the local sheikh and his people. The time was spent in working under great pressure, examining the magnificent structures of the Nabatean city which are described with Bankes's usual precise architectural detail. Plans were hastily measured out and inscriptions searched for and copied, in the hope of discovering some which recorded the names of the tomb-owners. The monuments contained many diverse and unusual architectural elements including niches with pyramids and obelisks evoking ancient Egypt. The effect of the astonishing remains was heightened by natural beauty: the riverside lined with carob, fig, mulberry vine, and pomegranate, and an aloe plant 'bearing a flower of an orange hue, shaded to scarlet'. Some had 'upwards of one hundred blossoms in a bunch'. To Bankes's disappointment the theatre did not contain any remains of its original scenery structures. He always hoped to chance upon one which did, since this would fill a gap in contemporary knowledge.

Bankes concluded that such wealth 'and such a taste for magnificence', coming after the time of the Roman conquest, pointed almost certainly to Petra having been a major trading centre. The realization that such astounding mausoleums belonged to mere private individuals and were due to 'the effect of vanity of some obscure individual in a remote corner of the Roman Empire, has something in it surprising and almost unaccountable'. The extraordinary colouring of what would become known as the 'rose-red city half as old as Time' added to the captivating effect.[14] The rock, which Bankes concisely if less romantically described, 'sometimes presented a deep, sometimes a paler blue and sometimes was occasionally streaked with red, or shaded off to lilac or purple, sometimes a salmon-colour was veined in waved lines and circles, with crimson and even scarlet, so as to resemble exactly the colour of raw meat; in other places there are livid stripes of yellow or bright orange and in some parts all the different colours were ranged side by side in parallel strata; there are portions also with paler tints, and some quite white … It is this wonderful variety of colours … that gives to Petra one of its most characteristic effects.'

That first afternoon they clambered up the steep path of Mount Hor to the highest monument, 'the Tomb of Aaron', strewn with votive offerings. They copied the Hebrew inscription at the tomb but were later disappointed to find that it was not an ancient one. The guardian had not been informed that they were Christians so they were permitted to descend into the vault, barefoot and rather anxious about scorpions (a few days later they noted one four inches long). From the mountain summit the expanse of the surrounding country could be seen, and to the north at some distance appeared the façade of another temple which was too far off to reach.

Bankes had used the time to advantage. In addition to his drawing of the Khasneh and his copy of the long Nabatean inscription (the first drawings of monuments and copies of inscriptions ever made at the site), he had made many significant discoveries deploying his usual methods: careful observation and inspired deduction. A Greek inscription on the back of a tomb provided the proof that Christianity had been established in Petra. He had noted the distinctively delicate style of the pottery, made comparisons between some architectural elements and pre-Islamic architecture, and found the remains of free-standing domestic houses, therefore establishing that not all habitations had been excavated in the rock. In examining the tomb now known as the Turkmaniyya tomb he spotted that the excavation process had been affected by the defective rock, and the lower section, now crumbled away, had been of built masonry. This showed that construction had begun at the top, contrary to usual building practice. Metal stains (now vanished) around the great Nabatean inscription carved directly into the rock pointed to the former presence of actual bronze studs imitating an attached plaque, as he had noted elsewhere at the site.[15]

Their Arab guides had by now become increasingly uneasy and insisted on their departure. A bathe in a hot natural spring relieved the cold on their return journey to Kerek. While the rest of the party explored the Dead Sea, Legh took himself off to hunt antelope and 'have further opportunities of witnessing the manners of the Arabs'. On 2 June the others reached the marshy backwater at the southern extremity of the Dead Sea on a scientific quest. Seetzen had reported finding shells there which proved the sea contained living creatures. The shore was minutely searched but all that could be found were the bodies of locusts, bleached and preserved by the salt, and some snail shells. At the shallow natural pools on the beach the local people were peeling off the solid surface of fine well-bleached salt. The travellers collected up lumps of nitre and sulphur which had been washed down from the cliffs. Around sunset an area of dark shade on the sea created the mirage of an island such as Seetzen had spoken of.

Moving on to 'Beit el Karm', Bankes thought he had found one of the monuments he was seeking: the Temple at Carnaim, mentioned in the Maccabees. Further on he found a number of standing stones which put him in mind of the Druid remains in England. Despite now being in a part of the country supposedly under the hegemony of friendly tribes, Bankes was attacked while examining some ruins in search of inscriptions at 'Oomarasass'. He received several cuts from a sword and his cloak was stolen, but fortunately the injuries were minor and did not dim his delight shortly afterwards at discovering, between Heshbon and Assalt at 'Arrag el Emir', the vast blocks and hanging gardens of what he correctly recognized as the palace of Hircanus, as described by Josephus. There was even a Hebrew inscription to be copied over its doorway. From the vantage points of the heights overlooking the Dead Sea they were also able to take bearings from Jerusalem, Jericho, the 'Frank Mount', and other visible points to complete their survey. They were now following a Roman road marked by milestones which brought them to the great ruins at Amman, the ancient site of Philadelphia. From there they returned to Jerash, where Bankes, now on his third visit, was able to finish measuring the public buildings with the captains' help. Several more inscriptions were discovered in the process. Beyond Jerash the country became picturesque and thickly wooded and the long grass concealed snakes. Camped one night, Legh discovered under the edge of his blanket an adder, which was quickly disposed of with his knife.

As well as inscriptions to copy and the curious phenomena of the Dead Sea to be investigated, the area had yielded much of botanical interest. Various species of plants and trees, some unknown to the travellers, were recorded. Amongst these was a strange pod-bearing tree growing near hot sulphur springs and an unusual type of large-headed wheat. Legh took back to England a sample which was successfully propagated and turned out to be a species called bearded wheat.

At the top of Mount Tabor near Tiberias they came across a place where earlier travellers had left their graffiti. Among these was that of a Mr Wright, first lieutenant of the *Tigre* with Sir Sydney Smith, and one by Sheikh Ibrahim (Burckhardt).

Passing Nazareth, they reached the port of Acre, where the party was to split up. On 12 July Irby and Mangles boarded a brig bound directly for Constantinople, advised by Bankes and Legh that it would be madness to contemplate a tour of Asia Minor in the heat of the season. Legh had already left Acre by land for Palmyra, Baalbec, Damascus, and Aleppo and, unknown to Bankes, to write up their journey for publication. Bankes himself took a few days to relax, walking and riding about Mount Carmel. It had been a satisfying, if uncomfortable, six-week tour, the food often unpleasant and the nuisance of fleas constantly present in their clothing from the infested tents and houses that they stayed in. (Shaking their clothes over a fire in camp at night was followed by the crackle of burning fleas.)

Relaxation not being Bankes's forte, it took only a few days for him to become restless again and he turned north to the Galilee once more, toward Safed, but his horse suddenly turned blind and it became impossible to proceed further. On his return to Acre, no boat was found to be leaving for Egypt, so he and Finati embarked instead for Jaffa. The gardens of Jaffa presented an attractive cornucopia of ripe fruits, but Bankes's over-indulgence in the watermelons and mulberries brought on a violent fever from which he was soon in great danger and often delirious. Finati was so alarmed that he hastened to Jerusalem and returned with a skilled Spanish medical brother from the Latin convent. Bankes's illness lasted for four or five weeks and reduced him to a very weak and debilitated state. The Governor of Jaffa even suspended the customary firing of the fortress gun so as not to disturb him.

Bankes had a secret reason for choosing to convalesce in the convent of Ramah, to which he was conveyed unseen in a covered horse-litter, the doctor having gone on ahead. Finati did not inquire what this might be, 'Mr. Bankes not liking at all to be questioned, and still less when long illness had rendered his temper irritable', although his suspicions had been aroused when the emaciated and reduced Bankes had ordered him to purchase a handsome new Albanian dress in the Jaffa bazaar. As soon as Bankes had recovered, he sent the doctor away and hired two mules to be readied at nightfall, specifying a Turk rather than a Christian conductor. 'After supper he shaved off all his beard, retaining only the hair upon his upper lip, and then calling for the Albanian suit, put it all on, with pistols in his belt, and a scarlet cap upon his head.' The ravages of the illness coupled with the loss of his bushy beard rendered him unrecognizable. Without further explanation from Bankes they rode to Jerusalem, presenting themselves at the military guard-post in the guise of two soldiers intending to enlist. While Finati took coffee with the guards, Bankes pretended to a dreadful toothache, concealing his face in a handkerchief and riding on. It was not until they reached the gate of the city that Bankes revealed his intention to visit the forbidden temple mount. Knowing that their discovery at the mosque would mean death not only for Bankes as a Christian but also for any Muslim who connived at the deceit, Finati was less than happy with Bankes's reasoning that no one there would understand Albanian or expect them to speak either Turkish or Arabic, so that the risk of detection, especially when a change in the government filled the city with strangers, must be very small. In addition, the soldiery seldom frequented the mosques and, at worse, the device of the toothache might be resorted to.

It says much for Bankes, as editor of the narrative, that he makes no attempt to present this episode in a heroic fashion, although he still manages to emerge from the story as cool and fearless. He allows Finati to point out the reality of the situation. If they were caught, Bankes, as a British subject and a man of substance, would undoubtedly be threatened but not touched, while Finati, who could actually have visited the mosque alone as a Muslim whenever he wished, would be made an example of. The whole episode is treated rather as an amusing prank, and Bankes's reputation for courage is debunked by his servant's protestations that true bravery was exemplified by his own loyal support.

While admiring the exterior of the Dome of the Rock they were invited inside to worship and so we also have a description of the interior of the mosque with its huge central mass of rock, and a report of the many different sacred legends surrounding it.[16] Although they had now achieved their object and remained in great danger, Bankes insisted on waiting until the customary certificate of his pilgrimage was prepared for him. It was usual for the deed to be placed on the pilgrim's head but this would have revealed Bankes's full-grown hair under his cap, announcing him as an infidel, so Finati placed both certificates on to his own shaven scalp. Bankes still lingered on the mount in order to enter the El-Aqsa mosque, and managed to complete his exploit by visiting another prohibited place, 'the tomb of David on Mount Sion', not once, but twice. This aspect of his travels provides a very revealing insight into Bankes's character since he assumes an almost foolhardy bravado which seems to invite discovery. One cannot help comparing this episode and its presentation with the reality of Bankes's later flaunting of risk in public places in London.

But now, outside the walls their waiting muleteer had at last realized their deceit and they were in imminent danger of exposure to the authorities. Fortunately they were well armed and made their escape to a desert convent where the muleteer was paid off. By the following day, however, their adventure was common knowledge, it was no longer safe to appear in public, and it became necessary to fly the country.

The truth of the mosque escapade is confirmed in the account of Mrs Belzoni, and also by the Vicomte de Marcellus, who found that the following year a view of the courtyard of the mosque from the Governor's window was all that he was permitted to see since the Mullah was still furious over Bankes's ruse. Marcellus had met Bankes in Constantinople, and later in London he would admire Bankes's portfolio and hear tales of his discoveries and they would laugh together over the affair.[17]

❧

Whatever Bankes's intentions, the descriptions of Syria, like those of Egypt and Nubia, remained unpublished. Perhaps this was because his journal notes, like those of Nubia, remained barely punctuated and almost illegible, and his Syrian discoveries were pre-empted and published almost immediately: Petra by Thomas Legh in 1819, and Jerash by Buckingham in 1821; Irby and Mangles produced their own book in 1823.

When Thomas Legh's previous travelling companion, William MacMichael, had left him in Constantinople to return to England, Legh had embarked for Jaffa in order to continue his travels into Syria alone. At Jerusalem he joined up with Bankes and the captains at his own suggestion. Legh's description of their subsequent tour was not published independently but was incorporated as the last chapter of MacMichael's book *Journey from Moscow to Constantinople in the Years 1817, 1818* (a title giving no indication that it also contained the detailed narrative of a journey to Petra). The book appeared in 1819, even before Bankes had returned to England. Legh did not inform Bankes of any intention to publish, although the book deferentially bows to Bankes's superior ability to describe Petra. Legh claims that his main object is to give the reader 'some insight into the mode of life followed by the wandering tribes of Arabs we fell in with and to relate the adventures of a journey not in the usual route of ordinary travelling'. After a general description of the monuments of Petra he adds: 'I abstain from attempting to enter into a more minute account of the wonders of this extraordinary spot.' Declaring himself conscious of his own inability to do the monuments justice, he was sure that the 'public will soon be favoured with a much more detailed and accurate description of them from the pen of Mr. Bankes, whose zeal, intelligence and unwearied assiduity in copying inscriptions, delineating remains of antiquity, and ascertaining points of curious classical research, cannot be surpassed'. Legh did not in fact write the chapter himself; he had simply provided MacMichael with the information and MacMichael wrote it himself using the first person as if by Legh.[18] Their praise was perhaps of little comfort to Bankes, whose energies were as usual channelled into a fit of choler at his rivals rather than into publishing his own work – thus ensuring that the extraordinary body of work from Petra would remain hidden from the scholarly world for two centuries. An aggrieved letter requesting withdrawal was drafted: 'read with great surprise … I invited you … mine has been a life of study … a man's discoveries are his own' etc. His friend David Baillie, Charles Barry's patron in Egypt, sympathized in Bankes's plight: 'I heard when I was at Constantinople that Mr Legh had advertised his journey around the dead sea; it immediately occurred to me that as you had planned the journey, it was not quite consistent with good taste or that tacit understanding which ought to prevail among gentleman, to anticipate you with so much haste … I knew nothing at that time about your exclusive property in the journal upon which of course depend … reasons against such a publication … But surely in whatever light you may view such a transaction, Mr Legh's work can not possibly interfere with … valuable information of which I presume you to be the sole depository, or contain much more than a summary of names and adventures.'[19] Charles Irby also wrote to deprecate Legh's haste in publishing, but bravely pointed out that most people who had seen the correspondence between Bankes and Legh on the matter did not share Irby's opinion, considering Bankes's letter too strongly worded for a book of little importance and a failing of 'delicatesse' only.[20] As in the case of Buckingham, Bankes's explosive reaction to the publication of a book he had not even seen was viewed by his colleagues and contemporaries as both intemperate and inappropriate. According to Buckingham, Bankes had again accused his companion, this time Legh, of copying his notes.[21]

The Monthly Magazine for 1 July 1819 carried an anonymous early report of Petra (also carried by *The Times*) based on 'brief conversational notices' with 'a recent British traveller' (presumably the author had spoken to one of their party) and states that 'Mr Bankes … intends, we understand, to publish, on his return home, an account of his excursion to Wadi Moosa … with engravings of the drawings he made of the hitherto-undescribed excavated temples there; as well as of the ruins of JERRASCH'. A brief narrative of the journey and discoveries of 'Mr. Bankes and his companions' follows. The magazine had received from 'the same source' a translation of a Bedouin Love song, a note on the inhabitants of Nubia, and some opinions on the monuments of Egypt. No mention is made of MacMichael's book.

This disturbing turn of events was followed by Irby and Mangles's publication in 1823. Their journals, in the form of letters written home to the family, were at first printed up by John Murray for private circulation only, but were eventually fully published and sold, becoming very popular. Recent research has shown that Bankes had collaborated on this work to the extent that the tour from Jerusalem to Madaba, which includes the description of Petra, was variously written, drafted, or dictated by him. The captains did not acknowledge this in their book, but it seems highly unlikely that such a form of collaboration was without Bankes's agreement. The cordial relations between the three men afterwards certainly imply that Bankes was happy with the arrangement, and both Irby and Mangles appeared in Bankes's defence at the 1826 libel trial. Nevertheless, in a letter of 1 May 1820, Irby, while offering his narrative on Abu Simbel to Bankes for 'your publication on Nubia', appears to deny any intention to publish. 'You may have seen Mangles' letters advertised, but it was a mistake of Mr Murray's we believe.'[22] An undated note to John Murray from 'the Miss Irbys' says that their brother 'has given up all idea of publishing as another Gentleman is going to publish upon the same Tour'. Buckingham claims (in *Arab Tribes*), speaking of Bankes's reaction to Legh, that 'A Captain Mangles, also, who was about to publish his travels, had received some accusations or threats from the same quarter'. Léon Laborde – who travelled to Petra with Bankes's former artist Linant de Bellefonds in 1828 and published an illustrated description, *Voyage de l'Arabie Pétrée* (Paris, 1830) – wrote that regrettably neither Irby nor Mangles could draw and, unfortunately for science, Bankes had not wished to give them his own drawings. Laborde comments that such miserable disputes should not enter into such noble matters.[23] Mangles himself wrote to Murray in 1832 in reply to a query on views in Palestine that 'neither Capn. Irby or myself are Draughtsman' and recommended that Murray approach Bankes hoping that Bankes 'will assist you, if he does you will derive great benefit from his valuable store'.

The full extent of the collaboration was only recently realized when Norman N. Lewis, who was cataloguing Bankes's Syrian journals, discovered the two notebooks which Bankes had headed 'Jerusalem round the South End of the Dead Sea to Karrack... and from thence to Shoback & Wadi Mousir – 1818 – taken down by the Honble. CL Irby from my dictation – William John Bankes.' and 'Journal No 2 Wadi Moosa and Dead Sea part dictated to CL Irby & part in my own hand'. By comparing the manuscript with the published text (no easy feat since many parts were field-notes and almost illegible) it was clear that pages 335 to 471 of the published work were Bankes's contribution. With hindsight, the architectural descriptions of the city are typical of Bankes's writing, although his opinions are still carefully inserted in the third person by the 'authors'.

In the same year that Legh's version of events appeared before the public, Bankes was dismayed to learn that his collaboration at Jerash had also been abused. The brief stay at Jerash, covering just five pages of Finati's narrative, stretches to over one hundred pages in Buckingham's account.[24] Buckingham's publication of his travels, which included a description and plan of Jerash, caused Bankes to explode with anger, precipitating events which were to go beyond his control.

Bankes's discovery of the acoustic devices in the theatre of Scythopolis are mentioned in an 1830 *Gentleman's Magazine* review of a new edition of Stuart's *Athens*, in which the Greek theatre at Mycenae is discussed. 'We find that J. W. [*sic*] Bankes, Esq. has discovered at the theatre of Seythopolis in Syria, a very complete example of the eccheia chambers under the seats, with a gallery of communication affording access to each chamber for the purpose of arranging and modulating the vases.'

Even as late as 1830 Bankes was still protesting his firm intention to publish his researches at Jerash and the cities of the Decapolis that year. Bankes desperately needed someone to take down his dictation or copy his notes, but the archive material shows no signs of arrangement with the exception of the inscriptions, which were prepared on lithographic stones. Did Bankes originally plan to publish these separately or were they intended to be the illustrations for a major work?[25] It was finally perhaps purely anger which prompted Bankes, in desperation, to put pen to paper, and to 'publish', but in an unfortunate and anonymous manner. Apart from Finati's account Bankes has almost unintentionally left us two of his

51 Rameses II offers incense to the god Ptah,
while the goddess Neith numbers the king's years
on a palm-frond. A scene from the Great Temple
of Abu Simbel. Painting by Ricci.

52 Rameses II kneels under a sacred tree
and offers incense to the god Amun Ra
at the sacred mountain of Gebel Barkal.
A scene from the Great Temple of Abu
Simbel. Painting by Ricci.

53 ABOVE Rameses II attacks a Syrian fortress. A scene from the great hall of the Great Temple, Abu Simbel. Painting by Ricci.

54 RIGHT The sons of Rameses II in their chariots of war. A scene from the great hall of the Great Temple, Abu Simbel. Painting by Linant.

55 ABOVE A scene showing Nubian captives from the Great Temple of Abu Simbel. Painting by Ricci.

56 LEFT Divine statues in the sanctuary of the Great Temple, Abu Simbel.

Two excursions in the Delta region were made from Damietta, where they stayed with the 'native Vice-Consul for the English'.[25] One was 'by Mansourah to the lake Menzaleh, and the other by Matarieh to San, where the fragments are lying of six great granite obelisks, and a very colossal sphinx of the same material'. (The latter, Bankes adds in a footnote, he believes to have been removed to Paris.) Bankes visited the ruins of San, which Hamilton and others thought to be ancient Tanis, but he considered that the true site was some thirty miles distant '& still retains its old name.[26] I visited it & found it as Strabo has described it, very vast; but without any interesting remains. At San there seems to have been a magnificent granite temple.' He passed up the Nile towards Cairo and went by a canal to further antiquities at 'Timei'[27] and then 'Bahbeit'[28] (which he found ruined but magnificent with very delicate 'sculpture'). Returning to Cairo, at the end of September 1818,[29] he was able to visit the recent discoveries at Giza with Salt. At the pyramids he inspected 'a new passage & chamber & the termination of the well in the largest, two passages & chambers (in one of which is a sarcophagus) in the second, & the forepart of the great Sphynx, which is now again almost buried in the sand'.[30]

At the beginning of October boats were engaged to visit the quarries at Tura, two hours away. The cost of a *cangia* and crew of twelve for Bankes came to 675 piastres monthly, while Salt hired a roomier two-cabined vessel at 900 piastres; both had awnings of palm-branch and matting. Walking to the ancient quarries (all the donkeys were occupied on the Pasha's service), he mused that in building the pyramids the Egyptians 'had not only the glory of creating artificial mountains but one that is uncommon in having visibly reduced the natural ones'.

After an attack of ophthalmia had forced Bankes to take what was probably a sensible rest, preparations were begun for their expedition up the river.[31] Bankes was no doubt comfortably installed with Salt at the Consulate. According to another traveller, 'although its outward appearance was not very promising, we found within airy and pleasant, containing some spacious apartments, and having the advantage of a good garden shaded by lofty palm-trees, and laid out in gravel walks and shrubberies in the English fashion'.[32]

The second Nile journey began in mid-October 1818. Despite Bankes's avowal that 'of all things in the world any thing in the shape of a party in travelling is to me the most disagreeable',[33] the original party consisted of Henry Salt, Beechey, Baron Sack, Linant, and Ricci. Salt wrote: 'As our objects were the same, to examine the antiquities and make sketches of them, nothing could agree better nor prove more agreeable.'[34] The serious task of drawing and recording was enlivened by 'the party consisting only of very *pleasant* and *agreeable* people: Mr. Bankes, a traveller who has much distinguished himself by his researches in Syria; Baron Sack, an old Prussian nobleman, fond of natural history; Mr. Beechey; Mr. Ricci, a young surgeon; Mr. Linant, an artist whom I had engaged to accompany me, and *myself*. Mr. Bankes is one of the most delightful companions I ever met with, high-bred, well informed, and possessing an inexhaustible fund of humour; the Baron Sack full of little anecdotes … of armadilloes, flamingoes, field mice, and monstrous snakes, which he had collected in the course of a long residence at Surinam; withall very credulous, and permitting himself to have a goose's egg foisted upon him for a crocodile's, yet infinitely amusing and *good-humoured*; the third, a traveller [Salt is referring to himself], still fond of gibes and merriment, and now and then when conversation slacked, introducing an *Abyssinian* story to while away the hour;

while the *secondary* planets were content to shine in their respective spheres, and looked up with *all due* deference to the more *brilliant luminaries*. All but the baron, who was chiefly engaged in killing frogs, snakes, beetles, and such like game, were enthusiastically fond of the arts, and really vied with each other who should produce the best sketches; being generally occupied *hard at it*... from nine o'clock in the morning till dark.'[35]

This convivial party was to be joined briefly by Belzoni to supervise the removal of the Philae obelisk at Bankes's request, and from Abu Simbel by John Hyde, encountering various other travellers along the Nile.[36] Finati accompanied the party as dragoman, taking 'some inferior attendants', among whom was numbered d'Athanasi, who is not named in the *Narrative*.

The four boats of their flotilla can be seen in Linant's drawing, moored before Abu Simbel (pl. 61). 'A large canjia with fourteen oars was engaged by the month for Mr. Bankes; a more roomy, but less manageable vessel called a mash, for Mr. Salt; an inferior sort of boat for the baron, and a fourth for riding-asses, milch goats, sheep, fowls, and such conveniences'; the latter was also used for cooking and the servants. Belzoni commented sarcastically on what he considered their luxurious mode of travel: 'for even at table we had not ice to cool ourselves after the hot repast, which was concluded with fruits, and only two sorts of wine'. What irked him were exaggerated accounts of hardship and starvation penned by travellers who had actually been living in style, 'like Sir John Falstaff'. Salt however reported that they were 'living during the whole time on board our boats, in a *frugal* way'. [37]

They progressed slowly up the Nile, examining every known quarry and tomb in Middle Egypt including the tomb of Djehutyhotep at Deir el-Bersha (pl. 13).[38] No doubt their thorough preparations had included an ample provision of ladders and candles[39] so they were able to examine and admire all the details of the *arts et métiers* scenes at Beni Hasan.

Some time was devoted to examining Thebes, where Salt's rival, the French consul and collector of antiquities Bernardino Drovetti, was also installed, the two camps having staked out their territorial rights. Despite some initial qualms the antiquaries, while residing at Thebes, managed to inure themselves to using the wooden fragments of antiquity, such as mummy cases, as seats and tables, shelves, and even fuel (following the practice of the local people). Any remorse was assuaged by the huge quantity of such items which were being brought up from the tombs at that time. One evening Finati and Bankes found three women lifting bull-mummies from a pit behind the Ramesseum. They purchased two of them, then descended into the pit themselves where they searched over stacks of embalmed bodies for papyri, uncovering only one.

For Bankes, copious academic notes now replaced the personal impressions of his early journals. Ricci kept a brief diary: just the date, the work accomplished, the winds, and stray details.[40] Linant also noted dates and places; he and Salt (probably with Sack) were to return separately to Cairo when Salt fell ill.[41] John Hyde's unpublished journal is informative, but he may have made the return journey separately.[42]

Armant, their first stop, was reached within a day of leaving Thebes on 16 November 1818. Their drawings of the temple and some of its more remarkable details are particularly important as it no longer exists. They went on to Esna, where on 19 November they drew some details of that temple and visited the local Bey, crossing the river to make two valuable plans of the Temple of Isis at el-Hilla (destroyed in 1828). At el-Kab they visited two rock-cut temples on the evening of their arrival, 20 November. At daybreak, Ricci visited the enclosure, after which he drew the temple reliefs, but at noon they left to do the more interesting drawings of the tombs. Here another attack of ophthalmia from the wind-blown sand prevented Bankes from working for two days until Ricci's treatment effected a successful cure.

On 22 November 1818 they travelled to Edfu and drew the temple. Becalmed, they revisited it on the 23rd. They finally arrived at Gebel el-Silsila on 25 November to see the rock temple and another small temple. On the river the small boat of Antonio Lebolo, Drovetti's Piedmontese agent, passed them; 'he was hailed but would not stop to speak'. This behaviour epitomized the rivalry and mistrust which had developed between the two camps of consul collectors.[43] Continuing on to Kom Ombo, they visited and drew the temple, and Ricci recorded the reliefs of the *mammisi*, the small temple celebrating the birth of the child-god, which has now vanished, leaving his drawings as the only evidence of the scene. Arriving at Aswan on 29 November at dusk, they paid a visit to the Casheff. The ominous behaviour of Lebolo had prompted Belzoni to set off for Aswan a day ahead of them, accompanied by his assistant Osman,[44] anxious about possible moves to prevent their securing the Philae obelisk, the ownership of which was disputed by the French.

Ricci spent three days working on the island of Elephantine, he and Linant recording the temples, which were destroyed soon after (pls 17 and 18).[45] The evening before they left, Bankes went off to visit a granite column some two hours away which carried a Latin inscription.

The lack of wind prevented them passing through the First Cataract area and they remained stranded a league from Aswan. The following day they succeeded, with local assistance, in getting three of the boats through fairly easily, each taking an hour and a half. The last boat was badly damaged against the granite rocks.

A prodigious output of 128 drawings was to be made at Philae (pl. 19), where they remained nine days, having put off their departure for a day because of the visit of four Englishmen: David Baillie, his artist Charles Barry, and the travellers Godfrey and Wyse. Ricci, who seems always to have been put to work the moment they arrived, was kept busy recording the vast temple. Bankes had begun excavations there, 'employing many hands in clearing the ground, both within and without the ruins, and in destroying the great masses of crude brick-work which had been built up against them. The laying-open of the pavement in one of the chambers of the principal temple discovered the secret entrance to some others, that were quite unknown before, but they are without ornament, and nothing was found in them.'[46] Belzoni, an expert in these matters, was now to remove what 'want of proper tackle' had prevented Bankes taking away in 1815: the obelisk and its pedestal. After some arguments with the local people over their rights to the obelisk, there followed the difficulty of its physical removal. Unfortunately the obelisk proved too heavy for the pier which Belzoni had built in order to load it on to its boat, and the result was that 'the pier, with the obelisk, and some of the men, took a slow movement, and majestically descended into the river [pl. 20]'.[47] Belzoni took the blame for this on himself, or rather on his having entrusted the building of the pier to others. He noted that Bankes, who was not present at this event, 'said that such things would happen sometimes; but I saw he was not in a careful humour himself'. As Finati put it, more bluntly, 'Mr Bankes said little, but was evidently disgusted by the accident'.[48] Fortunately it was eventually refloated and began its long journey back to Kingston Lacy. Meanwhile an accident during its removal left the pedestal grounded in the middle of the cataract, where it lay stranded until its removal four years later.

The architect and traveller Jean-Nicolas Huyot, wrote to the French consul Drovetti from Aswan on 13 December 1818 with the painful news of this British *fait accompli*. The obelisk, which Drovetti considered as his own, was already on the *cangia* and would leave the island the next day (although argument would continue over its ownership even after its removal).[49]

During all this intense activity, Finati, left behind with Belzoni to oversee the passage of the obelisk back through the cataract, took the opportunity of his month's stay at Philae to take a Nubian bride (and perhaps now chiselled his name on a façade of the temple). Belzoni then returned to Thebes, while Finati caught up with Bankes's party at Kalabsha and was promptly sent down to the banker at Esna for money to meet all these expenses, before rejoining them.[50]

Despite Huyot's leanings towards the rival French camp in the obelisk dispute, when he fell ill at Aswan Dr Ricci was sent back from Dabod to treat him. They returned together to Philae on 17 December, the day that, at seven in the morning, the obelisk began its successful three-hour crossing of the cataract. Catching up with the party at Dabod, their flotilla rested overnight before their arrival at Qertassi on 18 December. Huyot was to remain with Bankes's party right up to Abu Simbel, although his presence is, astonishingly, never mentioned in Finati's account, and remained unknown until Ricci's diary was discovered and translated. The obstacle of the First Cataract now behind them, the almost unexplored expanse of Nubia lay ahead.

CHAPTER SEVEN

THE NUBIAN EXPLORER

DABOD TO QUBAN

BANKES AND HIS COMPANIONS, intent on exploring and recording sites which had never before been seen or investigated, were not unaware of the precarious future safety of the ancient monuments, although the full extent of the eventual losses might have astonished them. Temples, often preserved only by having been adapted to Christian worship, had remained intact until their nineteenth-century rediscovery only through a combination of disuse, isolation, and a general lack of interest. From Bankes's first visit in 1815 until the present time probably more ancient remains were to be lost than in the previous centuries. While the rapacious depredations of rival early nineteenth-century European collectors were to strip Egypt of many of its treasures to the ultimate benefit of European museums, there was some justification for considering that leaving objects *in situ* would probably lead to their destruction. It was thus possible to argue that Egypt's ancient culture was being rescued rather than plundered, the modern concept of preserving archaeo-logical contexts being then unknown. In reality, it was unnecessary to offer any rationale, since neither the Turkish administration nor the Arab population were concerned about preventing the European onslaught. The indigenous population were in no position to do so, and from Bankes's account generally seem to have regarded the travellers as slightly mad but a useful source of income. They assumed any excavation to be treasure-hunting. Neither Turks nor Arabs regarded ancient Egypt and its remains as their own cultural heritage, while Europeans such as Bankes brought an entirely different aesthetic to the antiquities, seeking connections with the classical world which formed the roots of their own culture and civilization.

Within their own lifetimes our travellers in Egypt noted the disappearance of entire tem-ples at places such as Elephantine, the continuing collapse of standing elements of architec-ture such as columns, and the general lack of interest, or even active vandalism, of the Turkish administrators. In 1822 Linant could find no trace of the temple at Elephantine. He deplored the damage, which resulted, not from war, but because 'Mehemet Bey' deliberately destroyed the antiquities, hating Europeans, who annoyed him by visiting Aswan.[1]

Between 1810 and 1828 thirteen entire temples were lost and countless objects were removed from their contexts, not only as cultural icons to be admired abroad.[2] Ancient allu-vial mud-brick was recycled as a fertilizer, limestone was burned to produce lime, and, as in ancient times, stone was removed for other building work. Even in later years, it took consid-erable ingenuity and effort for Linant to dissuade Mohammed Ali from dismantling the pyramids in order to use the stones for a river barrage.[3]

In the twentieth century the increasing water damage to the ancient monuments of Lower Nubia, as the Aswan barrage was gradually extended, culminated in the threatened crisis of the erection of the High Dam. The creation of Lake Nasser, between 1960 and 1970, flooded the area between the First and Second Cataracts. Many of the Nubian monuments were submerged and destroyed although a major international effort was made to record the doomed area through studies and surveys. In extraordinary feats of engineering accomplished through international co-operation, many of the colossal stone temples, such as Abu Simbel and Philae, were cut up, dismantled, then reconstructed and relocated to safe positions above water level. In this great UNESCO-directed salvage operation, other monuments were transported to far-flung museums around the world in recompense for various countries' help. Both solutions displaced them from their original environment.

Even today, sites such as Qasr Ibrim are still threatened by the rising levels of the lake, and other sites in Egypt and Nubia are endangered by environmental changes, increasing industrialization, population growth, and the intensification of agriculture. The indigenous people of the Lower Nubian area, whose ancestors' cultural customs and everyday lives in the villages and towns along the Nile were chronicled by the early travellers, were also displaced by the new lake and forced to leave their ancient homelands. Bankes's portfolio provides modern archaeologists with otherwise irretrievably lost information on Egyptian and Nubian monuments, now damaged, moved, or entirely destroyed.

Since neither Bankes's own journals nor Finati's narrative provide an entirely coherent account of their journey, and it is evident that work was accomplished on both the outward and return voyage, it will be simpler to follow their progress site by site as they moved south through Nubia.

DABOD

The young Charles Barry, future architect of the Houses of Parliament, travelling artist to David Baillie, found Bankes's party busily engaged at the temple of Dabod (pls 23 and 24) when the two parties met up on 17 December 1818.[4] About twelve miles south of Philae, the temple lay in a traditional frontier zone: in Pharaonic times between Egypt and Nubia, later between Ptolemaic Egypt and the Nubian kingdom of Meroe.

The temple, Ptolemaic with Roman additions, was begun in the third century BC by the Meroitic king Adikhalamani,[5] a contemporary of Ptolemy IV. Adikhalamani, who is known only from this temple and a stela from Philae, constructed and decorated a chapel in which he is shown making offerings to twenty-four Egyptian deities. The whole temple is decorated in the traditional Egyptian style and was embellished by other Ptolemaic kings who inscribed a pylon and two naoi (shrines), and later by the emperors Augustus and Tiberius. The original chapel was incorporated into a smaller version of the characteristic Ptolemaic temple design like that at Dendera; a rectangular block with access to the roof and a façade with screen walls interspersed with columns. It was dedicated to Isis, Amun of Dabod was also venerated, and the temple was part of a ritual processional pilgrimage route which included the temple of Philae. Blocks inscribed for Sety II probably indicate the presence of an earlier construction, but the temple was apparently abandoned in Christian times.

In 1737 the Danish traveller Frederick Norden was unable to leave his boat for fear of the local inhabitants, and the Napoleonic expedition reached no further south than Philae, so there may have been no further visitors to the site until Burckhardt in 1813.

What Bankes found was a terrace platform (the ancient quay) and a causeway leading to three pylons, forming a sacred way from the Nile to the portico of the temple. The portico led to the chapel, a small vestibule, and the sanctuary, and the central section was flanked by side rooms, one to the left containing a staircase to the roof.

The symmetry was broken by the addition of a small chapel, or *mammisi*, at the south, which Bankes recognized as an undecorated subsequent addition while the chapel was the earliest structure. He spotted the sockets for the hinges of the portico doors and noted the weak brick foundations, deciding that what looked like an enclosure wall was actually the side of a great platform. Nearby tombs were planned, a necropolis with anthropoid coffins of red pottery and some quarries discovered, and ruins on two nearby islands examined and drawn.

The thirty-four drawings of Dabod offer a good example of Bankes's comprehensive approach to the recording of a site. Every possible aspect is covered: reliefs, inscriptions, objects, views, measured architectural plans (including the roof of the temple), individual details of architecture and decoration, relationships of individual structures, and secondary inscriptions. He copied a solar quadrant or gnomon drawn on a wall, described the temple, and sketched the fragmentary front part of a foot-high seated sandstone lion which was brought to him.

Beechey's record of the portico (pl. 21) is particularly important since it was entirely destroyed by 1868. Although there are other records of the architectural structure and parts of the inscriptions, his careful drawing constitutes a unique record of the complete decoration and hieroglyphic inscriptions of an entire missing wall.

The various stages of the monument's construction were detected by Bankes's observing where reliefs lay over the stone joints and elsewhere doors cut through reliefs; he differentiated between what was unfinished and what destroyed. He also deduced from the name of the island opposite, 'Barambroum', that Dabod was the ancient 'Parembole'.[6]

Travellers in the nineteenth century observed that the temple had remained unfinished and that up until 1827 it contained two shrines in its sanctuary, repositories for the image of the god. Following Bankes, a series of travellers documented the gradual disintegration of its fabric and its pylons.[7] In early photographs of the temple in 1843–44[8] and 1849–51[9] the portico columns still remained, although by 1868, according to the Baedeker guidebook, the portico had fallen. Beato's 1875 photograph and Borchardt's record of 1896 show the three pylons still standing, but by 1906–08 the third pylon was almost entirely robbed of its stone, and reconstruction was necessary. Much of what Roeder recorded in his fundamental 1911 study was destroyed by the prolonged submergence of the temple for up to ten months of the year as a consequence of the raising of the barrage at Aswan.[10] The colours were gradually eroded and the fabric crumbled.

Bankes's portfolio also solves the mystery surrounding the two shrines originally in the sanctuary. Some time between 1821 and 1827 the larger shrine disappeared and the smaller one now occupies the centre of the sanctuary in the reconstructed temple in Madrid. Roeder made extensive inquiries as to the identity of the Ptolemaic ruler who dedicated the missing shrine and where it went. One drawing (pl. 22) provides, apparently for the first time, a complete illustration of the lost shrine which includes its full hieroglyphic inscription, including the cartouches of Ptolemy VIII, Euergetes Tryphon. Roeder had attributed the missing shrine to Ptolemy IX and Cleopatra because he thought it was the same shrine which lay shattered at Gamli, some fourteen miles south of Dabod and on the opposite bank of the river, although he remained bemused as to why or how it got there. The portfolio provides the explanation that these fragments are not from Dabod but belong to the shrine of the ruined temple at Gamli.

Rescue came in 1960 through Spanish participation in the UNESCO project. Requiring much new stonework, the reconstruction of the remains in Madrid was based on other nineteenth-century records. Bankes's portfolio had been forgotten, despite containing a unique record of this monument, its decoration, and its texts.[11] The surviving inscriptions were revised in a 1960 study.[12]

The fact that the portfolio has been entirely ignored in the modern record is of potentially great importance, and the drawings contribute to a fuller understanding of Dabod Temple, now displaced and much depleted, a shadow of its former glory.

QERTASSI

After stopping briefly at Wadi Hedid, where Bankes painted the only surviving standing column of a small temple (pl. 27), they moved further south to Qertassi. The ravishingly delicate little temple of Qertassi (pl. 25) is a single-chamber peripteral kiosk similar to that at Philae, placed on an elevated position, overlooking the Nile. The site held no antiquities earlier than Ptolemaic and the place probably had no importance until the quarries, which supplied the stone for Philae, began to be worked. There had been a Roman garrison and the area had been inhabited by Greek quarrymen. One quarry contained a cultic area including votive stelae. In the rock face were some fifty *ex-voto* Greek inscriptions, various small carved figures and objects, two portrait busts in semi-circular recesses, and a niche shrine in the form of an Egyptian doorway (one shrine still retained deep yellow paint).[13] Bankes was in his element copying all the Greek inscriptions.

The massive enclosure on the river about one mile south of the temple was described by Bankes, although at first he failed to recognize it as a fortress. His detailed plan remains a unique record (pl. 26).

Because of its high position the temple was protected from the flood water of the earlier barrages. It was saved from the higher waters of Lake Nasser by the UNESCO project in 1960 and re-erected near the temples of Kalabsha and Beit el-Wali on a rocky height overlooking the High Dam where it remains, elegantly poised, still looking much as Bankes's party pictured it.

TAFA

Now about nineteen miles above Aswan, Bankes and his party reached the remains of Tafa, which occupied a strategic position at the mouth of the pass of a cataract, one of the areas of the river where granite outcrops make navigation difficult and sometimes impossible. The ruins were dotted around the one-mile-wide bay and in the hills set back from the river. On the east bank was the Roman fort of Contra Taphis, and on the west bank Taphis. Bankes was familiar with both sites from the Itinerary of Antoninus, which gives their distance from Talmis (Kalabsha). No remains predated the Roman occupation, and the buildings were later used for monasteries and churches.

The ruins consisted of two temples, one having almost entirely disappeared by 1906–07 (pl. 29), and several houses built of large stone blocks, with Egyptian-style doorways carved with the winged sun disk and rearing heads of the cobra goddess, Wadjyt, known as *uraei*. Near the river the undecorated North Temple held a single chamber, its roof supported by six columns with floral capitals. The South Temple, which was still standing in 1870, was on the south-west of the bay. It was later destroyed and its stones were reused in the village houses. The detailed plans and fine views capture a number of details otherwise unrecorded, including the vanished structures once abutting the North Temple.

Bankes illustrated some of the strangely fashioned fragments he discovered (pl. 28). His 1815 plan and description are also important evidence for the position of the doors in the North Temple. Seven pages of his notebook hold plans, architectural details, and inscriptions from Tafa (which he referred to variously as Taefa, Tayfa, Teyfa, Teffa, and Taffa; there being no common spellings for the place-names encountered by travellers).

Any sighting of a ruin merited a stop and an inspection. Just above Tafa they landed at two islands, noting on the northern one ruins of crude brick and two fragments of sandstone architrave. A plant similar to a geranium grew there and 'some sort of melon growing (I believe) wild', while 'Durkhan' was being sown (the cereal Penicillaria, known as *dukhn*). On the second island Bankes found 'another brick ruin over fragments of a lintel with snakes and one architrave as at Tafa – neither in their places'. Landing on the west bank opposite, they made out coarse hieroglyphs scattered over the surface of the granite rocks. A pottery sarcophagus and many Roman coins were brought for his inspection, and he purchased a copper stamp.

Tafa had been visited and described by many travellers from Norden onwards but by 1906–07 the bay was already suffering flooding as a result of the Aswan barrage, and the ruins were deteriorating.[14] The North Temple met a remarkable fate as it was struck by a ship and collapsed inwards.[15] It was dismantled and saved in the UNESCO rescue project in 1960 and eventually donated to the Netherlands, where it now graces the specially constructed forecourt of the Rijksmuseum van Oudheden, Leiden.

With the South Temple destroyed, the North Temple dismantled and moved, and the site itself lost under Lake Nasser, Bankes's detailed record of this site, with plans, orientations, and distances, is especially valuable.

KALABSHA

The massive temple of Kalabsha (the largest in Lower Nubia after Philae) came into view on the west bank of the Nile about thirty-four miles south of Aswan.[16] Bankes noted that it resembled Edfu in plan, 'tho probably much later', and correctly identified the site as the Roman Talmis. Nearby, further up the hillside, was the earlier Ramesside rock-cut temple of Beit el-Wali. Between them were the remains of the ancient town, largely ignored by the early nineteenth-century travellers as being of less interest than the temples.[17]

The present temple was built under Augustus for the local god Mandulis and augmented under later emperors but records the tradition of earlier kings. Amenhotep II's name appears on reliefs, and Bankes himself drew an inscribed statue of Thutmose III, which he found near the quay, possibly moved from elsewhere by the Romans. This statue was once considered lost, and its existence in the Museo Egizio of Florence was only confirmed through the accuracy of Bankes's drawing.[18]

The Romans abandoned Talmis to the Blemmyes in about AD 300 and it was then conquered by Silko, the Christian king of Nubia, and both Kalabsha and Beit el-Wali were used as Christian churches.

Henry Light, one of the many early nineteenth-century visitors, spotted a row of sphinxes on the paved approach from the quay in May 1814 but they were never seen again. Perhaps briefly exposed by the low waters of May, they remained hidden to winter visitors. Light, who had taken advice on Nubia from Bankes's future litigant, James Silk Buckingham, was interested in possible connections between the ancient cultures of Egypt and India, citing the presence of 'pyramids and hieroglyphics amongst the Mexicans' who also used pictures as their earliest form of writing. He also noticed Christian remains in the temples of Nubia. 'The travels of Mr Bankes and Buckhardt [sic] will, perhaps, prove whether [Light] was right in imagining Christianity might be thus traced to Abyssinia ... the field is still left open for speculation and discovery.'[19]

Bankes copied the many Greek inscriptions, mostly from the second and third centuries AD,[20] and he also noted a Meroitic inscription on a column. The famous inscription of King Silko recording his conquest escaped Bankes's notice on his first journey and was first remarked on and copied by Salt. They considered it certainly post-Diocletian but prior to the conversion of Nubia to Christianity. 'The boastful style of the whole record is very remarkable ... it is evident that it comes from the dictation of a barbarian translated literally into very indifferent Greek.'[21] One inscription was an order for driving pigs out of the temple and it was 'surprising to find that the authority of the military command of Ombos and Elephantine extended up this far above the cataract'. Another inscription dating to Hadrian confirmed his view that 'the style of the temple so evidently betrays the decline of Egyptian architecture'. Bankes observed that much of the temple remained unfinished and undecorated although in part richly decorated and brightly painted; some of the work was 'abominably bad & very unfinished ... It is very remarkable how superior the structure of this temple is to the style and sculpture of it.'[22]

The intense cold of late December did not prevent Bankes's party from beavering away for six days on the forty-two drawings recording Kalabsha temple and the rock-cut temple of Beit el-Wali. Just before their departure their interest was aroused by the capture of a hyena which had entered the village in search of prey. The hyena was an animal little known at close quarters, and Bankes industriously penned a detailed description. Christmas Day came and went unmentioned.

Ricci, capturing now-lost colours and detail, chose to copy the southern walls of the temple because the colours opposite had faded from exposure to sunlight (pl. 30). Bankes admired the blue 'star' ceiling of the inner vestibule and mentioned the unusual use of deep violet: 'which seems to stand in place of black. This might seem natural in Ethiopia but is not found elsewhere.'[23] The possibility of gilding was mentioned by other travellers, including Champollion, who thought the colour violet part of a surface treatment intended to receive gilding,[24] but Bankes did not discover any despite a 'search for gilding on front observed by Mr Baillie'.

Unlike other travellers who unquestioningly assumed that the inner chamber columns were original, Bankes, finding them oddly positioned, realized that they did not support platebands but 'the roofstones themselves & are probably put afterwards, a very ineffective contrivance since each could only support that particular roofstone that rested on it which was in no more danger than the rest'.[25] He was proved correct for, during work on the temple in 1905 and 1907, Gaston Maspero discovered that the Copts had moved the shafts of columns from the rock-cut chapel in order to consolidate the ceilings and that none of these chambers had ever originally possessed columns.[26]

A quay led from the river to the two terraces of the Great Temple which were linked by a causeway: 'in the long terrace Dromos some stones with hieroglyphs on them & figures that do not seem of an early style'.[27] The vast pylon of the temple led into a forecourt, originally colonnaded on three sides (pl. 32). Within the inner enceinte wall of the pylon was a separate building consisting of a hypostyle hall, two vestibules (the outer one with a staircase to the roof), and a sanctuary. The outer enceinte wall held a rock-cut chapel in the south-west corner and a small Ptolemaic chapel in the north-east (now thought to be of Ptolemy v or Ptolemy x).[28] The portfolio provides two additional examples of the Ptolemaic cartouche-name in this chapel, the subject of much academic speculation. The existence of Bankes's copies remained unknown during the debate and during Gauthier's major study of the temple.[29]

The greatest deterioration of the temple fabric had occurred between 1875 and 1907, by which time part of the terrace of the dilapidated structure was flooded in winter as a result of the Aswan barrage. Fallen stones from the roof and walls filled its rooms. Many wall-reliefs had been hammered out and destroyed and others covered over with frescos by the Copts (pl. 9).

Even before the construction of the High Dam, Kalabsha temple was almost submerged for nine months of the year, provoking international action under UNESCO auspices. The temple joined Beit el-Wali and the Qertassi kiosk on a new site near the High Dam.[30] Daumas augmented Gauthier's study in 1956,[31] and the Ptolemaic chapel was also studied in depth.[32]

During the dismantling process between 1961 and 1963, earlier blocks and the ground plan of the Ptolemaic structure were discovered. A smaller chapel with a landing quay, and a portico of imposing dimensions emerged, together with some blocks of the Meroitic king Ergamenes. The rediscovered early Ptolemaic temple was erected on Elephantine island and the portico given to the West Berlin Museum in recompense for the rescue.[33]

The *wabet* (purification chamber) on the temple roof was excluded from Gauthier's study, probably hidden behind the Nubian houses built on the roof in an area which he did not have time to explore. A very fine plan and section of the staircase and *wabet* in the portfolio (pl. 31) is so detailed that Bankes even observed the draining function of the waterspout from the *wabet* chamber.[34]

Daumas considered that the rock-cut chapel in the south-west corner of the great enclosure was the *mammisi*, refuting Gauthier's opinion that a *mammisi* would most likely have stood in front of the pylon. Interestingly, Bankes's plans reveal an apparently hitherto unidentified structure in this very area.

BEIT EL-WALI

Cut into the rock about three hundred yards from Kalabsha was the temple of Beit el-Wali, one of the earliest of the seven temples built by Rameses II in Lower Nubia, each larger than the one before it. The reliefs illustrate his military prowess: defeated foes to the north and south of Egypt bring him rich tribute.

Despite the attraction of the well-preserved historical scenes, the small temple had lost its façade, and was not very accessible to early travellers; the area soon acquired a reputation for inhospitality. The aggressively armed local population demanded payment in return for access.

The rock-cut temple was of irregular and careless structure, consisting of an entrance hall, a transverse columned hall, and a sanctuary.[35] Bankes noted that the side doorways from the columned hall to the entrance hall were introduced secondarily, cutting through the decorative relief scheme (although they still show the early form of Rameses' name).

Roeder's 1938 study[36] suffers from poor-quality monochrome photographic recording for the reliefs and standardized, printed hieroglyphs, but the later epigraphic study of the joint US/Swiss expedition achieved better results with methods not dissimilar to Bankes's.[37] Greener and his artist colleagues manipulated a series of mirrors to reflect sunlight into the dim inner recesses of the temple, their experiences replicating Bankes's working conditions.[38] Despite their covering the entrance with a large black cloth to facilitate the photography, the chill 'devil-driven wind' still whistled into every corner of the temple and shook Greener's drawing board. At midday they warmed their hands on mugs of strong tea, emerging to thaw out in the sun to the noise of the river's waves beating on the rocky shore like a sea.

Greener found the site, like many in Nubia, denuded of objects by the Egyptian antiquities traders.[39] All the remaining colour had been removed from the temple's historical reliefs by Bonomi who, working for Robert Hay in 1826, took the plaster casts which are now in the British Museum. Greener could see the scratches on the temple made by the knives used to cut away the plaster. All twenty-eight of Bankes's drawings are outline only without the interesting painted details shown in the tribute scenes which now appear on the Bonomi casts. However, the casts were repainted in the 1960s and show more colour than the originals had in the early nineteenth century.

To save it from the waters of Lake Nasser the temple was dismantled, cut up, and transferred to the rocky heights overlooking the High Dam between 1962 and 1965.

DENDUR

After being temporarily stored on Elephantine island, the temple of Dendur now stands in the Metropolitan Museum, New York, in recompense for American help with its rescue. Bankes found it about twelve miles south of Kalabsha, close to the river's west bank, abutting the low cliff face and surrounded by the ruins of the ancient town.[40]

The temple was built by the Roman emperor Augustus over an existing shrine and was dedicated to two deified local brothers, Petesi and Pihor (post-Twenty-sixth-Dynasty names).[41] Their titles show that they drowned – a venerated death putting them among the deities shown being worshipped by the pharaoh.[42]

A terrace and monumental pylon led to the main temple (pl. 33) with its successive chambers of the pronaos, the vestibule, and the sanctuary, which concealed a crypt. Bankes had broadly plotted the temple in 1815, and now sought out details: a ceiling decoration of alternating winged vultures and cobras, the north door which, while well cut, was certainly not in the original plan, and remains of paint on the cornice of the pylon.[43] He observed that the terrace could not have been a quay since the river had never reached up to it (this fact, and his view that the damage to the pronaos resulted from its conversion to a church, are agreed by the report of the Centre d'Études et de Documentation sur l'ancienne Égypte (CEDAE)).

Bankes believed the terrace area might have been a burial ground and suspected that the rear rock-cut chapel had been a tomb as there was a row of small tombs nearby, one with a stone mummy case and uninscribed lid. He sketched the pattern on the column bases and drew the sphinxes on the drums. The reliefs were 'not of the best & lightest sort, yet better than Kalapshé [Kalabsha] and possibly earlier'.

The twenty-six drawings hold details of missing reliefs and some interesting architectural information including remains of what he considered the church conversion and a perhaps previously unrecorded structure near the end of the terrace. Several drawings shed light on the exterior part of the mysterious rock-cut chapel behind the temple. Bankes appears to be the only source giving measurements for this external anteroom, which, like the interior chamber, he found uninscribed.

This curious small undecorated chapel, containing a hollowed-out bench, was cut into the cliff behind the rear wall of the sanctuary of the temple. There were traces of a construction in front of it, but whether it had ever been joined to the temple could never be ascertained, even when the foundations of the temple were examined. It is not on the main axis of the temple and may have been the original shrine. Its door had been restored and strengthened when the temple was built.[44] Bankes noted that the built section of this 'grotto' seemed to have been constructed later than the excavated part.[45] On the stela in the sanctuary, Petesi and Pihor are said to be 'entombed in the Holy Hill' so perhaps this was their tomb with the temple as their funerary chapel.[46] When Barsanti restored and consolidated the temple in 1908–09, he only partially rebuilt the chapel's antechamber as many of the stones of its walls were missing. He filled the cracks in the rock-cut chapel which had become the nests of serpents.[47]

The temple was fully published by Blackman in 1911 and, during the UNESCO rescue in October 1962, dismantled and extensively documented by CEDAE using many of the systems and principles practised by Bankes and his artists some 140 years earlier. Many of the CEDAE comments echo those made by Bankes.

GERF HUSEIN

A further journey of about nine miles took them to Gerf Husein, the coarse rock-cut temple of Rameses II, a provincial pastiche of Abu Simbel. Arriving on 30 December 1818, they found a temple already in decay which by 1909 had become filthy, blackened, and infested with bats, its reliefs practically indistinguishable.[48] The grotesque Osiride figures with their shiny blackened surfaces looming out of the darkness of the hall induced feelings of fear and terror rather than awe (pl. 35). No wonder few travellers chose to carve their names there.

The temple was dedicated to Ptah, and the town, which lay opposite on the eastern bank, had apparently ceased to be important by Roman times. It is not known for certain whether the temple was later converted to a church.[49]

The temple had an open court with walls cut from the natural rock (pl. 34). There had been a pylon near the river and from this an avenue of sphinxes led to a flight of steps which mounted the hillside to the gateway of the court. On three sides of this court was a covered colonnade, the columns flanked with colossal statues of Rameses II. A small door-way led from the court into a hall, excavated in the rock, which contained square pillars on either side with colossal Osiride statues of Rameses II. The temple niches portrayed Rameses II between various gods. Beyond the hall, a vestibule led to a sanctuary and four further undecorated chambers. The sanctuary contained a pedestal, probably to support the sacred boat pictured in the wall-reliefs and used for the ritual transport of the image of the deity.

Near the village which Bankes called 'Ghirsi Hassan' lay a small inscribed fragment of sandstone, 'interesting as being the sole morsel of Greek characters that I have met with there'. He examined the remains of a brick-built 'church' (probably a monastery), and 'a very considerable city in ruins' on the opposite bank.[50]

Of the temple approach, he reported '3 pairs of sphynxes not all alike – 1 colossus fully intire ...[51] head & mitre of another, perhaps from the peristyle rolled down – there was cer-tainly a flight of steps but I suspect not a wide one ... a sort of gateway may be seen ... Immense antiquity apparent throughout – the building dropping to pieces from decay even in the very interior rooms ... the surface was never smooth – yet the style of sculpture is not bad except in the colossi & some of these in the interior.' Satisfyingly, 'Mr Legh' was 'quite mistaken about the round part at the ends of the side-chambers'. Nor were the four sanctu-ary figures as described by Strabo, and the temple was too old to be of Serapis as Legh had suggested.

He was amazed that just two wooden dovetail joints within the upper part of one of the interior colossi were sufficient to hold such a huge mass in place. Near the exterior colon-nade he sketched a mutilated statue of Setau, Viceroy of Kush under Rameses II and responsible for the temple construction (now Berlin Museum Number 2283).

Owing to its poor condition (and to perceptions of its poor artistic quality), on the eve of the UNESCO rescue project the temple of Gerf Husein remained the least documented of all the threatened rock-cut temples. The walls could not even be cleaned for fear of losing the remaining colour.

In 1955 the first programme of ground photogrammetry was initiated there, including the recording of the colossi. The finest colossus was probably the work of a court sculptor and served as the prototype for the others to be carved by provincial sculptors. It was removed to safety, but the temple itself could not be moved because of the friable nature of the sand-stone. In 1961, with time pressing, recording and cleaning took place, and with no other alternative available the rescue team resorted to cleaning the temple using the scouring power of the alluvial silt, a successful operation which restored the bright colours. Soon the rising waters of the lake forced the final dismantling of elements of the temple which could be removed. The rest was submerged for ever under the waters.

The sad loss of this temple can be judged from the forty-one sheets of the portfolio, which include some haunting views of the interior. Two of the drawings show the area near the Nile where blocks of stone may represent the ruined portal.

DAKKA

Now poised serenely on high land overlooking the lake, Dakka temple is the result of collaboration between Meroitic kings of Nubia and Ptolemaic kings of Egypt.[52] In 1818 it lay in an open sandy area, probably cultivated land in ancient times, on the west bank close to the Nile, roughly sixty-five miles from Aswan.

Bankes recognized it as Pselchis, the Greek rendering of the Egyptian name *Pa Selk*, 'The Abode of the Scorpion', although the scorpion goddess Serket is not found in the reliefs, and the temple is dedicated to Thoth of Pnubs (pl. 38). Unusually, there were visible remains of the town. At the site the names of earlier kings showed continuity through the Pharaonic period. The central chapel was built by the Meroitic king Ergamenes, a contemporary of Ptolemy II, III, and IV, and the temple was embellished by Ptolemy IV and Ptolemy IX. The temple is full of Greek inscriptions, which Bankes copied, and the sanctuary was built by an unidentified Roman pharaoh.

Bankes read a mutilated inscription on the pylon as referring to the expedition against 'Queen Candace' in the reign of Tiberius, not realizing that Candace was the term used for the Meroitic Queen. Dakka had been the site of a famous battle between the Romans and Meroites in 24 BC. According to Strabo, the Meroites were forced to flee to a nearby island when Nubia was invaded by a Roman army which sacked Napata under the leadership of Petronius.

A rectangular terrace and avenue led to the pylon, where only a few reliefs remained. There had been a construction between the pylon and the temple which consisted of an *enfilade* of four main chambers on a central axis. The pylon encloses chambers and staircases leading to the roof, and there is an internal staircase off the inner court of the temple. Off the chapel of Ergamenes lies a small Roman chapel.

Bankes's party spent 2–7 January 1819 hard at work on the thirty-nine drawings, some showing details of texts and reliefs now destroyed. One shows the doorway breaking through the back of the sanctuary (pl. 36), another a pylon east of the east entrances to the inner court (in question on a plan of 1842), another the enclosure wall. All demonstrate the usual very astute and concise observation of the different stages of temple building. Bankes's own plan marks emplacements for what he thought obelisks and statues (perhaps a sphinx avenue) running to the pylon, and between the small east pylon and the temple.

By 1907 three chambers were in ruins, the enclosure wall destroyed, local cemeteries robbed, Christian frescos damaged, and digging into the foundations had damaged the temple, scattering loose blocks. Before the UNESCO rescue it was mainly flooded, leaving only a short period available to remove stones and investigate the site.

QUBAN

The town and temple of Quban, on the east bank a short distance south of Dakka, had a magnificent and impressive ruined Middle Kingdom fortress, probably built about the time of Senusret III in order to safeguard the caravans which set out from here to the gold mines of the Wadi Allaqi. These gold mining operations continued on into the New Kingdom.

Only half a mile to the south of the fortress were the remains of a small temple. Little remained of this by 1907–08 but it originally comprised a small hall with six columns, a sanctuary, and a courtyard excavated in the rock. Another temple, of Rameses II, lay outside the south-east corner of the fort.

Excavations in the 1930s showed that Quban was 'probably the most complete Middle Kingdom fortress in existence' yet discovered.[53] An earlier fort, which probably dated from the opening of the gold mines by Senusret I, was uncovered below the foundations of the main building. The report said: 'The inscribed material from Kuban was very limited and of little interest. Sufficient evidence remains, however, among the fragments to confirm the theory of the existence of a small Ramesside temple built within the fortress area.'[54] The existence of this temple is now proved by Bankes's very valuable record of it: a drawing of the battle reliefs from the propylon (pl. 45), and a plan and description of both the fortress and pylon, showing the remains of columns.

At Qurta, on the west bank about two miles south of Quban and opposite the large island of Dewar,[55] Linant made a charming watercolour (pl. 39) and three drawings of the little temple of Isis. By 1906–07 this uninscribed Ptolemaic or Roman monument was reduced to a single rectangle, one block high. The ruins were not saved from the lake, but, before they were finally submerged and lost, investigation proved that the temple lay over an earlier New Kingdom temple.

CHAPTER EIGHT

VESTIGES OF ANTIQUITY

WADI ES-SEBUA TO THE SECOND CATARACT

THE LARGE, PART-ROCK-CUT TEMPLE of Wadi es-Sebua, the 'Valley of the Lions', was crudely constructed for an elderly Rameses II and dedicated to Amun Ra, Harmachis, and Ptah. The temple (pl. 42) was approached by royal statues, an avenue of sphinxes, and a pylon, leading to an open court with relief decoration. The court had roofed side galleries running behind five pillars with standing colossi. Cut into the rock behind the court was a vestibule, leading to a transverse antechamber off which were the main sanctuary and four other rooms. At the rear of the sanctuary was a niche holding statues of Rameses II, Amun, and Harmachis.

Bankes found that access to the interior was blocked by wind-driven sand, which had part-buried the temple and seeped through its roof into the chambers. In five days, his team cleared the entrance and internal chambers, revealing very well preserved paintings including 'some of the sacred boats with their colours entire [pl. 43]' which 'had escaped all other travellers'.[1] No earlier visitors had ever penetrated the sanctuary where the Coptic fresco of St Peter was flanked by two earlier painted figures of Rameses II, giving the curious impression that the pharaoh was adoring the saint. Bankes was even more struck by what appeared to be the sudden abandonment of the church with its sacred vessels still in use.

His description is lengthy but barely legible.[2] The pottery-strewn surface nearby indicated the ancient city, and he examined stones inscribed with hieroglyphs and an odd vitrified substance in the back wall of the temple. A mitred sphinx carved on the relief of the inner face of the pylon resembled one from the sphinx avenue whose mitre now lay detached on the sand. The remains of plaster on the stone architraves told him that the stone was of a poor quality. These rock-cut temples led him to believe that the earliest Egyptian architecture began not from wooden constructions but from 'grottoes'. A small pylon recorded as two to three hundred yards south-west by south of the temple 'with 2 lions sitting up before it' fails to appear in other travellers' plans.

On 8 January 1819, after examining the roof, they deemed it impossible to effect entry by attempting to clear the great door since the temple must have filled up with sand, and so: 'after clearing sufficiently to ascertain the proportions of the entrance doorway we proceeded to dig in the centre of the end of the great chamber & with 20 men at work towards evening succeeded in entering – it gave us access to 6 chambers which resemble in their disposition & some details to a certain degree those of Girshe [Gerf Husein] – Derr – & at Ipsambul [Abu Simbel]. The altar standing… statues in end niche have been cut out intirely, from the abhorrence of the Greeks … in the place is St Peter as fresh painted as the 1st days … boats on side walls … raised benches … were not these places of sepulchres? … small pieces of wood & rags on the floor & palm leaves which fell to powder on being moved – many little saucers on the altar for lamps – quite black near St Peter – the wall much discoloured with smoke … There is great appearance that the place was suddenly deserted or perhaps all massacred as I judge from the things found. The lamps were ranged along the seat in the sekos where evidently were originally 3 deities sitting – wicks of these lamps were found – quite sound & intire though every thing wooden was quite reduced to powder. – [the red earthenware chalice eerily remained on the ground hardly broken] – in one of the side chambers a large thick piece of pottery with a cross in relief, the material has much the appearance of being part of a coffin of pottery … but it seems too shallow … charcoal was found with that yellow gum adhering to it which seems to have been used for incense. – the mummy pit was nearly full – we cleared to the bottom – bones were found in it & the upper part of a human skull so that it could easily have served as a burial place but it is not easy to conceive that it was inhabited otherwise than as the entrance to a Catacomb since it is neither big enough nor wide enough to lay a body at full length & (in spite of Mr Legh's account) there is no example of bodies found upright either in Egypt or Nubia.' On his plan he marked the external emplacements of the sphinx removed by Lord Belmore and the sphinx found by Mr Salt – 'there were never more than these two'.

Thirty-six drawings include superb coloured views and reliefs showing minute colour details: a valuable and graphic description of their excavations and discoveries as the first travellers to open, excavate, and record the inner temple. Bankes also astutely noted the resemblance of Sebua to other structures of Rameses II, not merely making a general distinction between the Ptolemaic/Roman and the Pharaonic temple types.

No one fits the bill better than the architect Franz Christian Gau for Finati's derisive description of the 'German artist' who was following often only days behind them and taking advantage of their endeavours, but despite gaining access to the inner chambers which had remained free of sand, Gau's description is full of errors. After 1819 the shifting sands almost immediately returned to render the temple once more inaccessible. Cailliaud made no effort to enter in 1822 merely to satisfy his personal curiosity, convinced that the sagacity and erudition of Salt had left nothing for him to glean.[3] Nor could the excavator Jean-Jacques Rifaud enter, although he stated that Salt and 'Beinks' had succeeded in visiting the interior rooms and seeing the sculptures and paintings with ease.[4] Surprisingly, neither Champollion (who thought the quality of the work poor) nor Rosellini entered the inner rooms of the temple. Familiar with the work of Salt and Bankes but quite unaware of the existence of Bankes's archive, Gauthier lamented in his 1912 study that neither had left any record of their visit, and he remained mystified as to when the temple had been cleared.

His brief two-month recording session revealed monuments to Setau, the Viceroy of Kush, who probably organized the construction, inaugurating the building in regnal year 44 in the absence of Rameses, himself perhaps too old to make the long journey.[5] The temple fabric was in such poor condition that Egyptologists relied heavily on the reports of the nineteenth-century travellers.

The original rescue plan of 1955 was to remove the statues only, but the whole temple was eventually cut out, dismantled, and moved in 1964 to a higher site nearby, near the temples of Dakka and Maharraqa.

On 13 January 1819, between Sebua and Amada, they again spent the day with Baillie's party, now returning from the Second Cataract. Their already substantial pile of drawings was admired. Barry wrote: 'We breakfasted together on the low flat sandy bank. Mr Salt showed me the whole of the sketches that have been made since leaving Philae. They were all in pencil and very numerous. They are the work of himself, Mr Beechey (whom he calls his Secretary) and a French artist named Linant. I looked over Mr Bankes's drawings, which, on account of their great number, he kept in a basket. They principally relate to detail such as hieroglyphs, ornaments etc. and are executed by himself and an Italian doctor in his employ [Ricci]. All the drawings made by Mr Salt and his employee, belong to Mr Bankes.'⁶

Abu Hamdal and Amada

About an hour's journey below Amada Beechey made two drawings of a fortress with twenty-foot walls on the east bank of the Nile at a village called 'Abou Hamdau' (Abu Hamdal). Bankes noted that it had the air of a station. This may be Korosko which was an east-bank caravan station for the journey to the Sudan.

Amada temple (pl. 44), consecrated to Amun Ra and Re Harmachis, was constructed and decorated by three successive kings of the Eighteenth Dynasty, Thutmose III, Amenhotep II, and Thutmose IV, during the finest period of Egyptian art.⁷ Akhenaten's heretical denial of the god Amun removed the name of Amenhotep II, which was restored by Sety I and the Nineteenth-Dynasty pharaohs. The Ramesside restorations were in a crude local style, perhaps by the same team who carved Gerf Husein.

The end wall of the sanctuary holds an important historical text of Amenhotep II mentioning that he had brought back seven captive princes from a war in Asia, six of whom he slew by his own hand in Thebes while the seventh was hanged on the wall of Napata in order to strike terror into the hearts of the Nubian inhabitants. On the entry door are inscribed the name of Rameses II and a stela of his successor Merenptah.

When the temple was converted to a church, with perhaps a brick monastery attached, the Eighteenth-Dynasty reliefs were covered with plaster, helping to preserve them, and a cupola was raised on the roof, remaining there until 1860 or 1870. At some point between the Nineteenth-Dynasty restorations and Christian times, openings cutting through the decoration were made between the two originally separate rooms either side of the sanctuary, giving access from one into the other.

Bankes's plans show that the ruins of the small temple of Sety I at the south-east had nine 'bud' columns, with hieroglyphs on the abaci: 'it seems to be of the highest antiquity & destroyed by the mere action of time'.

They had perhaps worked somewhat anxiously on the seventeen drawings of this well-preserved and well-documented temple, as close to their boats were the imprints of a very large hyena. Bankes delved into the construction of the temple and admired the delicacy of its painting, noting the restoration work: 'in one instance [the painting] has scaled off & the figure has been repainted & formed with a different outline'. Gauthier found no trace of the pylon entrance (later restored) but Bankes recognized that the entrance had been flanked by a pylon: 'tho' such a disposition as attached immediately to the pronaos is without example'. The curiosity of the decoration was that 'all the intaglio painted plain yellow – all the rest is bright colour'. He believed that the repeated cartouches represented the name of the founder with a coat of arms or device as found in Gothic buildings.

In 1965 the temple was moved about two miles to a higher site to preserve it from the waters of the High Dam, its decoration undamaged by earlier water levels. In a spectacular endeavour the entire rear section of the temple was moved in one piece on rails to avoid cutting the walls, whose joints had been plastered over and painted in ancient times. During the reconstruction the ruined front pylon of brick was rebuilt. Finati left another graffito here which dates from his return with Linant: 'G—v— Finati Ferrarese / 1822'.[8]

DERR

Bankes's party covered the seventeen miles or so to the temple of Derr in two hours. Set back from the river, behind the town, it contained two pillared halls, a sanctuary, and two side-chapels, constructed by Rameses II and dedicated to Ra, Harmachis, and Amun Ra.[9] Except for parts of the first hall, all the chambers were cut into the low cliff (pl. 46). With the exception of the sculpture in the first hall, the cut relief was clumsy and coarse, and the pillars and the second hall were all considerably out of true. The position of the Osiride statues, facing the entrance, was unique in Nubian temple design.

In the second hall and the inner rooms, blackened from the infestation of bats, only the outlines were cut; the rest was moulded in plaster with painted details. The Osiride statues and the statues of seated gods had all been deliberately hacked out, and the wind-driven sand had destroyed most of Rameses II's battle scenes in the roofless first hall, and stripped off all the painted plaster. The rock-cut parts followed the natural profile of the hill, and the original builders had added a masonry superstructure, but all the additional stone blocks had been quarried away. The church conversion had been placed across the first hall in order to run east–west, and this no doubt accounted for the partial removal of the Osiride figures.

Bankes made thirty-one drawings and watercolours, and perceptively compared the reliefs to Beit el-Wali and Wadi es-Sebua, other temples of Rameses II. 'The 4 gods at Derr are too much mutilated to be quite certain but believe them the same & in the same order with those at Ipsambol' (Abu Simbel: also Rameses II). He suggested that the small relief figures shown carrying the sacred boat were intended to represent boys; adding 'nor in any instance in Egyptian sculpture is the character of a child otherwise expressed than as a little man'.

By 1907–08 the temple was beset by the dilapidations of faulty rock and neglect. In 1965 it was moved near to the new site of Amada, and studied again.[10]

ELLESIYA

On the return journey, Ricci was to make four numbered drawings (number 3 is missing) of the small rock temple of Ellesiya, on the east bank about half a mile from the Nile between Derr and Qasr Ibrim. Ellesiya is the most ancient rock-cut chapel known from Nubia, constructed by Thutmose III in year 52 of his reign. Behind the temple façade, inscribed by temple officials, lies a transverse chamber with a niche at the end. The reliefs were in the best

Eighteenth-Dynasty style, but by 1907–08, filthy and evil-smelling from bats. The slightly vaulted roof of the chamber had fallen in, and the reliefs, on which no colour remained, could barely be made out.

Following the first raising of the old barrage, the temple was regularly under water for nine months of the year and was not studied and published until the 1960s.[11] After its rescue the temple was reconstructed in 1967 in Turin.

QASR IBRIM

Today the great rock-spur site of Qasr Ibrim, to Bankes's party such a striking landmark, is largely hidden beneath the waters of Lake Nasser. The archaeological investigation of the site by the Egypt Exploration Society still continues, but today's traveller on a Lake Nasser cruise sees only a small island covered with ruins. The site, continually under threat from the rising water of the lake, has yielded a mass of diverse material from different periods, including many texts.

Ibrim, on the east bank, comprised three massive barren headlands of sandstone, rising perpendicular to the river and separated by rocky mountain clefts (pl. 47). The central cliff contained the ruins of a fortified enclosure largely of Roman construction, the Latin 'Primis'. Qasr Ibrim means the fortress or castle of Ibrim, the name of the local village.

The fortress was occupied by the forces of Petronius, the Roman prefect of Egypt under Augustus, in 23–22 BC, but later returned to the possession of the Meroites from whom he had conquered it. The Meroites were themselves ousted by a people known as the X-group, and, on the conversion of Nubia to Christianity, Ibrim became an important religious centre. It was a bishopric, and a large church was built within the fortress at the centre of the hill. The Roman and later history of the site was well documented and was known to Bankes and other early nineteenth-century travellers. The early history of Ibrim is less well documented.

In 1815 Finati had written that 'Ibrim is very unlike most other situations upon the Nile, being perched upon a very bold rock, in the perpendicular face of which are some small painted chambers so difficult of access that our traveller was drawn up into them by a rope round his body [pl. 49]'.[12] Near these inscribed and decorated New Kingdom shrines they sighted a monumental royal stela of Sety I which had been cut into the cliff-face. They were unable to copy it at that time but Bankes had it drawn on his second voyage by Beechey (pl. 48). The area was probably the administrative headquarters of the viceroys of Kush and other officials commemorated in the shrines.[13]

Bankes himself drew some nineteen of the thirty-three drawings and, intrigued by this spectacular place with its monuments almost out of human reach, he uncharacteristically ventured to speculate on how it once appeared. All three very fine and accurate copies of the stela of Sety I were, however, made by Beechey. Bankes attempted some hieroglyphic inscriptions but his watercolours show only schematic versions of the shrine texts. However, the stylistic resemblance between the decoration of one shrine (of Usersatet, Viceroy of Kush under Amenhotep II) and the temple of Amada did not escape him. Other standing monuments visible on 21 January 1819 were the fortress and the pylon of the Egyptian-style temple (probably Roman) 'nobly perched' on the northern peak of the rock.[14] Bankes scoured the buried remains of a village on the opposite bank for clues to an ancient site, and found a granite tablet to the north. Ricci supplied a series of fine watercolours of reliefs which recorded some details lost by the 1960s, and there are fine views by Beechey and Linant.

Caminos' study-expedition of 1961 recorded texts and representations which would be lost under the lake.[15] Almost uniquely among Nubiologists, he was aware of Bankes's copies through Porter and Moss's *Topographical Bibliography of Ancient Egyptian Hieroglyphic Texts, Reliefs, and Paintings* although he did not consult the originals. Caminos considered Bankes 'probably the pioneer of epigraphic work at Ibrim', as earlier travellers had failed to spot or record the shrines or stela. The chapels and many of the rock inscriptions and drawings were cut out and saved by an Egyptian team as part of the UNESCO rescue process.

ABU SIMBEL

The two imposing rock-cut temples of Rameses II at Abu Simbel still inspire the 'awe & astonishment' experienced by Bankes in 1815. The Great Temple was dedicated to Ra-Horakhty and the deified Rameses II, the Small Temple to Hathor and to Rameses II's wife Nefertari. Threatened with imminent submersion under Lake Nasser, they became the focus of the greatest of all the UNESCO salvage operations. After many different schemes had been considered (including underwater viewing platforms), they were cut out of the rock between 1962 and 1968 and reassembled above the new water-level against artificial cliffs.

The small doorway at the centre of the façade, below the striding figure of the hawk-headed Ra-Horakhty facing into the sunrise, leads into the great hall of the temple with its lines of colossal Osiride figures of the king. The hall is decorated with reliefs of his triumphs, including the vast panorama of the Battle of Qadesh. The main axis of the temple leads through a second hall and vestibule to the sanctuary, at the end of which sit the figures of the gods Ptah, Amun, the deified Rameses II, and Ra-Horakhty. Off the halls are eight side-rooms.

The Great Temple (first stumbled upon unexpectedly by Burckhardt in March 1813, sketched by Bankes in 1815, and opened by Belzoni only in 1817) inspired Bankes to excavate one of the colossal figures down to the feet, having speculated in 1815 that the four great seated colossi, of which only the heads were visible under the great sand-drift, might be standing. It took them fourteen days of working with thirty hands to uncover the first figure (pl. 62). Despite Bankes's initial opinion that the sand could easily be carried to the Nile and thrown in, this method proved unworkable, and it was possible to uncover the façade only a section at a time.

'A few letters scratched on the surface of the legs had excited Mr. Bankes's curiosity so much from the antiquity which he was disposed to ascribe to their form, that, judging it likely that those legs which were nearer to the door would be likely to furnish fuller examples, he undertook to pursue the inquiry further; but for this purpose it was necessary so far to undo what had been done, that the sand was rolled down again on much of that lower half which had been uncovered, in order to lay bare what was wanting of the adjoining colossus, since we were too far removed from the Nile to get rid of the mass altogether, without a much greater expenditure of time and labour. Within three or four days accordingly a large and long inscription first began to make its appearance, and to show itself above the surface by degrees, yet it lay so deep and the position was so aukward for opening it, that it was a work both of difficulty and time and contrivance to obtain the last line, which was only at length brought about by consolidating the sand with immense quantities of water poured upon it. The discovery, however, which seemed to delight all concerned in it, was considered to be an ample recompense for the toil. So soon as that had been copied, it became its turn to be covered again, part of the sand running in directly upon becoming dry, and part being rolled down upon it in clearing the fourth colossal head [pl. 57], (which had never before emerged at all above the surface,) for the sake of making a general drawing of the whole: and the exterior was thus left greatly disencumbered for travellers who might come after, the level of the drift having been lowered many feet throughout its whole extent, where it encroaches upon the temple.'[16]

Bankes proudly reported: 'The inscription relates to the King Psammeticus, and is certainly among the very earliest extant in the Greek language.'[17] It was one of the earliest Greek inscriptions that had been found at that time, dating to the seventh century BC, and told him that Greek mercenary soldiers of the Egyptian King Psamtek (whom Bankes called 'Psammeticus'), on a Nubian expedition during the Twenty-sixth Dynasty, had left their graffiti at a level which implied that this ancient temple was already in disuse and partly covered by the drifting sands.

In celebration of these discoveries the thigh of the colossus to the left of the entrance was carved with an inscription recording their joint excavation, for which they shared the expenses (pl. 58). Bankes, uniquely for him, inscribed the leg of the southernmost statue with his own name (pl. 59). They left the temple exposed by several feet more than they had found it, but Bankes, in covering up the inscriptions he had discovered, deliberately or not prevented Gau, who arrived only days after the party had left, from finding the Psamtek inscription, despite having been informed of its position by Huyot.

Their labours were inspected by the 'Defterdar Bey', son-in-law of Mohammed Ali and governor of the upper country, who was positive that so much effort could be exerted only in search of treasure, and remained unconvinced when their true motives were explained to him.

They remained at Abu Simbel from 23 January until 18 February 1819. On 14 February John Hyde arrived at Abu Simbel with his Greek servant and interpreter Kyriaco Porithi, the former dragoman of Lord Belmore. Hyde, a Manchester man, had arrived in Cairo on 16 December 1818 two months after leaving London. He and Porithi had already seen Rifaud at Luxor, encountered Belzoni's boat bringing the Sety I sarcophagus to Europe, met Baillie's party near Edfu, and met Captain Ducane and his companion Curteis at Philae. Arriving in the evening, Hyde formally presented his letters of introduction to Salt, 'from whom I received the most friendly reception – this gentleman introduced me to Mr. B: son of Sir Wm. Beechy [sic], Mr. Bankes, late MP for Truro – Dr. Ricci'. Hyde (and his journal) now joined their party.[18] The two anonymous Frenchmen who, according to Ricci, departed on 8 February, were undoubtedly Huyot and his companion Lachaise.[19] Bankes and Ricci were both more interested to record that at ten o'clock that day two large dead fish floated down the Nile and were caught and eaten by the crew: 'a vulture sitting on one, both stink but eaten by the Nubians with relish – supposed killed in passing the Cataract'.

The interior of the temple had never before been recorded. Once inside, Bankes's party braved the appalling heat by stripping off, and rigged up sufficient light to begin work. 'As for the interior, that, during all the time of our stay, was lighted every day, and almost all day long, with from twenty to fifty small wax candles, fixed upon clusters of palm branches, which were attached to long upright poles, and, spreading like the arms of a chandelier, more than half way to the ceiling, enabled Mr. Bankes, and the other draughtsmen, to copy all the paintings in detail [pls 50 to 55], as they stood, almost naked, upon their ladders.'[20]

It was only on their return that Bankes improvised a satisfactory method of lighting the vast relief-scenes of the Battle of Qadesh of which Ricci's paintings preserve lost details. For Bankes, the heat and the exertions of copying brought on a severe fever so that Beechey was obliged to take over the architectural recording from him.

Bankes interpreted the historical reliefs by equating Qadesh, shown encircled by the river Orontes, with the island of Meroe. The fortress certainly depicted the enemy but he was less sure about the camp, although he knew that the shields that made up the palisades were Egyptian. He could not account for the non-appearance of the camel in such scenes (it was unknown in Pharaonic Egypt), nor for the absence of elephants in battle. He theorized about the battle tactics, recognizing that the hero single-handedly fighting and driving his chariot was unrealistic iconography. He realized that the hero, when shown with the gods, was the deified king (Diodorus stated this was the Ethiopian custom). The ancient writers also supported his conviction that the rock-cut temples were tombs. He wrote down Beechey's first-hand account of discoveries on first entering the temple in 1817, from the details of statuary to 'a light & black substance resembling decayed wood … in every apart-ment. in some to the depth of 2 feet – & various pieces of timber which fell to dust on being touched'.[21] He postulated that a wooden floor might have accounted for this. Finati, also pre-sent at the first opening, told him that a skull and some bones were found in one of the long rooms.

Recognizing the figure of Hathor, the cow-goddess, on the reliefs of the Small Temple, he thought it likely that the sanctuary was used for the burial of sacred cows and dedicated to the goddess (pl. 63). He explained the predominance of the female figure in this temple by the high position of the 'Candaces of Ethiopia'. The façade of the Small Temple had remains of red and yellow paint, and 'on the top of the wall that engages the 2 last colossus-piers – is a mass of the black decayed matter – at least 2 foot in thickness standing up per-pendicular as if it had been some chest or possibly wooden sarcophagus laid there'.[22]

Every part of the Great Temple façade was carefully drawn and measured down to the toes of the statues. The hieroglyphs on the thrones and frieze of the façade had been coloured yellow '& the little figures the same outlined in red – the great colossuses were prob-ably red – a strange effect they must have had'. Perplexingly, on one he discovered 'holes found in the body as for beams that it is probable some shed or hut has been built in his lap'. As in many Egyptian temples the decoration inside was unfinished: 'one wall is not even painted & on the other the last figure inwards is sketched in black & only a very small part cut in'. The background colour for the wall-paintings in the first rooms was quaker grey, the sanctuary walls yellow and reddish, but how realistic Ricci's vivid colours are we cannot be sure. While Irby and Mangles in 1817 found the colour 'injured' although sufficient remained 'by which to judge of what is lost', Gau, in contrast, defined it as brilliant.

News reached them that violent rain had broken into Belzoni's newly discovered Theban tomb (Sety I) causing great damage and confirming Bankes's opinion that the wells in tombs were built to remedy this problem. There was also, alas, a small accident to the sanctuary statues at Abu Simbel to be declared, when an arm of the blue figure came off while Bankes drew it (pl. 56). Before leaving Bankes purchased a five-string lyre which 'wants nothing but the tortoise to be like the ancients'.

The magnificent record of 155 drawings demonstrates the temple's remarkable state of preservation, while interestingly capturing the various stages of excavation. This revealed the proportions of the colossi to be very heavy but there was still a most beautiful effect by moonlight when the shadows were cast in an opposite direction to sunlight. Beechey painted the scene: the façade bathed in moonlight and partly lit up by the fire of their Arab crew (pl. 60). (Barry, perhaps not by coincidence, painted an identical view, according to his father.) Because of the great interest in the temple, several of the watercolours were produced as highly finished copies for show.

ABAHUDA

The cluster of far smaller monuments, stelae, and inscriptions nearby were no less worthy of their attention, and excursions were made into the desert to examine a quantity of Coptic writings. Just south of Abu Simbel, the multi-layered decoration of the rock-cut chapel of Abahuda of King Horemheb (1319–1292 BC) encompassed 'many saints on Horseback as at Dakke – there are scrawls also in Arabic & the saints have been carefully effaced [pl. 64]'. Beyond it lay Gebel Adda, topped by a medieval fortress overlooking the island of Shataui where they sheltered from a storm. The scenery had a 'very singular character of abrupt and detached mountains rising out of the plain near it – some pyramidical – some with many sharp spires & fantastical tops'. The double-peaked hill of Gebel el Shams contained the stela and niche of Paser I, Viceroy of Kush under Ay and Horemheb. Paser was carefully drawn as he sits receiving the homage of his relations and kneeling to worship the seated statue of the god. Some daring was required for this since the shrine and stela were difficult of access, and it was later remarked that 'the archaeologist who is not accustomed to climbing might find his attempt to reach them terminated by a fall into the river'.

The temple of Abahuda proved impossible to dismantle and move in the 1960s, so only fragments of the ancient reliefs covered by Christian frescos were cut out and rescued. Bankes left a very detailed and complete record of them in their twenty-four drawings encompassing both his visits.

FARAS

The strong north wind carried them on past pelicans, tamarisk, fields of lentils, wheat and doura, and brick ruins, towards Faras. On 20 February they passed the 'remains of several Greek, or early Christian churches, mostly situated on the Western [side of] the Nile – all of which Mr B examined with the most minute attention to find out any inscription or Date that could at all throw a light upon their history – but ineffectually'.[23]

Faras had occupied a vast and complex ancient site spread over what was then an island in the Nile. It had had a long occupation, and the 1910–12 excavation recovered Palaeolithic tools.[24]

Earlier travellers noted a small niche or grotto of Setau, Viceroy of Kush under Rameses II, built on the south-east face of an isolated rock situated south of the Meroitic enclosure and known as the Hathor Rock.[25]

The archaeologist Karkowski, to whom the existence of Bankes was unknown, remarked: 'The localization of Faras between two of the most attractive sites of Lower Nubia, Abu Simbel and Wadi Halfa, was the reason why a number of early travellers and scholars who risked the journey south of the First Cataract did not stop to visit this place. On the other hand the vast area over which the Pharaonic remains were scattered, resulted in the fact that even those who stopped at Faras were not always able to localize all the places in which Pharaonic material could be found in their time.'[26]

This comment is certainly true of the disjointed prose of Bankes's description in which the structures described are hard to locate on maps, and clarity obscured by his unspecific use of the name 'Farras'. Of the nine drawings, his plans of tombs are recognizably those of the rock-cut New Kingdom tombs,[27] and the lintels which he drew are probably the 'Egyptian doors' observed by Horeau in 1837 among the ruins of walls, granite columns, and door-ways in the area of the Great Kom (the Meroitic enclosure).[28]

Bankes examined the ancient frescoed church remains; the (Meroitic) enclosure with its high walls, towers, and houses within; fragments of architrave (too small for doors), a frieze with grapes and another of 'Eagles bearing crosses on their heads'. Small granite columns lay scattered among the debris. A mass of rock and ruins (perhaps the Hathor Rock?) resembled a quarry and at the rear was a small tablet inscribed in an unknown language. Entering a four-chambered tomb with a sarcophagus and a well, 'some of the bats frightened out of it by us into the daylight were immediately seized by hawks'. Faras was the first point above the Cataract with plentiful cultivation: a lemon tree bloomed among lentils, lupins, and wheat. In the village, which boasted a school, a pilgrim was being rapturously greeted on his return from Mecca. The desert was scattered with onyx, agate, and carnelian, '& a sort of stone like petrified wood & another species which the Dr [Ricci] believes bones'.

Prior to the eventual submersion of the site, the Polish archaeological expedition (1961–64) made many new discoveries in the area including churches with remarkable frescos.[29]

WADI HALFA

Reaching Wadi Halfa at half-past three on 21 February 1819, 'Mr Salt pitched his tent to remain some days; this completes our journey by water as the rocks of the second cataract are much more numerous and intricate than those of the first'.

The following day they visited the travellers' rock of Abusir, the point of return for most travellers. Hyde inscribed his own name and recorded in his journal the other graffiti he found as 'it is customary with travellers to inscribe their names upon the rock'. Here, where they captured a rather fierce lizard, Bankes's eye caught traces of older inscriptions on rocks in the desert and by the river.

Exploring the area below the Second Cataract, their boats passed groves of date trees, the 'Palma Christi', and a natural hedge of tamarisk, hung with a creeper which was new to him. Here and there a few lupins edged the river. Goats abounded, a few cows, a camel was seen, and a rare sighting made of two horses. The islands in the river glimmered black or dark purple and held curious plants. Sandstone rock lay just beneath the surface of the desert, which was strewn with lumps of 'agate & jasper & black basalt & a stone with green veins like copper… Mr Linon picked up near the buildings one jasper that seems to have been wrought to a clumsy ring.' Among the hieroglyphic inscriptions in what Bankes took to be a quarry there were some very singular ones, a little like Greek, which he conjectured were simply hieroglyphs turned the other way.

The days followed close and hot without sun or blue sky and a storm blew up; quite a hurricane with clouds of sand. A lone clap of thunder was followed by a little rain. Some of their Nubian crew swam down the Cataract and the river swirled with large particles of golden mica.

Wadi Halfa was always strategically important. Situated north of the Second Cataract, it marked the frontier in ancient times between Wawat and Kush (Lower and Upper Nubia), and in modern times between Egypt and the Sudan. The Cataract stretched over twenty-five miles, known as the Batn el-Hagar, 'the belly of the rocks', an area impassable to shipping. Here stood the ancient Egyptian fortress town of Buhen; one of the great chain of Middle Kingdom fortresses which, by controlling the river passage north into Egypt, formed a security cordon against what the ancient Egyptians called the threat of Kush. The forts held garrisons of troops to protect the rich gold routes and other Nubian trade, and were centres of administration from which to source Nubian manpower for mining and for the Egyptian army. After a period of Egyptian withdrawal and a Nubian occupation during the Second Intermediate Period, Buhen was again inhabited in the New Kingdom when two temples were constructed over older ones within the fortress.[30]

Bankes and his party were not the first to notice the unpromising ruins opposite Wadi Halfa, barely visible above the sand, but they were the first to investigate them closely and to excavate them. This pioneering undertaking, organized in an orderly fashion approaching modern methods, was prompted by his frustration when faced with the conundrum of the South Temple in 1815. Unknown to Bankes, this temple, the core of which was built by Hatshepsut, had been radically altered and enlarged by Thutmose III, and then restored and rebuilt in the time of Taharqo.[31] Bankes was at a loss to explain the plan, confused by the juxtaposition of incompatible architectural features, and puzzled to discover that the front entrance was not where his experience told him to expect it, at the centre of the axis. He was aware that there must be a buried vestibule and sanctuary complex at the rear, and recommended its excavation to future visitors. Now, ten days were devoted to the dig which had 'chiefly been resorted to as a pastime, during a tedious negociation which was carrying on to induce the Kashief… to furnish camels and an escort for Mr. Bankes and some of his companions, so far as Dongola, a journey which had long been determined upon'.[32] The Khamsin winds whirled outside as they pressed the Casheff, but he proved reluctant to provide camel transport or any help for the rest of their journey. Finally he grudgingly presented them with a letter of recommendation to his son and an Ababde escort, allowing them to continue the journey south, leaving da Costa to oversee the work in their absence. During a brief stop on their return they examined the 'chambers and small monuments' which had come to light.[33]

It was not an easy site, being choked up with sand and masses of ruined brick which formed a high mound above the desert surface. The digging exposed the ruins of both temples, which were encircled by the river and the massive Middle Kingdom fortifications. Other remains in the vicinity were examined which were perhaps temple walls; two large detached stones which may have been part of the entrance doorway to the quay, and long lines of foundations which relate to the external fortifications.

Bankes rewrote his lengthy descriptive notes three times, adding finally: 'it only remains to explain what the excavation & researches have brought to light'. Unfortunately, his lack of understanding compounds the illegibility of hurried notes making it hard to decipher, although graphically explaining his inability to transcribe his notes later for publication.

The larger South Temple was recognized as decorated in the style of Amada (i.e. New Kingdom) but the plan was incomprehensible. The deterioration of the poor-quality sandstone Bankes put down to the rigours of time. The difficulties of the plan did not finish with the entrance doorway; columns and piers corresponded with nothing, and one was so far out of line that he had to dig down to ascertain it was actually in situ rather than detached. Many of the piers remained 'complete to the very summit & the columns still crowned with their Abacus'.

On the thick stuccoed walls of the North Temple they made out the remains of paintings 'in a tawdry taste', a seated female Egyptian figure and a sacred boat, brilliantly coloured but not harmonious and badly finished. There were inscribed and decorated 'tablets' (stelae) and niches where others had once stood. On one 'a man seems to be presenting captives – with their names written under each – to a god'. This would become known as the Buhen stela, a historically important monument recording the victories of General Mentuhotep in year 18 of Senusret I and showing the captured Nubian towns. In some chambers nothing remained but borders and architectural decoration, in 'other apartments it may be traced that the walls have been previously painted in colours & patterns somewhat different from the present'. In the centre of one room stood 'a plain & rather rude altar table of stone', another had 'a long couch of brick raised about a foot & plastered – I suspect it provided for a body'. The upper part of the temple was eroded away – 'the painted figures are uniformly cut off about the waist' – but he believed the roof to have been arched.

Bankes was aware that the sand concealed more than the remains of the four unintelligible structures he had planned, but he guessed the mud-brickwork had been mined away for fertilizer or to build elsewhere.

The site was excavated in 1909 and 1910,[34] then re-excavated and published by the Egypt Exploration Society for the UNESCO campaign. The New Kingdom temples were recorded by Caminos as part of the Egypt Exploration Society project in 1960–61.[35] By then the northern temple was an utter ruin, almost levelled to the ground.[36] Bankes left not only a long and explicit description of his findings but also an annotated measured ground plan (pl. 67). The detailed plan and decorative scheme of the North Temple are known only from his portfolio.

The great mud-brick fortress is sadly submerged below the lake, but the South Temple was re-erected in the grounds of the Khartoum museum.[37] The South Temple remains did not indicate to Caminos whether or not the court had been open or roofed, and no column capitals were found nor any columns, pilasters, or pillars which had not 'lost their upper ends'.[38] No capitals were recovered by Bankes either (he almost always noted the architectural style of capitals). He certainly found many columns 'quite intire to the very top' and noted on his plan whether the abacus remained in place or not. He concluded that the court had been roofed but gave no archaeological evidence to support this theory. The type and position of the columns simply suggested to him an analogy with Amada, which was roofed.

Bankes was clear that the screen walls of the North Temple interrupted the decoration and therefore were a secondary construction. They are possibly Coptic.[39]

The three Middle Kingdom stelae carefully copied among the eleven drawings are of immense historical importance. All were left in situ within the North Temple and soon disappeared under the encroaching sands. The pair of inscribed stelae of Deduantef, a commander of Senusret I, were rediscovered by H. G. Lyons in 1892 exactly where Bankes had found them, on either side of the central sanctuary. Although both were said to have been sent to the British Museum, only one was actually received; the other stela is lost and its text known only from Bankes's copy. The text of its pendant, now BM 1177, is also more complete on Bankes's drawing (pl. 65).[40] The famous Buhen stela was carefully copied by Ricci for Bankes but left in situ (pl. 66). By 1828–29 when Ricci revisited the site with the Franco-Tuscan expedition of Champollion and Rosellini, it too was buried. It was Champollion's main objective at the site; its great importance obvious from the original drawing but frustratingly impossible to relocate. Fortunately Ricci recalled its position but only the upper part was found; the lower section was not rediscovered until 1893 by Lyons. Both sections are now reunited in the Museo Egizio in Florence. Senusret is shown standing before the god Montu, who holds the ropes which bind the captive figures surmounting the fortified ovals representing towns. By following the order of the town-names his expedition route can be reconstructed and information on the topography of Upper Nubia obtained.[41]

Using the drawing of the hieroglyphic inscription around a doorway it is now possible to link the temple to the goddess Isis, although not to show securely that the temple was founded for her or dedicated specifically to her – questions which Caminos was unable to answer without seeing the lost format of the inscription which Bankes recorded. An unplaced fragment found by Caminos is now revealed as from the lintel.

On the overcast morning of 26 February 1819 Bankes and his party crossed to the west bank to begin the slow overland journey south, the Second Cataract preventing further progress by boat. They left without Salt, who had fallen ill with a complaint so violent that it almost killed him (probably dysentery).[42] It was judged prudent for him to leave the party before the rigours of the overland trek, taking Linant (and probably the elderly Sack) with him. Hyde names the remaining party as Bankes, Beechey, himself and Ricci, three servants, six Ababdes, the Sheikh of Wadi Halfa, a native, and Hassan, Bankes's pilot: sixteen in total (d'Athanasi again included anonymously under 'servants'). They had ten camels and the Sheikh of Wadi Halfa's donkey.[43] Having successfully reached the Second Cataract, Bankes now dreamt of reaching Dongola and 'even upon penetrating to Meroe'.[44] From this point few travellers had ventured south.

CHAPTER NINE

ROBBERY AND OBSTRUCTION

THE END OF THE JOURNEY

THEY FOLLOWED THE CATARACT, riding along the river bank and sleeping out in the open. Passing Mirgissa, Beechey drew a panorama of the very extensive fortress where they found fragmentary hieroglyphs.[1] The construction was of brick 'with wood introduced, and remaining here and there as a bonding'.

SEMNA AND KUMMA

More impressive still was the great river barrier where twin Twelfth-Dynasty fortresses, Semna and Kumma, spanned the southernmost point of the Second Cataract, guarding caravan and river traffic.[2] 'There is nothing at all like it in Egypt. The fortress itself is square, and of brick, resting upon stone foundations, but on the three land-sides (for the fourth is precipitous to the river) there is a broad dry trench carried all round, faced on both sides with granite, and beyond it a great slanted rampart of the same to the exterior. Upon the granite cliff towards the Nile, a low and narrow covered way descends, which secured a safe access to the water. Within, upon the summit, is a very small temple, in the Egyptian manner, profusely and delicately sculptured, and a mutilated statue or two, and some finely wrought and polished tablets [stelae]. An ancient strong hold of similar construction stands directly opposite, across the Nile, which is very narrow at this point, and interrupted by a chain of rocks, which seem as if they might almost furnish footing for a bridge.'[3] At low water there was a narrow passage through; at high water turbulent rapids. Burckhardt's name, witnessing his presence at the fortress, impressed upon them all his courage in venturing there alone. Their twenty-three drawings of Semna and fifteen of Kumma record the drowned mud-brick forts and the two temples now reconstructed in Khartoum.[4] Linant's drawing of the temple at Semna shows the temple in its original position (pl. 68).

They met two caravans coming from Dongola but none which they could join going in their direction. The Mamelukes escorting one of the caravans were alarmed at first on seeing them 'in Oriental garb' but then reassured by the sight of Bankes and Hyde, who were wearing European dress.[5]

☙◯☙

On 7 March 1819, at Mograka below Amara, they stopped to rest, and Bankes and Beechey stretched out under a tree while the rest bathed.[6] They had been told by their Ababde guides and interpreters that the stop was necessary 'on the pretext that the river could not be crossed upon a raft higher up', and, while they relaxed, the guides secretly made off with their camels. They were pursued in vain. D'Athanasi thought that their guides were motivated by anxiety for the safety of their camels after Bankes had intimated his intention to cross the river.

Finding themselves stranded at least 150 miles above the Second Cataract, with no guides or local interpreters, no transport for themselves or their baggage, and no village nearby, they 'necessarily remained stationary for this night and were supplied with a Lamb and Milk by a neighbouring Cottager'. This disaster still did not dampen their enthusiasm for exploration since the following day Hyde remarks: 'having been informed of ruins at a little distance… they were inspected but did not seem to be of any great antiquity'. Following communications in a combination of sign language and Arabic with the sheikh from the island opposite, a makeshift raft was constructed by the natives 'of 7 or 8 Domb trees [palms] tied together with ropes formed of green rushes and Domb leaves, a skin filled with wind being attached on each side'[7] and they and their baggage were ferried across in ones and twos, the rafts being pushed along by swimming 'natives'. Bankes and Beechey were first to cross.[8] The operation took all day because of the current and they got soaked through. Hyde was almost swept away by the strength of the current; 'the accident so alarmed him that he fell seriously ill, and was within an ace of dying'.[9] Hyde stoically fails to mention his own health although Finati and d'Athanasi agree that he became extremely weak and that his life was in danger.

Since they were only four or five miles from Amara, Finati was sent ahead to seek assistance from the son of the Casheff of Wadi Halfa, but this was not forthcoming. Meanwhile the rest had managed to find two Nubians, one of whom had worked as a servant in Cairo, who were prepared to hire them two asses, enabling them to reach Amara. This sufficed for their baggage, but they were forced to make the fatiguing journey through the deep sand to Amara on foot. This time they received a better welcome, although their host helped himself to Hyde's supply of spirits.[10] Bankes, 'who still would not abandon his favourite object of proceeding much further, did his utmost' to persuade the 'young Prince' to provide them with help, but without success for he said that even the very next islanders (of Sai) were his enemies and he would not trust 'either us or his animals with the Mameluks at Dongola'.[11] Moreover, 'should we persist in going forward to the upper country we should find 'our graves were already dug for us'.[12]

Through Bankes's absolute refusal to relinquish the idea of seeing Sai island ('Mr Bankes had caught sight of a small sail in that direction… and was bent on throwing himself on board…') money changed hands and they were finally permitted, on horseback, to view the ruins of Sai island from the bank.[13] Ricci may well have believed, as he later wrote, that they were looking at the inaccessible ruins of Meroe, but Hyde wrote more prosaically, 'the ruins are supposed to be a work of the Sultan Selim 2nd… no vestige visible of remote antiquity'.[14] They lingered, hoping a boat might pass to carry them onward, but on 13 March 1819 Hyde resignedly wrote, 'Returned towards Egypt from this date'. Tantalizingly, at Amara, 'the cachif and his people without the name being mentioned to them spoke of Meroe as a place with many interesting remains'. They even encountered a camel-driver 'who pretends to have resided there fourteen years, he spoke of it as an Island two days journey in length formed by the junction of two rivers'.[15]

The Casheff's son, having earlier promised them camels if they would return north, now reneged even on this offer. They accordingly then dispensed with any baggage which was not absolutely necessary and which could not be carried by their single remaining ass, and set off on foot. 'Dr. Ricci pronounced it, quite impossible, that Mr Hyde could have strength to walk the journey; therefore, with considerable delay and difficulty a single hired camel was found for him, which served also to furnish now and then an occasional ride to one or other of our number, perched up behind.'[16] Reaching Dal island the next day, they stopped for the night opposite the island of Kulb.

By necessity they now became bandits; stealing any unladen transport animals they met with which were refused to their hire (although paying for them later) and by this means managed to accumulate some five or six animals. Four camels enabled the gentlemen to be mounted for the tiring journey back to Semna. Chancing on the leader of those Ababdes who had been responsible for all their difficulties, they cheerfully revenged themselves by giving him a good beating, 'even the sick man, Mr. Hyde, sliding off from his tall beast to take his full share in this administration of summary justice'.[17]

'Hussein Cachief' of Wadi Halfa was in temporary residence at Sarras, near Semna, and, perhaps embarrassed by his son's behaviour, furnished them with a good dinner of boiled or stewed meat with dates, feasting them on milk and mutton, and entertaining them with the loud music of kettledrums.[18] Shortly after passing the large islands of 'Omki' (of which Bankes painted a panoramic view) and 'Dahby' (Dabenarti) opposite Mirgissa, which straddled the two-mile width of the Nile, they descended into the plain and reached their boats at Wadi Halfa.[19] Though all were disappointed, Finati felt that continuing up-country could have proved dangerous since there was talk of Mohammed Ali organising an expedition against the remaining Mamelukes who had fled beyond the cataract.

AMARA AND WADI HALFA

'In this long scramble upon the eastern bank, we had met with no other ancient remains in the Egyptian style, excepting eight or nine pillars at Amarra' and the small temple opposite Semna.[20] Ricci eventually recorded the reliefs and (rather inaccurately) the Meroitic inscriptions on the columns. Linant's measured plan differs from other descriptions by showing a total of sixteen columns differently arranged and, if not hypothetical, may perhaps solve the question of the position of the entrance to the temple.[21] By 1934–35 all that remained visible of Amara's Meroitic temple were 'one granite column-base and traces of mud-brick foundation walls'.[22]

Next they spent four days (20–3 March) examining the excavations at Wadi Halfa which had been carried on in their absence by Antonio da Costa.

On 21 March John Fuller, travelling with Mr Foskett and Nathaniel Pearce, arrived at Wadi Halfa on his journey up-river. Fuller had left his travelling companion the Reverend Mr Jowett[23] with the Reverend Mr Connor at Aswan on 7 March to await the imminent arrival there of Salt. Three days later Fuller, continuing his journey, had arrived opposite the temple of Kalabsha 'and saw some tents pitched near it … Mr Salt, though labouring under severe indisposition, received me with great politeness'[24] and was able to offer him some useful information for his journey. Fuller had been overtaken on the river by Foskett's eight-oared *cangia* which then towed him up to Abu Simbel. When they arrived at Wadi Halfa they

57 Linant's drawing of the third and fourth colossi on the façade of the Great Temple of Abu Simbel.

58 ABOVE This sketch by Linant is entitled 'Colossus of Abusumbel during the process of excavation'. The square plaque commemorating Salt's order to open the temple in 1817, and Bankes's excavation of the southern colossus in 1819, is just visible on the right.

59 RIGHT Bankes's graffito on the leg of the southern colossus at Abu Simbel, which reads 'Wm BANKES OPENED [THIS] *traces* [COLOSSUS] *hammered out*'.

60 OPPOSITE ABOVE Moonlight on the Great Temple of Abu Simbel, by Beechey.

61 OPPOSITE BELOW The party's flotilla at Abu Simbel in 1819, with a top-hatted figure in the foreground boat and a tent on shore. Drawing by Linant.

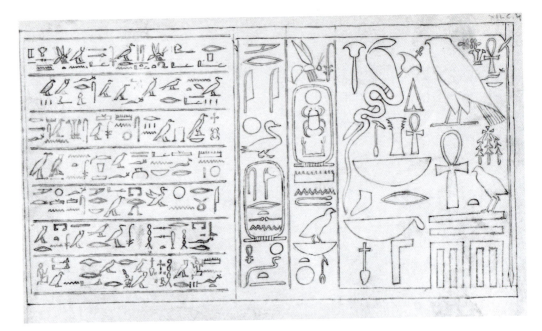

65 Bankes's drawing of the lost inscribed stela of Deduantef, a commander of Senusret I, from the North Temple at Buhen.

66 The stela recording the victories of General Mentuhotep in year 18 of Senusret I. This drawing, by Ricci, shows the stela in its original position in the North Temple at Buhen.

62 ex Te in Be

63 pla int Te Sin

[134]

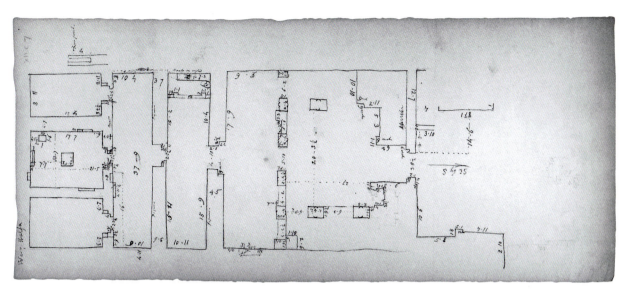

67 An important detailed plan of the lost North Temple at Buhen, by Bankes.

68 A view of Semna temple, by Linant.

69 A pencil sketch of Bankes in Oriental dress, by Maxim Gauci, c.1820.

70 The Hon. Charles Irby (1789–1845), by J.-B. Borely, 1820.

71 James Mangles (1786–1867), by J.-B. Borely, 1820.

72 A house with a
tower at Sanamein,
Syria, by Bankes.

73 Frescos in the funeral chapel at Sidon, Syria. Painting by Bankes.

74 The oval piazza at Jerash,
Syria, by Bankes.

75 James Silk Buckingham
and his wife,
by H. W. Pickersgill, c.1816.

76 The rock-cut Khasneh at Petra. Drawing by Bankes.

77 The narrow defile
entering Petra, by Bankes.

79 Alessandro Ricci, sketched by
Salvatore Cherubini, on the
Franco-Tuscan expedition of 1828–29.

78 Linant de Bellefonds in middle age.

80 Linant's view of the ruins of Soleb temple.

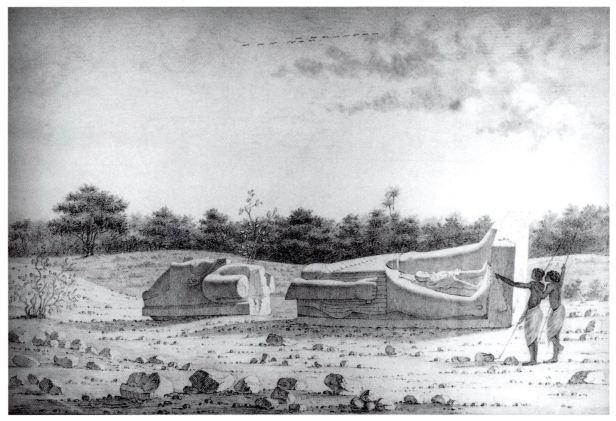

81 The broken colossus at Tabo on Argo Island, by Linant.

82 ABOVE Camel riders
in Nubia, by Linant.

83 RIGHT A scene showing
Queen Nawidemak from
a destroyed pyramid
chapel at Gebel Barkal.
The Meroitic text on the
small plaque above is
from another wall.
Painting by Linant.

84 The exterior of the 'Typhonium' at Gebel Barkal, by Linant.

85 The interior of the 'Typhonium', by Linant. The columns are carved with images of the god Bes and cartouches of King Taharqo.

'found there a little flotilla of boats belonging to Mr. Bankes, Mr. Beechey, and Mr. Hyde, who had just returned from an unsuccessful attempt to penetrate … above the second Cataract'.[25] After having 'passed a very pleasant evening in company with these gentlemen, and learned the particulars of their adventure', the account he heard of their robbery and their failure to reach further into Nubia caused him to lay aside all intention of making a similar attempt.

Maharraqa

Returning through Maharraqa, Bankes decided he would like the granite platform there as a base for his obelisk. The heavy stones were removed with some difficulty by Linant in 1822 and brought to Kingston Lacy in 1829. The exact date of Maharraqa, a late Roman temple dedicated to Isis and Serapis, is unknown. The Roman town was called Hierasykaminos, and marked the limit of the Dodekaschoinos (the territory which stretched from here north to the First Cataract).[26]

Between the temple and the river stood an isolated wall bearing a remarkable relief in a mixed Egyptian and Roman style (pl. 40). By 1906–07, with the temple in a pitiful state of collapse, it was unclear how this wall had related to the main temple. Fortunately Bankes's 1815 plans show the remains of the linking walls, and Ricci completed a more detailed plan of the temple and this second structure in 1819.

The temple was already ruined (pl. 41) when Bankes, stopping on their return journey, recorded the Greek inscriptions on what he identified from its position on the Antonine Itinerary as Hierasykaminos. He was inclined to the idea that the open peristyle of the temple stood around the sacred sycamore tree depicted on the isolated wall. Two peacocks were painted in a Christian altar niche: 'a bird which never occurs in more ancient Egyptian painting'. Other odd features for an Egyptian temple were the spiral staircase at the north-east corner, square plinths to the column bases, and the bizarre mixture of styles in the reliefs of the isolated wall. Some sixty local tombs were also investigated. A mile below Maharraqa[27] a villager proffered a legless statue of dark white-blotched granite. The style was not bad but the finish poor. However, when Bankes wished to draw it he was obstructed by the local men: 'the object was to get money. The fragment measures about 2 ft 6 inches high, it had been buried in sand but dug up & removed to prevent its being seen without paying. The owner said that he found it in the Nile.'

Although at first considered beyond rescue, the temple was substantially reconstructed by Barsanti in the aftermath of the water-damage from the early barrage. Eventually, in 1961, Maharraqa was saved and re-erected with Dakka and Wadi es-Sebua, near the former site of Wadi es-Sebua. The decorated wall was moved to Cairo Museum.

Philae

Now back at Philae, Bankes discovered that, as at Kalabsha and Esna, 'by placing himself in a side light, he could trace the indication of letters cut in the surface of the stone under the stucco, which induced him to scrape this away, and to bring out the inscriptions, which proved to be Greek'.[28] Bankes knew that the same method had been used by the architect

Sostratus on the Pharos at Alexandria. It proved that some of the texts he had found were as late as the reign of Commodus.[29] Hyde noted at Philae that the chapel before the second pylon of the main temple 'is a small temple which Mr B thinks is the most ancient in the whole Island' and that 'much … rubbish has been removed by Mr B who has entirely cleared out the area of this beautiful little Sanctuary'.[30] All the travellers' graffiti at Philae, many in the year of his own journey, went into his own notebook. Hyde may not have travelled back with the party, since he remained at Philae only twelve days, while Bankes lingered for thirty. Hyde arrived back at Thebes on 5 June 1819 and shortly after made 'my first visit to Carnac and spent the day with the French and Prussian artists Mr Huyot & Mr Gow [Gau]'.[31]

<h2 style="text-align:center">THEBES</h2>

On reaching the Luxor area of Thebes, Bankes wrote to Salt in Cairo on 11 June, hoping he was in better health and sending news of their latest discoveries and a gift: a live ostrich for his garden, but perhaps untrustworthy among his shrubs, 'being a mortal enemy to blossoms of all sorts … this is the only inhabitant of our cangia that you are unacquainted with'.

Above the rough draft he scribbled a memorandum: 'Dr – Garden' (for Ricci to draw this famous tomb scene? (pl. 16)), 'Belzoni', 'Mr. Hyde', 'Mr. Sloman' (perhaps the Reverend Mr Slowman, *en route* to the Second Cataract), 'Mr. Eliot & Gow' (Huyot and Gau), 'Frediani', and, ominously, 'Buckingham – write Constantinople'. The following day Bankes penned an acrimonious letter to Bombay, retracting an earlier recommendation, and demanding that patronage of Buckingham be revoked.

With his Nubian journey now behind him, Bankes could feel some satisfaction at his discoveries. He now believed Maharraqa, rather than Derr as Burckhardt had thought, to be Hierasykaminos; and he had identified most of the other sites on the Antonine Itinerary. He had also made 'a very curious discovery' of a long verse inscription at Kalabsha which was an acrostic. Philae was well recorded, with 'three more chambers and a staircase leading to them in the principal temple' discovered, and other parts cleared out. Interestingly he considered that his most gratifying discovery was not from Nubia but below the cataract: Greek inscriptions from the portico of the little temple near Esna, supporting his theory that 'the zodiac of Esne is of the time of Antoninus Pius and consequently later than the zodiac of Dendera'.[32]

The dating of these ancient zodiacs was one of the great controversies of the day, as it was believed that they might represent the actual night sky at the date of the temple construction. The arrival of the Dendera zodiac in France in 1821 rekindled the debate. Churchmen were particularly interested in its relevance to the date of the Creation, for according to Edmé Jomard, one of the original Napoleonic Commission in Egypt and an editor of the *Description*, Dendera gave an age earlier than the six thousand years in the Bible. The matter was complicated by the inaccuracy of the hieroglyphic copying in the *Description* itself. Although the architecture was reasonably reproduced, many texts were added randomly or transposed from other monuments. Champollion was to discover for himself in 1828 that the Dendera cartouches were all empty, although they had been published with the title of a Roman ruler erroneously inserted. He also realized that the stars attached to the astrological symbols were simply what he called 'determinatives' of the script: explaining the type of word. Bankes considered that Dendera was a Late Period temple by his usual simple process of observation and deduction. The columns holding up the ceiling had Greek inscriptions, therefore the ceiling had to be of a late date.[33]

Having arrived back in Thebes, Bankes 'was successful in detaching the stucco from one of the most interesting and best preserved of the lesser tombs, so as to be enabled to send several groups to England, and especially a large one of musicians, with harps and other instruments, as fresh as when first painted'.[34] There were also opportunities to purchase other pieces to add to his collection. Fuller, two months earlier, had complained that 'a great number of antiquities were brought to me by the Fellahs for sale, but I was not fortunate enough to meet with anything of much value'. He believed that as soon as a new tomb or pit was uncovered 'all that is most valuable is immediately bought up by the agents of the European collectors at Cairo or Alexandria'.[35]

A relaxing round of social activity greeted the travellers assembled at Thebes. Hyde 'crossed over the river to the western side to dine with Messrs B. B. & R [Bankes, Beechey, and Ricci?] upon a fine crocodile which an Arab had caught, – in taste and appearance the flesh of this reptile greatly resembled veal – the fat had however a somewhat more fishy taste'.

Two days later there was a funeral to attend. 'Count Maloze died this day about noon, in the hut of Mr Lobelau [Lebolo], and was decently intired at Medinet Abu [Medinet Habu], the body previously to its being committed to the grave was placed in a mummy-case. The Coptic priest performed the service.'[36] On 21 June 'the Arabs this day brought to Mr Bankes 2 crocodile Eggs, they were not much larger than duck's Eggs, but the skin was as rough and nearly as thick as the skin of an Ostriches Egg – the colour was a pure white, like that of a common Hen's Egg – one of these eggs when broken was found to contain an imperfectly formed crocodile'.[37] Hyde dined with Lebolo at Gurna, and 'visited the tombs with Dr. R[icci?] and afterwards dined with Mr Bankes'.[38] The temperature, registered every day, rose to 110°.[39] On 24 June, 'Mr Bankes and his party left Thebes this day for Dendera'. On 27 June, Huyot and Gau dined with Hyde on board his *cangia*, and on 5 July 'Mr Linon [Linant] arrived from Raramoun' (near Beni Hasan). Hyde visited a mummy-pit at Gurna and then 'In company with Mr Gow [Gau] and Mr Huyot I this day [16 July] paid my last visit to the Royal Tombs'. He recalled that the tomb known to him as number five 'contains a large granite sarcophagus in the finely proportioned saloon so greatly admired by Mr B[ankes?]'.[40] On 18 July he dined with 'Mr R[ifaud?]' and supped with Lebolo.

Hyde left Thebes for Coptos on 19 July 1819 after a stay of forty-four days. He was at Dendera on 24 July 'in company with Messrs Huyot, Gow [Gau], & LaChaise' and after various stops made his way back to Cairo, arriving there on 5 August. Unlike Bankes he did not make a detour to the Fayoum. Bankes's party 'continued our work homeward, stopping a short time amongst the ruins and ancient temples by the way, we reached Ben Isuaf [Beni Suef], through which we passed on to the river named Fium [the Bahr Yusuf?]. On arriving at this river we went to see the Lake Birket Haroun, and the temple adjacent, and then returned by land to Cairo, where we found Mr. Salt; and in a short time afterwards we all proceeded to Alexandria.'[41]

A polite letter from Belzoni hopes that Bankes's 'journey in to the Faium no doubt has been productive of many good Discoveries and Observations', adding mischievously in the nature of competitive travellers: 'I am sorry you missed the town of Baccus on the North side of the lake a little on the East of the iland and about two miles inland.'[42]

CAIRO

John Fuller found Salt reinstalled at Cairo when he arrived back at the consulate on 29 March 1819. Because of an outbreak of the plague, Salt placed them in a detached apartment for two or three days' quarantine, before they were permitted to join 'the rest of the party which had sought refuge on the consulate. It consisted of my old companion Mr Jowett, the Baron Sack a Prussian, and two English gentlemen (Mr Stevenson and Dr Armstrong), who were on their way from Bombay to England.'[43] All were confined to the consulate, and strict procedures were observed. Bread, iron, and wood were allowed in, but no meat or other animal substances. Coins were washed, and letters, books, and papers purged by smoke. If it was necessary to sign papers, a plate of glass was placed between the paper and the writer's hand. Cats were slaughtered and 'even the flies are objects of alarm'.

Fuller, Jowett, and Pearce left on 1 June heading for Jerusalem, but were forced to return only three days later, having been robbed of all their valuables on the road. However their re-entry into quarantine at the consulate was enlivened by the comfort of 'a house with spacious and cool apartments, a shady garden arranged in the English style, a library well stored with books, an endless variety of drawings and sketches [perhaps Salt and Beechey's own work for visitors to browse through] a large collection of Egyptian antiquities; and though last, not least in our esteem, an excellent billiard table'.

'Soon after the expiration of quarantine, our domestic party was increased by the welcome arrival of Mr. W. Bankes and Mr. Beechey from Upper Egypt; and it was occasionally enlivened by Belzoni.' Hyde dined with Salt on 7 August and met Bankes, Beechey, Ricci, and Sack there.[44] The heat was intense; outside up to 110°, and 84° indoors. They rose at 4 am and rode for an hour or two before sunrise, dined at midday, then slept or rested for two to three hours. After this they 'walked out' or paid visits, supped after sunset and went to bed about midnight. Hints from the more experienced travellers were welcomed; Bankes recommended a guide for Fuller's forthcoming visit to Jerash.

Sadly, Bankes's ostrich fared less well. They were intrigued to discover the bird's fondness for eating iron, but unsurprised to find that, indulged in this habit by the servants, it soon died, having ingested knives, blades, and buttons. Perhaps at least Salt's shrubbery was spared as a result.

Hyde dined at the consulate with Bankes, Beechey, and Linant on 1 September. Hyde was travelling on to Mount Sinai, and Bankes gave him a commission to make an unspecified purchase from the monks at St Catherine's and perhaps also entrusted him with the four books he had obtained from the convent which Hyde would return to the library shelves there. The following day Hyde called to say farewell to Bankes.

It was after Ramadan, and, perhaps 'induced … to remain longer than he would have otherwise done' by the conversation of Pearce,[45] Bankes, accompanied by Beechey, left for Alexandria and Trieste.[46] They had remained in Egypt to celebrate Salt's wedding, and Bankes presented the bride with a gift of diamond earrings. Bankes's Eastern travels now came to an end, but not his involvement and interest in ancient Egyptian matters.

CHAPTER TEN

RETURN TO EUROPE

PROJECTS AND PLAGIARISM

AFTER LEAVING EGYPT IN 1819, Bankes spent a leisurely winter rambling through Italy. With his companion Beechey 'not disturbing me much by the liveliness of his conversation' he amused himself by composing doggerel poetry which he posted off to Byron. From Trieste, where he sat out his quarantine at the beginning of November 1819, he had written immediately to Byron, who although unable to join him there had 'not been ignorant of your progress nor of your discoveries'. In the seven years since their last meeting, 'you have employed better for others & more honourably for yourself than I have done'. The first two cantos of *Don Juan* were out, and Byron hoped to see him in Venice, longing to hear of his travels which he expected soon 'to *see* – at length'. 'You have had better fortune than any traveller of equal enterprise – (except Humbolt) in returning safe – and after the fate of the Brownes – and the Parkes [*sic*] – and the Burckhardts – it is hardly a less surprise than satisfaction to get you back again.'[1]

Bankes went first to Florence, then on to Venice to admire the art and add to his collection. The two friends were reunited in the rented Palazzo Mocenigo on the Grand Canal where Byron had begun his translation of Luigi Pulci's fifteenth-century heroic poem *Morgante Maggiore*. A visit to Bologna was followed by a return to Florence at the end of January 1820 and a further invitation from Byron, this time to the Palazzo Guiccioli in Ravenna. 'I have room for you in the house here, as I had in Venice, if you think fit to make use of it; but do not expect to find the same gorgeous suite of tapestried halls. Neither dangers nor tropical heats have ever prevented your penetrating wherever you had a mind to it, and why should the snow now? – Italian snow – fie on it! – so pray come. Tita's heart yearns for you, and mayhap for your silver broad pieces; and your playfellow, the monkey, is alone and inconsolable.[2] I forget whether you admire or tolerate red hair, so that I rather dread showing you all that I have about me and around me in this city.'[3] He is to entertain himself during the day with Dante's tomb and the magnificent Byzantine mosaics of the city since Byron rises late: 'the lark, that rouses me from my slumbers, being an afternoon bird. But then, all your evenings, and as much as you can give me of your nights, will be mine. Then, there are more cantos (and be d—d to them) of what courteous reader Mr. S[aunders][4] calls Grub Street, in my drawer which I have a little scheme to commit to your charge for England; only I must first cut up (or cut down) two aforesaid cantos into three because I am grown base and mercenary, and it is an ill precedent to let my Mecaenas [Maecenas], Murray, get too much for his money.'[5] 'I have more of Scott's novels (for surely they are

Scott's) since we met, and am more and more delighted.[6] I think that I even prefer them to his poetry, which (by the way) I redde for the first time in my life in your rooms in Trinity College. There are some curious commentaries on Dante preserved here which you should see'.[7] A week after his first letter from Ravenna Byron wrote: 'Pulci and I are waiting for you with impatience; but I suppose we must give way to the attraction of the Bolognese galleries for a time. I know nothing of pictures myself, and care almost as little: but to me there are none like the Venetian – above all Giorgione. I remember well his Judgement of Solomon in the Mariscalchi in Bologna [pl. 106]. The real mother is beautiful, exquisitely beautiful. Buy her, by all means, if you can, and take her home with you: put her in safety: for be assured there are troublous times brewing for Italy; and as I never could keep out of a row in my life, it will be my fate, I dare say, to be over head and ears in it; but no matter, these are the stronger reasons for coming to see me soon.'[8]

The collection in Bologna formed by Count Marescalchi, a high official under the Napoleonic empire, was being broken up, and the Velasquez portrait of *Cardinal Massimi*, and the 'Giorgione' (today reattributed to Sebastiano del Piombo) were on the market. Byron was persuasive and Bankes finally sure of his own taste: the 'Giorgione' joined the Spanish work as his single greatest purchase.

Byron introduced him to the 'cards, talk and coffee' of Ravenna life and whisked him off to a ball to meet all the 'Ostrogothic Nobility', presenting him to his mistress, Countess Teresa Guiccioli, the third wife of one of the richest noblemen in Ravenna, a man forty years her senior. The theatre and a lottery after the opera provided other diversions. Their meeting again after so many years renewed their closeness. He declared Bankes 'a wonderful fellow'; yet another of his early friends to become celebrated. The gift of an Italian seal marked his appreciation of Bankes's generosity of spirit towards him. 'I never met but three men who would have held out a finger to me…one was Wm Bankes.' It was offered 'from goodwill – but I was not in need of Bankes' aid – and would not have accepted it if I had (though I love and esteem him)'.[9]

After seven and a half years of travel, Antonio da Costa now left his master's service in Florence and returned to his native Portugal. Bankes joined his sister Maria in Rome in March and did not arrive home until April 1820.[10] News of his Nubian discoveries, trumpeted in the *Quarterly Review*, preceded his return.

'I find the world very much as I left it, not indeed perhaps the same people, but the same *sort* of people; very dull, very meddling, very silly, & very false. The Sothebys flourish, the Wordsworths write, the Hobhouses speak, the Agar Ellises marry… For my own part, with almost all perhaps that this country can give me, I am pining for the sunshine & intense blue skies of the East, for those enticements to curiosity & interest which abound there, & for the free & vagrant life which I led. It is not so easy, I find, to commence a journey as to protract one, & Heaven knows whether I still have the spirit & resolution to plunge again.'[11]

To celebrate the return of his much-travelled son, Henry gave a dinner at their London house at Old Palace Yard, in the shadow of the Houses of Parliament, so that William and the Duke of Wellington could renew their acquaintance. (Wellington's party continued on to Lady Bessborough's to meet the other famous traveller in town: Belzoni.) Bankes was lionized by society hostesses as 'the Nubian explorer' who, Byron announced, had 'done *miracles* of research and enterprize'. Now his energies were to be thrown into Soughton Hall. The eighteenth-century Flintshire house of his great-grandfather Bishop Wynne, inherited from his great-uncle, was to be rebuilt in the Italianate style. Young Charles Barry, encountered on the Nile, had set up as an architect in Holborn in August 1820, but had become so anxious and despondent at the lack of work and his failure to win any public competitions that he was considering abandoning his profession. Barry's father believed there was talk at this time of a possible collaboration between the two men in a work on Egypt. Barry presented him with an excellent drawing of the temple at Karnak which Bankes reckoned 'would cost at least twenty or thirty guineas in a shop' in gratitude for recommending him to the Archdeacon of Cambridge, Commissioner for the erection of churches; the beginning of a series of such projects which launched his career. Bankes invited the 'very nice architectural draughtsman' to Kingston Lacy to make plans of 'alterations there which I have only roughly sketched upon paper'.[12] These were not the first changes to be suggested, but nothing was actually carried out until he inherited the house in 1834. Meanwhile an intriguing experiment saw Bankes as the principal architect of the work at Soughton. Barry was involved but does not appear to have made a major contribution to the redesign. Unlike Kingston Lacy, it is not listed among his principal works in the Italianate style.

Finati left an account of Soughton, which was still in the throes of rebuilding at the time of his visit in 1824. It reminded him of the old villas in northern Italy with its towers and ornamented stonework, 'walled courts about it and lines of trees in all directions'. Impractically for the climate of Wales, the house (later altered in the 1860s) had the open lofty rooms and galleries more suited to the heat of Italy.

✧✦✧

In the year following his return there was talk of his returning to Egypt.[13] Mrs Arbuthnot wrote, 'Mr William Bankes… told me he meant to go next year again to Africa & that he wd. try to get to the sources of the Nile, & was quite determined to return to Europe by the Cape of Good Hope. I am afraid if he goes he will never return.'[14] He was elected to the Society of Dilettanti, and dinner tables were regaled with endless entertaining tales of his adventures, with more serious comments on the state of the East being discussed amongst the men. Stratford Canning, cousin of George Canning and later ambassador to the Porte, wrote in his diary for 29 May 1820:[15]

'I dined at Brompton with Mr Frere [Bankes's erstwhile companion in Constantinople where he had been in charge of the embassy]. Wood and Mr. Bankes were of the party. The latter particularly entertaining – a various reader, an enterprising traveller, with great fluency & liveliness, more memory, I should think, than judgement, more singularity than wit, and yet with a sagacity and promptitude that might often pass, and occasionally with reason, for those more valuable qualities. – I found him talking on my arrival at a quarter after seven, and it was his voice that concluded the conversation at eleven, his power of utterance unwearied, and his stores of memory to all appearance undiminished. He talked of his travels in the East. Cairo, he says, is visibly wasting away under the effects of the commercial monopoly exercised by the Pasha of Egypt. He being almost the only merchant in his territory, that valuable class cannot exist under his government, and their former habitations are consequently deserted and going to decay. The distress caused by this extends to the country, and the Mamluk Beys are regretted, unpopular as they were in the time of their power. At Jerusalem there is no similar appearance of decay; that city is the great market town to the surrounding country. Mr. Bankes had seen Lady Hester Stanhope in Syria; she was living in a small but comfortable house, at the foot of Mount Lebanon, in full persuasion of her being one day called to the assembling of God's chosen people, in the capacity of Queen of Jerusalem. This fancy, which Mr. B. represents as having taken full possession of her mind, arose (as she herself relates) from a prophecy which the famous Brothers made to her many years ago when her superstitious curiosity led her to try his oracular skill. He then predicted, she says, that she would pass some years in the East and reign at Jerusalem. She has already exceeded the probationary term by two years.

'Mr. B. most amply confirms the account given by the Quarterly Review of Count Forbin's veracity. [Virtually nil according to the *Review*, which, enraged by the French museum director's disparagement of English travellers, had railed: "it would be difficult to find any 'rich Englishman' travelling with greater celerity, or passing the most interesting objects with greater indifference, than the Count himself."]

'Porson's name was mentioned. Mr B., who had been frequently in society with him at Cambridge, spoke rather slightingly of his powers. He described him as having read for conversation and as having been surprising only when he could take the lead in topics; his quotations, he said, had by no means the variety and extent which were commonly attributed to them. He had once sat between him and Matthias, the reputed author of the *Pursuit of Literature*, in which Porson was rather severely treated. Matthias proposed to drink wine with him; the offer was accepted, but this did not prevent Porson from muttering between his teeth, according to his usual practice when much irritated, and loud enough for Matthias to hear, every sort of abuse *against a rascal whose name began with such and such letters, and who had had the baseness to write an anonymous lampoon against him.*'

The irony of Bankes's criticism of Porson for faults which he himself amply displayed may have struck his listeners. Frere, for one, spoke up in Porson's support, giving examples of his deep knowledge of ancient Greek and Latin literature.

⌘

On his return to England, Bankes presented Thomas Young with his copies of Greek and hieroglyphic inscriptions for Young to work on, and they corresponded about the grammatical possibilities of the texts. Young was more interested in 'the temptation that your hieroglyphical tablet [the Abydos king-list] holds out: I wish you would have it engraved and publish it with a few other select materials as pledges of your future intentions.' Given access to Bankes's papers in London, he joked from Welbeck Street, 'I hope on Saturday or Sunday to make another attempt to break into the temple at Ebsambal [Abu Simbel]. Pray tell me if I shall find it accessible about 3 o'clock.'[16]

When he had proposed that Dr Meryon might become his secretary in 1816 Bankes was already aware that 'My miserable indolence about writing grows upon me every day', and in addition to the prospect of 'a good deal of business' from his great-uncle's death, his 'many notes & memorandums which it was almost a duty in me to have made in my travels' meant that he was 'in real and almost daily need of an amanuensis'. 'I begin to have some thoughts of drawing up some small memorandums of the strange places & strange people that I have seen.'[17] Following Dr Meryon's refusal he considered approaching Charles Barry in 1820, but Baillie thought he would decline, preferring to pursue his architectural career.[18]

The immense amount of material which he brought home from his travels, with the further addition of Linant and Ricci's papers, must have been overwhelming. He wrote to Byron in 1822 of publishing: 'I am always thinking of it, &, from a strange mixture of indolence with industry always deferring it. I hate, & always did, method & arrangement, & this is what my materials want.'[19] Even a letter to Murray in 1829 begins: 'According to usual habit, I have been deferring writing to you from day to day for some time past.'

In 1830 Bankes was still protesting his intention to publish at least his drawings of Syria and Palestine: 'The plans, elevations and views, taken … during my several visits, were arranged some years since, so as to be almost ready for publication, but other matters carrying me off from them, it has been delayed.'[20] Although he doubted the fame was worth the candle, 'A large collection of Inscriptions however I shall certainly edit, & that soon.'

Copious protestations of his own indolence aside, the organization and publication of such a mass of detailed material would have been a daunting task for the most energetic individual. His own fastidious nature and his colleagues' expectations required no less than an outstanding work.[21] Even so, he clearly just put off the concentrated effort it would have required. Meanwhile, others published. Young suspected that the scholar and traveller John Gardner Wilkinson, one of the founders of Egyptology, had 'borrowed' Bankes's own copy of the Abydos king-list: 'You will have all your things … anticipated if you do not fairly publish them without delay.'[22] Young continued working on Bankes's copies of inscriptions and, eventually realizing that nothing would be forthcoming from him, offered to publish 'as a Specimen of your Egyptian Collections a Series of the Kings of Egypt, consisting merely of 3 or 4 large folio plates, or perhaps rather 5 or 6 quarto plates, with a few explanatory pages of text. Of this little publication I could take the whole labour: it should bear your name, as being copied from your drawings … The risque of the publication should either be undertaken by a bookseller or by yourself or I would share it with you.' But the offer was not to be taken up although he had use of the copies for his publication of the Rosetta inscription.[23]

Nevertheless, a considerable amount of work was carried out to prepare for the publication of the inscriptions, which Bankes undoubtedly considered the most important and useful part of his portfolio. Rescued from an outhouse and now conserved and stored on racks in the attic of Kingston Lacy are fifty-six lithographic stones containing the plates for this project (pl. 110). They feature the many different scripts collected in Sinai, Egypt, Nubia, Syria, and Asia Minor, and include some of Linant's drawings. Much of the inked preparatory work for the plates and many copies of proofs from the stones are to be found amongst Bankes's papers. Most plates are inscribed 'Published Nov. 27. 1821. by John Murray, London. Printed by C. Hullmandel', with Scharf as the artist/lithographer. The plates are unnumbered, with the inscriptions arranged in individually numbered groups by location, except where examples of the Nabatean script from Petra and from Sinai are placed together on one stone, to point up their similarity.

John Murray's accounts ledgers show that £25 was paid to Scharf on 22 August 1821 for 'Bankes's Inscriptions – Author' (this form of title designating a work commissioned and paid for by the author rather than the publisher, though it was more customary to raise a subscription for such privately printed books). On 29 November 1821 a further payment was made to Scharf for engraving. Unknown delays in 1825 caused Bingham Richards to take 'some decisive steps to procure the stones from Hullmandel for Scharf to work upon, who has been some days waiting their arrival'.[24] Hullmandel was paid £56 9s 1d in June 1824 and Scharf £56 in February 1825; the final ledger entry was abruptly crossed through with a line and the single word 'Loss' when the great work was abandoned. No text appears to have been written to accompany the plates.[25]

Copies of a set of three prints showing the obelisk, the pedestal, and their inscriptions were actually produced and circulated, one print bearing the annotation which was to be responsible for the fiasco over who was first to decipher the name of 'Cleopatra'. The British Museum received a copy bound under the title '*Geometrical Elevation of an Obelisk*, by W. J. Bankes, 1821'. Cambridge University Library also received a set as well as four prints showing Bankes's transcription of the Stratonicea Inscription.

Byron received a roll of the proof engravings of the obelisk in January 1822 with a rather plaintive note beginning: 'I do not know whether you have forgotten your Greek as entirely as you seem to have forgotten me' and hoping that even if they were never read 'the mere act of receiving them may call me to your mind; & I am satisfied'.

Beechey wrote on 29 May 1822 from his North African expedition that he was glad to hear that Bankes was 'getting on fast with the inscriptions – they cannot fail to be very interesting – but I wish that I could hear that the other parts of your immense collection were equally advancing – But so it is – those who have most are often most backward in producing it – while any fool who has been to France thinks that it absolutely incumbent on him to let the world know the mighty fact as soon as possible'.[26]

Perhaps intended for a frontispiece for the great work was a pencil portrait by Maxim Gauci (1774–1854) (pl. 69). Gauci was working in London at this time and contributed regularly to Hullmandel's publications. The style of the portrait is similar to that which he drew of Belzoni, used for the frontispiece of his *Narrative*. It shows an elegant figure, wearing a turban and diaphanous loose Oriental trousers under a lightly draped, tasselled cloak.[27] A bare arm emerges, leaning nonchalantly against twined palm-trees and holding aloft a rolled document. A faint vista of a great pyramid looms beyond him. Romantic curls peep out from under the turban, tasselled and plaited to form a diadem, and the neck is bare. The figure's rather effete pose has his left hand against his hip, and he crosses his small, delicate, bare feet, which are encased in finely strapped Greek sandals. The effect is very similar to the orientalizing and antique Greek female fashions of the French Directoire: loose, gauzy, and revealing. Portraits of Irby and Mangles are, in contrast, considerably more robust (pls 70 and 71). Both moustachioed men were painted wearing magnificent blood-red Oriental costume, creating a striking effect very different to this languorous pose and costume. Here, the features are strongly reminiscent of the Sandars's miniature, in particular the cupid's bow lips, suggesting that the unnamed portrait, dated c.1820, is of Bankes.

⋘⊙⋙

The arrival of the obelisk in London in September 1821, the 'first ever brought to England', was reported in *The Times* with an account of its recovery by Belzoni and provoked a further bout of interest. Mrs Arbuthnot dined at Vansittart's (the Chancellor of the Exchequer) 'and saw Mr W. Bankes, who told me that an Egyptian Obelisk was just arrived which he has brought from Philia, far above the cataracts, 1200 miles from Alexandria. He says it is a very curious one, being the only one the object of which is known. This one was raised to commemorate a revision of taxes in the reign of the great Ptolemy & Cleopatra. We proposed to Mr. Bankes to give this obelisk to Mr Vansittart as an instructive lesson; but Van said *no*, that one to commemorate an *imposition* of taxes wd. be more in his way.'[28] The Duke of Wellington arranged for it to travel to Dorset on a converted gun carriage; the weight would be worked out from its dimensions.[29]

On 28 June 1822 Mrs Arbuthnot was to spill out in her journal the intimate confidences of an affair which was to create sufficient scandal to affect Bankes's parliamentary career. She also recorded Bankes's opinion of Byron. 'In the evening we came back to town & went to a concert at the Duchess of Wellington's. I there saw Wm Bankes, who makes me the confidante of a love affair of his which, I am afraid, will end by his getting into a scrape. It appears he is very much in love with Lady Buckinghamshire, a very young & very handsome woman who has been married about 3 years to a man she cannot endure, & who is still more desperately in love with him. She is about to be separated from her husband, not about Mr. Bankes, but because their tempers & tastes do not suit, & she is excessively anxious to induce Mr. Bankes to go off with her & to take her with him disguised as a boy into Africa, where he has some thoughts of going. As he has told me of this intrigue I have entreated & urged & implored him not to listen to a scheme fraught with such ruin to both &, as he is not so blindly & madly in love as she is, I hope he will resist the temptation. He is endeavouring to prevail on her to return to [her] husband &, if once she goes out of town, he will, I hope, have too much reason not to avoid meeting her again till he can do so without danger to either. She is very clever & eccentric, which suits him exactly.[30]

'[July] In the morning I had a long visit from Mr. Bankes. He first talked to me of his distresses about Lady Buckinghamshire, who is now quite separated from her husband & is very anxious to go & live abroad & take him with her. This he resists, feeling that it wd. ruin her & himself, too. He afterwards talked to me of Lord Byron, who he has been extremely intimate with all his life. They made acquaintance at Cambridge, & Mr. Bankes said that in spite of his vices he could not help liking him, that he believed Ld. Byron had been more attached to him than he had ever been to anyone else & that, in the eccentric parts of their characters, they had many points of similarity. He told me he thought Lord Byron was vicious from the mere love of vice; that he had often heard him say that he wd. be sorry to die before having committed every vice that was ever heard of, that he had been the lover of Lady Caroline Lamb & afterwards of her mother-in-law, Lady Melbourne, that he had lived in Switzerland with two sisters, the daughters, I think, of Godwin; & he, Mr. Bankes, said he thought it lucky that his [Byron's] own daughter, a child of 5 years, had died, as it might have become his victim. He says that to all his other vices he has now added that of stingyness, to a degree he never saw in any human being.'[31]

Bankes's wit was renowned among the famous and fashionable. Samuel Rogers, the banker-poet, recalled among his anecdotes about Sidney Smith that, 'Witty as Smith was, I have seen him at my own house absolutely overpowered by the superior facetiousness of William Bankes'.[32]

Anecdotes about Bankes were legendary. 'As a member of the Travellers' Club, on a question being started as to the best mode of dealing with a foreigner admitted to its society, who was addicted to spitting, he moved as an amendment to the recommendation that the offender should be sent to *Coventry*, the substitution of *Spitalfields*. He was quite at home in the College Hall and Combination Rooms, and capable in an easy good-humoured way of keeping up the ball of conversation with Whewell, Sedgwick, or any other professed talker.'[33]

His reputation as a great talker gained him two entries in the undated collection of unconnected anecdotes, 'Gossip redeemed by the speakers and the subjects', published by Frances Wynn, a well-connected lady who moved in high circles. 'I have heard this evening a strange wild romantic story from Mr. Bankes, almost too improbable for a novel, and yet the leading facts seem established beyond a doubt.' *The Pretended Archduke* is a tale of a mysterious stranger who arrives at the house of the British consul in Jaffa, tips lavishly, and confides that he is the brother of the Emperor of Austria, travelling incognito. Overawed, the consul lent a large sum of money. Promises of advancement for the consul's son, if he would travel with the stranger, lured him into extending an even larger loan. The stranger moved from place to place, accompanied by whispers of his secret rank, and extracting larger and larger sums from his hosts. Even when rumours of fraud spread, his ingenuity masked the deception. Returning to Europe, the truth was at last uncovered, he was imprisoned, audaciously seducing his jailer's wife to effect his escape. Bankes is said to have heard the story in Italian from the consul's son, when visiting Jaffa, and been so impressed by the young man's continuing loyalty in the face of such deception, that he engaged him as his servant. The circulating story of this adventurer, now set in Greece, was confirmed by Sir William Gell in his *Memoirs*. According to John Barker it was 'romantic tho true'.[34]

The second tale, *Anecdotes of Dénon* (*sic*), resulted from an intimate meeting between Denon and Bankes in Paris. Denon had by then been removed from his position as Director of the Louvre Museum by Louis XVIII on the Restoration, and the great museums and botanical collections had been stripped and destroyed by war and neglect. Bankes wished to visit Roustan, the Mameluke servant who had been given to Napoleon in Egypt by one of the pashas and who had remained at his side and been treated with the greatest generosity by the Emperor. Bankes hoped to quiz him on the domestic life of Napoleon, but Denon replied that their friendship would end if Bankes were to honour such a traitor, who had abandoned his master, preferring to run a small shop in Paris rather than join him in exile in St Helena.

They met when Bankes was invited to Paris for the 6 May 1821 baptism of the Duc de Bordeaux in Notre-Dame. Denon arranged a meeting with Count Forbin to examine an interesting inscription, and presented Bankes with a set of prints of masterpieces from the art gallery of Florence as a souvenir of his esteem. The anecdote records what must have been a fascinating encounter with the most celebrated of the savants who accompanied Napoleon to Egypt, and one whose best-selling book accompanied Bankes's travels.[35]

'The great traveller' was still 'excessively entertaining' in 1821, although Henry Edward Fox declared that he had 'a tiresome voice'. Although 'full of knowledge and originality', the *raconteur* was 'unceasing, his voice is painfully unpleasant'.[36] By 1826 even Mrs Arbuthnot's ardent enthusiasm was waning. The famous traveller so delightful and agreeable in discussing his travels according to the Duke of Wellington[37] 'provoked us excessively by engrossing as much as possible all the conversation, & talking so loud as quite to drown Sir Walter's [Scott's] conversation. I never saw such bad taste in my life, I almost thought he was drunk.' By 1829, she was describing his humour as 'coarse & sometimes tiresome'.[38]

෨෧෨

Following his travels Bankes had returned to Parliamentary life, representing one of the two seats belonging to Cambridge University from 1822 to 1826 alongside Palmerston, then Secretary of War. Having started late in canvassing for the seat, in opposition to the Prime

Minister Lord Liverpool's protégé Lord Hervey, he was 'hurried & harassed' but hoped his friends were 'canvassing in all directions', urging Murray to 'Lose not a moment in thinking of any body not only that has a vote but that has a Brother or a fifteenth cousin *& compel them to come in!*' He had just received news of Linant's acquisition of a rare portion of a second-century Greek papyrus roll containing part of Homer's *Iliad* in Elephantine, 'upon the utmost borders of the ancient civilised world', and had acceded to his friends' clamours and announced the discovery in the Cambridge papers to excite interest among the learned body, 'though it is an odd thing to get Homer canvassing for me!'.[39] Mrs Arbuthnot too was pressed into service in canvassing, to the annoyance of her husband, who was a supporter of Lord Liverpool. On his being chosen, Bankes presented the University with a gift of valuable books and subscribed a hundred guineas towards the erection of their observatory.

Bankes won his seat with such a large majority that it was common talk in London that Palmerston might have to look for another seat at the next General Election. Palmerston himself was surprised at Bankes's success. He recognized the strength of 'Protestant' (i.e. anti-Catholic) feeling, but knew the 'Protestant' majority of rural clergymen were mainly non-resident voters and difficult to turn out on polling day. Even visiting Cambridge at Christmas 1822 and finding Bankes 'feasting with his constituents', he still considered that his supporters would not turn against him.

Palmerston had moved away from a High Tory position and favoured Catholic Emancipation, voting for it in the great debate of May 1825 when the House of Commons passed the resolution put forward by the Irish MPs, only to have the bill thrown out by the House of Lords. He was informed by Dr Wood, the Master of St John's who owed his appointment as Dean of Ely to Palmerston's patronage, that Bankes had become unpopular in Cambridge and his moral conduct was causing concern. The reason given was his shocking pursuit of Lady Buckinghamshire. (Wood was apparently oblivious to Palmerston's own philandering activities.) Mrs Arbuthnot's earlier fears had been realized. On 6 January 1823 Lord Clarendon declared: 'The principal news of the day, I suppose, is the elopement of that wonderfully travelled high-churchman (so recently deemed a fit – and the only fit – representative of the extreme high church of Cambridge) Bankes with Lady Buckinghamshire. She is young, rather particular looking in dress and face, tho' prettyish, and had a strong case of flirtation with him all last year. I can't recollect who she was but I know I have heard that her family traced their descent in a strait line from King Alfred, and I believe all eat oatcakes in honour of him ... I have just been so interrupted by visits I must curtail my letter. First, Tierney [George Tierney (1761–1830), a government minister] but he told me no news, only that I was wrong about Lady Buckinghamshire. She was a natural daughter of Sir Arthur Pigot's. He (Lord B.) was originally a clerk in one of the public offices, but on coming to the title retired from public life. He perceived improper intimacy between Bankes and Miladi, brings an action against him [on a charge of "criminal conversation" as adultery was then called] and employs Scarlett (his Cambridge opponent) against him!'[40] Indeed the prosecuting counsel was ironically none other than his former rival in the Cambridge election, James Scarlett KC, a celebrated lawyer and later first Baron Abinger. Many years later comes a hint that Bankes had abruptly abandoned the lady.

In November 1825, with an election expected the following summer, Sir John Copley, the Attorney General, and Goulburn, the Chief Secretary for Ireland, both High Tories, decided to stand against Bankes for the seat. They were not officially standing against Palmerston, but as there were only two seats for Cambridge University their success would mean his defeat. Palmerston, who had held his seat for fourteen years, was astonished and infuriated to have two other government colleagues standing against him. Some assumed that the only explanation for this was that Palmerston would be given a peerage and Bankes ditched by the government. Although Palmerston was not supported by Lord Liverpool, Bankes, Copley, and Goulburn all opposed Catholic Emancipation so that the High Tory vote would be split between them, and Palmerston would have the united support of the Whigs, who were not contesting the seat, and the pro-Catholic-Emancipation Canningite Tories. The young Thomas Macaulay attempted to discredit Goulburn, accusing him of cruelty to the slaves on his West Indies estate, in order to encourage Bankes to remain in the field and inadvertently play the role of a spoiler. Bankes, trailing last, attacked Goulburn as a tool of the government, and Goulbourn was delighted to witness Bankes's discomfiture when at a dinner of the Society for Promoting Christian Knowledge Bankes jumped to his feet to announce that he himself had founded a branch in Cambridge, only to discover he had confused the societies. Bankes wrote a violent letter demanding a comparison of strength with Goulburn: 'ungentlemanlike & unfair' according to Palmerston. This prompted a clever ballad including the lines: 'Bankes is foolish in Reviews / Goulburn foolish in his speeches. / Choose between them, Cambridge, pray, / Which is weakest, Cambridge say. / Bankes, accustomed much to roam, plays with truth a traveller's pranks; / Goulburn, though he stays at home, Travels thus as much as Bankes.'[41] The poll took place in June 1826. Bankes rejected last-minute demands to end the extravagance of paying voters' travelling expenses. He saw it as a trick to reduce his support but after tumultuous debate the practice was abandoned. Palmerston requested his supporters to wait until the last moment and use their second vote tactically to ensure his success; Bankes asked his supporters to vote early hoping to get a sufficient lead to persuade the anti-Catholics to vote for him, rather than Goulburn, to prevent Palmerston getting in. At one point Bankes was ahead of Palmerston by four votes and, confident of beating him easily, insisted on a fourth day. However, in the event, Copley won 772 votes, Palmerston 631, Bankes 508, and Goulburn 437, putting Bankes out of Parliament until 1829.[42] Hobhouse was delighted to see Bankes and 'No Popery' defeated, declaring, 'He is exactly the same rattling grinning fellow as ever and he talked at the hall table today the same sort of nonsense as he used when a pupil at College.' None of the candidates came out of it well, being lampooned as Profligacy (Palmerston), Knavery (Copley), Bigotry (Goulburn) and Buffoonery (Bankes). Undaunted, Bankes stood again in 1827 after Copley was elevated to the peerage, but lost; the supporters of 'our glorious, our Protestant, Bankes' inspiring Macaulay's *The Country Clergyman's Trip to Cambridge: An Election Ballad.*

Bankes had indeed spoken vehemently against Catholic Emancipation in the House on the many debates on this issue in the 1820s. He even managed to inject this grave subject with his customary wit, raising laughter in the House over his fellow member of Parliament Dr Lushington, an ardent reformer and a staunch churchman, who had complained to the University Club that their library stocked the scandalous memoirs of Hariette Wilson, the well-known courtesan, but excluded the Bible. In 1831, despite Bankes's 'most successful speech', the Catholic Relief Bill was passed.[43]

Bankes's architectural interests and 'indefatigable exertions' saved some of the finest monumental remains in Westminster Abbey, preserved Eltham Hall, and interfered to prevent the demolition of some fine early priests' stalls. It seems likely to have been William, rather than his father, who was Chairman of the Select Committee of 1824 considering the rebuilding of the Westminster Courts of Justice, presenting a report which was a plea for good taste and excellence. He also gave evidence to the House of Commons Committee valuing Claudius Rich's collection of antiquities (for purchase by the British Museum), particularly advising the purchase of examples of cuneiform script to facilitate its decipherment.[44]

Having lost his seat in 1826, Bankes turned his attentions to putting the adventures of 'Mahomet' (Finati) into print. Mrs Arbuthnot wrote encouragingly, 'I hope you will persevere with yr. intention to publish Mahomet for I long to see the conclusion of his adventures.'[45] Editing Finati's *Narrative* enabled Bankes to insert brief erudite footnotes (and to include parts of his own journal material that he perhaps considered too frivolous to appear under his own name) without the responsibility or *gravitas* of a major undertaking. He also helped Lady Caroline Lamb compose the Oriental and Turkish sections of her novel *Ada Reis*.[46]

Burckhardt's volumes and the 'pilgrimage of Ali Bey' happily proved the 'minutest accuracy of Mahomet's recollections'. Murray was requested to send Bankes a copy of Niebuhr, and Burckhardt's manuscript of his pilgrimage to Mecca, 'as I have now much leisure & am in the humour for working hard'.[47] Exactly three years later he was eager to have the title of the almost completed Finati book (over which he had taken great pains) advertised in the *Quarterly Review* – his own name, 'which I have added with some hesitation', to be printed in small characters. Two 'pretty little' volumes of six chapters each was his own choice, although he was worried this might prove a little small for the maps. His earlier protestations to Byron that he cared little for praise are not borne out by the obsessive care with which Murray was instructed to get the reviews written for the *Quarterly*. Having decided against writing them himself, Bankes suggested some background details on the politics and military aspects, and a few words on the sad death of the young Pasha from the plague (caught of a female slave he had purchased in Constantinople); perhaps Major Felix (Lord Prudhoe's artist) might be prevailed upon to add a few words about their own journey with Finati. Murray must have been relieved to hear he was at least pleased with the reviews in the *Monthly* and in the *Asiatic Journal*. The final draft was to be put into shape speedily 'or in the mean time I may relapse into inveterate idleness & not like to put the last hand to it which is wanting'. It should be published after the elections are over and 'Best of all when the new Parliament comes to London'. To his chagrin, the appearance of the finished book was delayed, provoking the usual effusions of disgruntled spleen. He was 'excessively surprised that in *not one of the papers* either of last night or this morning is there any advertisement or the slightest notice…insisting on its being published today… When I have worked hard to my own inconvenience to get it ready on time…vexed at finding delay…' etc., etc.[48]

⁂

Back in June 1819, Thebes had offered Bankes leisurely sightseeing in the company of other travellers and an opportunity to catch up with the post and peruse copies of the *Calcutta Journal*. Enraged at discovering in this an advertisement for the imminent publication of his own journey and discoveries in Syria written by his former companion James Silk Buckingham, Bankes immediately penned a series of inflammatory letters which were to prove to have a devastating and unforeseen effect: a libel action in 1826.[49] Buckingham, a mere merchant-seaman adventurer of no birth, wealth, or social position, had been his companion, no, rather his assistant, at Jerash, and now here he was advertising at length the publication of Bankes's own discoveries. An intemperate letter to Buckingham himself was followed by another to his father, Henry Bankes, in London, urging him to prevent John Murray from publishing the book, and one to the authorities in Bombay, demanding that Buckingham should be immediately dismissed and ostracized. As a result of Bankes's letter, Buckingham was banished from India.

Buckingham was a man who lived off his wits and schemes, an able, prolific writer who was to prove impervious to the superior forces of wealth and power that Bankes could bring to bear on his career (Bankes threatened: 'You will find that you have not duped an *obscure individual...*'). Buckingham was to become a man of pamphlets and projects, an irrepressible figure with a talent for self-advertisement. While Bankes fulminated in Thebes, the manuscript of *Travels in Palestine, through the countries of Bashan and Gilead, east of the River Jordan: including a visit to the cities of Geraza and Gamala in the Decapolis*, with its illustrative drawings and engravings, was already with Murray awaiting publication.

Henry Bankes successfully brought pressure against John Murray to refuse the manuscript and also demanded and received the illustrations. At sight of the book, which appeared in 1821, published by Longman & Co., William sounded off jubilantly to Murray, citing the numerous 'gross blunders & ignorance' of 'that swindler Buckingham's Quarto... You see that I am preparing for the review which I have not yet begun, but you shall have it within a very few days.' He needed 'to know whether it be a certain fact that this man has been imprisoned in India for a libel, when, & upon whom, & how long' and hoped that Murray would acquaint the *Edinburgh Review* writers 'of the nature of his transactions with me'. William John Bankes and William Gifford were said to be the anonymous authors of a 'malignant' review published in the *Quarterly Review*. (Gifford, with a reputation as a rather sour man, was its pro-Tory anti-Radical editor.)

In July 1825 Buckingham brought a legal action against Bankes's father Henry, for attempting to suppress the book by a libellous letter to Murray. Henry withdrew his defence and a nominal shilling was accepted as 'damages', with Buckingham's costs met. (Henry was also subpoenaed in the case against his son, but did not appear in court. Buckingham's Counsel scathingly remarked at the trial that, although £10 was paid to defray Henry's travelling expenses, 'Being, however an accurate accountant in these matters, (to which perhaps is to be partly attributed his son's similar care in pecuniary affairs) he made a stand for £20' (and was using his own carriage to boot). Action against Henry was followed by a charge of 'false and malicious' libel against William, which was to dog both parties until it finally reached court in London on 19 October 1826, seven years after the first inflammatory letter was written. The delays in bringing the action were caused by the difficulties of bringing Finati and Antonio da Costa from abroad as witnesses for the defence (for which the court ordered Buckingham to pay the expenses). Henry William Hobhouse seems to have avoided giving evidence as long as possible but was finally subpoenaed by Buckingham while in England.

Bankes's original letter to Buckingham had accused him of copying, without permission, Bankes's notes and plans of Jerash, referred to his 'notorious' reputation in Egypt and Syria, and threatened to blacken his character likewise in India. Buckingham, it continued, had falsely represented himself as an intimate of both Colonel Missett and Burckhardt to insinuate himself with Bankes; Bankes claimed that Burckhardt had referred to Buckingham as a 'villain'. The expedition was planned and paid for by Bankes; Buckingham was more employee than companion.

The great mistake made by Bankes was to copy the letter in cold blood some months later and, on his return to Europe, give it to Henry William Hobhouse in Trieste, unsealed and with instructions to show it to Barker, the British consul at Aleppo, and Claudius Rich, the East India Company's Resident at Baghdad, and then to make what use he thought proper of it, 'intending to injure the plaintiff in the sale of the said book'. Hobhouse showed it to John Palmer, a respectable merchant in Calcutta, and Mr Erskine, a high officer of the Supreme Court at Bombay. Bankes denied the charge of 'publication' necessary to a suit of libel and contended that the contents of the letter were true. The dispute centred on the recording work at Jerash, when Buckingham scarcely spent a week together with Bankes, but Buckingham claimed to have returned alone for a second visit upon which the observations in his book were based.

The matter was tried in the Court of the King's Bench at the Guildhall in London before Lord Chief Justice Abbott and a special jury. It took place on a single day. Bankes's character was smeared by the biting sarcasm of the plaintiff's Counsel, who accused him of a jealous and irritable over-reaction to someone who dared 'to tread on the ground hallowed by the footsteps of Mr Bankes' or 'to make any observations upon places ever described by his pencil, or even in his private conversation'. The libellous letter accused Buckingham of copying, effectively stealing (the word 'larceny' was used by Counsel), Bankes's own notes, drawings and plans: 'above all … the plan of ruins at D'Jerash was constructed and noted with my own hand, and that all the assistance I derived from you … was in *your* ascertaining for me the relative bearings of some of the buildings with *my* compass'. How fortunate, sneered Counsel, that Byron had not borrowed Bankes's pen to write *Childe Harold* or Bankes would surely claim that that also as his own. It was not disputed that Buckingham had traced a copy of the plan against the window of the Convent at Nazareth, and Bankes must have believed that plans made jointly between travelling companions were common property (as were observations and discussions) since he permitted it *knowing* why Buckingham wanted a copy. The fact that Bankes, though travelling for as many years as he and Buckingham had spent days together, had failed to produce a single line of his own travels was brought up several times.

Bankes's defence alleged that Buckingham joined him at his invitation, 'having previously agreed to take down any notes and the journal when I should wish it'. This was unfortunately at odds with the testimony of Bankes's servants, who stated that Buckingham never drew or copied anything himself, being ignorant both of ancient languages and of the skills of draughtsmanship. The letter had suggested that Buckingham was so ignorant that he failed even to distinguish between Turkish and Roman architecture. Tellingly, the original notes that Bankes claimed were copied by Buckingham were never produced in court. Bankes had, however, written much 'journal' material in the form of letters to Buckingham. They had all been returned, as requested, save for a single letter which Buckingham claimed had accidentally stuck to some sealing wax inside the portmanteau. In this letter Bankes wrote in friendly, if patronizing, terms, of a future publication in which 'I do not think you will be ashamed of having your name associated to what I may one day or another throw together into form'. Bankes had not seen a copy of *Travels in Palestine* when he wrote his letter and was not to know that no attempt was made to disguise the narrative of their journey together, and the book was full of praise for him. Curiously though, the book contained no details of Buckingham's alleged second visit to Jerash when his own plan, subsequently published, was said to have been made. Evidence was brought by Bankes to show that the deviations on this from Bankes's plan were as fictional as the second visit itself. Disparaging letters from Burckhardt, now dead, impugning Buckingham's character in lively terms ('a most barefaced impostor and swindler') were also produced.

Bankes's two servants, brought to England specially (Antonio having retired to his native Portugal and Finati coming from Egypt) and no doubt well rehearsed, did not produce the desired effect in court. Their evidence not only contradicted Bankes's own testimony, since Antonio asserted that Buckingham was expressly forbidden by his master to draw at all, but their reports of conversations between the two men in English were undermined by their inability to understand the questions put to them in court in English which had to go through an interpreter. Bankes had been in the habit of using the Italian language with both of them.

Charles Barry gave evidence about the inaccuracy, and therefore the fictitious nature, of the published plan of Jerash presented as Buckingham's own work, and Captains Irby and Mangles, Colonel Leake and Henry Beechey also appeared for Bankes.

The judge's summing-up to the jury was brief and clear. He accepted that the libel had been published, and found that the defendant Bankes had failed to prove two or three material parts of the letter's allegations and therefore failed to prove the facts of the letter true. The defendant had failed to prove that the character of the plaintiff was 'notorious' in Egypt and Syria, and essentially failed to prove that Buckingham had stolen what was Bankes's property. The jury took three-quarters of an hour to return a verdict for the plaintiff and £400 damages.

To rub salt into the wound, the affair was not then laid to rest. Buckingham added an appendix to his *Travels among the Arab Tribes*, published in 1825, which resurrected the affair in the most minute and extraordinary detail. It is packed with vituperative (and repetitive) denunciations of Bankes, his father, and the late Burckhardt. In addition, Buckingham himself published the proceedings under the title *Verbatim Report of the Action for Libel in the Case of Buckingham versus Bankes* in the same year as the case. It is peppered with footnotes which expand (especially when the defendant's witnesses are examined) to overwhelm the text of the 'verbatim' proceedings. Indeed at one point, a single line of text just manages to appear above the voluminous footnote text where Buckingham roars off in pursuit of every perceived slight or inaccuracy. Not content with *The Times* having supported Buckingham over the issue and its editor's pronouncement that 'The Bankes's make but a sorry figure in this affair', he deluged the newspaper with letters (which the editor, perhaps protecting the Establishment, refused to print). He represented himself as the victim of an injustice, his fortune entirely destroyed, his prospects gloomy. Presumably the publicity did not hinder the sales of his book.

Curiously, Buckingham chose to include with the *Verbatim Report* his defence against the 'Slanders of *Punch*' about his establishment of a 'British and Foreign Institute for the interchange of national hospitality with foreigners'. *Punch* had, he alleged, accused him of fraud, of feathering his nest at the expense of its members, and claimed his protests were 'only another instance of his matchless ingenuity to draw upon himself and his establishment the notice of the public'. It seems the 'Lectures, Soirées, Conversazioni, and Discussions' were mainly provided by himself. *Punch*'s final jibe that his was a life 'full of projects' is accompanied by his own proud list of projects accomplished. This eclectic list reads: 'Establishment of a Free Press in India, Liberty of settling in India for all British Subjects, Power of purchasing land by English Colonists, Establishment of Trial by Jury in India, Abolition of the burning of widows, Opening the Overland Route to India, Immediate Emancipation of British Slaves, Establishment of Temperance Societies, Providing Public Baths for the people, Opening Public Walks & Gardens for the same, Establishment of Provincial Museums, Forming Public Cemeteries, Annual Grant to Polish Exiles, Abolition of Impressment for the Navy, Seamen's Homes, Society for Suppression of Duelling, and Reduction of the Tax on Authors and Publishers'. There was already another project in the pipeline: 'a Voyage of Discovery, Civilisation and Commerce'.[50]

The venomous review penned by Bankes, probably the cause if not the legal basis for the libel suit, produced an unforeseen side-effect. In order to dismiss every archaeological and historical claim made by Buckingham, as well as impugning his qualifications to write about such a subject at all, it provides us with a rare example of a published description of Bankes's own opinions on the archaeology of the Decapolis region, and in particular of Jerash. This has enabled modern scholars of the region to use it, together with Bankes's notes, to reconstruct an early and important survey of the site.[51]

CHAPTER ELEVEN

THE MEROE EXPEDITION
AND THE OUTLAW

'THERE ARE TWO YOUNG MEN of great talents Mr Linant & Mr Ricci gone up at Mr Bankes' expense from whom we may expect most accurate views of everything in the way of antiquity if Mr Bankes *can only be persuaded to publish them.*'[1]

Thwarted himself in the quest for Meroe, Bankes left for the pleasures and responsibilities of England having commissioned Linant to explore in his stead, leaving Salt in charge of the arrangements. Much to Bankes's irritation, Linant, a wilful young man, failed to leave immediately for Nubia; instead he and Ricci joined an expedition to the Siwa Oasis, and later visited Sinai. Bankes still nursed this grievance in 1830 when, in the Finati book, he published the fact that Linant was left 'with a salary, upon condition of his taking the very earliest opportunity of following up the discoveries upon the Nile to the southward, with a view especially to fixing the site and examining the remains of Meroë. How far the injunction had been punctually complied with, of setting out the soonest that circumstances should permit, it is not my place to inquire, but full twelve months had elapsed before I heard of any preparation at all for the journey.' Bankes's tart footnote adds: 'I am as much at a loss upon this point as the author can be, since the departure of the Egyptian army … for the expedition which was to open the upper country, took place in the autumn of 1820, and Monsieur Cailliaud and Monsieur Jomard seem to have gone up at that time.'[2] Mohammed Ali had sent an army into Nubia in pursuit of the last escaped remnants of the Mamelukes, whom he had massacred in Cairo in 1811. Under the leadership of his sons, Ismail and Ibrahim, his troops successfully invaded and annexed the Funj kingdom of Sennar.[3] The mineralogist and explorer Frédéric Cailliaud with his companion Letorzec, and George Bethune English, an American officer in the service of the Egyptian army, accompanied the train of the army led by Ibrahim Pasha, as it travelled south.[4]

Linant eventually left Cairo on 15 June 1821 with Ricci, supported by the stalwart Finati and two servants. Following in the wake of the army, they found villages denuded of supplies and were forced to draw down illicitly on army reserves.[5] Along the way Cailliaud and Linant were to meet up in amicable rivalry extended over genial dinners and periodic squabbles. They even exchanged drawings, yet privately derided each other's achievements.

Hardly the ideal companion for a gruelling trip into dangerous little-known regions during a war, Ricci was moody from the start and sulked, refusing to speak to his companion. Finally in November, at the market town of Shendi, he threatened to leave, only lack of money and provisions having prevented him earlier. Linant retorted that only Salt's insistence accounted for Ricci's presence. It was quite against his own wishes, and Bankes had been expecting him to record tomb paintings instead.[6] Ultimately Ricci would have to explain his conduct to Salt and Bankes. Ricci complained of being slighted and treated as a servant, which Linant denied. 'Everybody knew that he was my equal and my friend. But those were always the ideas that he imagined; not just with me but with everyone.'[7]

Salt's explanation for sending Ricci without Bankes's permission did not assuage the latter's displeasure and annoyance, although Salt cleverly hinted at saving expenditure and the danger of yet again being pre-empted by another traveller, hitting both Bankes's weak spots. 'I am sorry that you continue to regret that Ricci was sent in to Nubia but I think if you will consider the matter you will be satisfied that all was for the best. When Linant left us his health was in such a weak state that I felt afraid to trust him alone as a relapse would probably have proved fatal, and the Doctor's presence on that account was very desirable. Besides it had come to my knowledge that very advantageous proposals had been made by Baron Minutoli to Ricci to undertake this voyage on his account & though Ricci said nothing of this to me I saw such a resolution on his part to make the voyage that I felt assured if I did not let him go with Linant he would go on his own. Besides, to tell you the truth, as Linant had already become somewhat extravagant in his expenses, according to my way of thinking, I judged that Ricci, from the instructions I gave him, would be rather a check upon him than an additional expense, as was in fact the case. The money I advanced to the Doctor for this trip was little and I made no engagement for his salary, explaining to him most clearly that I had no authority from you to send him up. Thus, at little expense in fact to you, I insured all he could do in this voyage for you. As it turned out, the voyage made his fortune – he saved Ibrahim Pasha's life & the Father together with Ibrahim Pasha presented him as a recompense with the sum of eight thousand dollars, with which he is now gone to Europe. This sum was in hard cash. Before he went he gave up to me, for you, all his sketches made in Nubia which were very interesting as they express very correctly the different character of the sculpture found there from any existing in Egypt which with all Linant's talents he was not so capable of doing. These sketches I shall make up in a small case and send by the first safe conveyance.'[8]

This he did, after carefully annotating Ricci's work by inserting a key to the ground plans. 'When you receive the beautiful drawings made by the latter [Ricci] of all the hieroglyphic monuments they met with, which I have in hand, you will not be sorry that I sent him up as it will make your work very complete.' Linant had been 'a little extravagant' but 'when the whole comes to be laid before you – you will have great reason to be satisfied.'[9]

⁕

The two men had proceeded south, accurately planning and drawing everything of interest and always clearly identifying the subjects, whether fragmentary remains of great temples at Soleb (pl. 80) and Sesebi, an overturned colossus and stelae at Tombos, or the huge brick structures of Kerma, thought to be ruined pyramids. What were perhaps the largest surviving Meroitic sculptures, two fallen twenty-three-foot colossi now in the Antiquities Museum at Khartoum, were drawn in situ at Tabo on Argo Island, at the head of the Third Cataract (pl. 81).

Now well beyond the tracks of most travellers, they approached the earlier of the two ancient capitals of the kingdom of Kush, an important religious centre with many temples and two groups of pyramids (pl. 86).[10] Napata, once an Egyptian New Kingdom administrative seat, lay around the foot of the striking 'Holy Mountain' of Gebel Barkal, a flat-topped rock rising from the plain (pl. 89). Napata became prominent from c.900 BC to c.270 BC; the capital then shifted to Meroe, with its more indigenous culture and language, until the fall of the kingdom in c. AD 320. The nature of this transfer is still not understood, but Gebel Barkal has been well documented by modern archaeologists.[11]

In examining the pyramids of Nuri, a nearby royal cemetery, Linant attributed their ruined condition to structural weakness caused by their material and fragile shape. He correctly observed they had always been truncated, rather than pointed, and were originally topped by small platforms. The rubble of one surprisingly revealed an earlier pyramid within (pl. 90); smooth-faced and of a finer, lighter-coloured stone but not on the same axis.[12]

The quantity of temple ruins, explored between 7 and 15 October 1821, convinced him that this was an ancient town. Among the debris he recorded two large red granite lions (brought in ancient times from Soleb, later removed by Lord Prudhoe and presented to the British Museum). Unlike other travellers he did not believe this to be Meroe, despite a similarly named place (Merowe) further downstream, and hoped to verify the ruins as Napata by astronomical observations. He copied Meroitic inscriptions and, after investigating the pyramids and their chapels (taking care to portray them with great exactitude), decided that the burial chambers must be underground. They 'set a number of natives to excavate in one of them, but after a good deal of labour, failed of discovering any passage into the interior [pl. 87]'.[13]

The second pylon of the great temple concealed curious (Meroitic) relief-figures representing battle scenes: soldiers, horses, and chariots. Nearby, the headless statue of a hawk was recognized as similar to a wooden one in Salt's collection. Linant refrained from drawing badly preserved reliefs, fearful of conveying a wrong impression, but sketched a strange pedestal. A square altar of fine blue granite, showing four figures of King Taharqo holding up the sky, graced one sanctuary; in a further chamber, which he thought was that of a separate building, he found a second granite altar or pedestal, but broken in two.[14] Both Linant and Ricci drew a sandstone Meroitic dais showing bound captives. Riding over to Merowe, Linant discovered some reused hieroglyphic blocks in the wall and in front of the door of the house of the local dignitary, the 'Melek Chaous'.

Linant was to return to Gebel Barkal in 1826 to find the site much depleted, aggravated by the heavy rains of that year, and bearing evidence of deliberate damage. The 'Typhonium' (Temple B 300),[15] of which he had made such a beautiful watercolour (pl. 85), was now ruined, having suffered the fall of a pillar and a large part of the ceiling, also altering the exterior view that he had drawn (pl. 84). Poorly organized and pointless excavations, including some under the blue granite altar, he attributed to 'Mr Broski',[16] or Turkish treasure-hunting.

Both men made meticulous copies of the pyramid chapel reliefs and texts (pl. 83), and Linant drew a superb series of views of the pyramids and temples; in all seventy-two valuable drawings of many monuments, now vanished. They drew one group of pyramids not recorded elsewhere and soon reduced to rubble (pl. 87).[17] Their important drawings of the remaining reliefs of Temple B 500 record the exact position of otherwise unknown and lost images which extend our knowledge of the decorative scheme of this temple.[18]

⟳⟲

Ricci finally abandoned Linant on 7 November 1821, after yet another argument, at Damer, just south of the confluence of the Nile and Atbara. He returned briefly a few days later but then left once again and went on alone to Sennar. They were to be reconciled later when they met near 'Sirvi' in Fazogli, the kingdom south of Sennar.[19] Ricci was now physician to Ibrahim Pasha and returned to Cairo with him when he was taken ill with dysentery. The drawings of Meroe, Musawwarat, and Naqa are therefore by Linant alone, who travelled on with Finati.[20]

Linant's journal presents a vivid picture of these months of travel along the Nile between Gebel Barkal and the sites which lay south of the junction with the Atbara. As commissioned, he explored and mapped the river and surrounding areas, correcting previous errors and recording the unknown monuments, many for the first time. But his journals and drawings are also redolent with the desolation and silence of these abandoned places, still verdant then and full of wildlife. Precise archaeological surveys are enlivened by descriptions of the land and its people: villagers and local sheikhs, caravaneers, European adventurers, and army personnel, all passing against the backdrop of heightened tension and outbreaks of violence from Ibrahim Pasha's military campaign; events which remain peripheral to his work, mentioned only when they impede his travels. At the southern headquarters, Sennar, Europeans had gathered in the Pasha's employment. Here, Linant compassionately befriended his former companion on the journey to Siwa, Frediani, who was suffering from a nervous breakdown, and found time to paint the Pasha's pet giraffe (pl. 103), a shy young animal who licked his hand with her soft tongue.

Linant was charged with 'following up the discoveries upon the Nile to the southward, with a view especially to fixing the site and examining the remains of Meroë'.[21] Having passed through the ruins of ancient Meroe on 9 November 1821, hurrying on his way to Shendi for the Saturday bazaar, it was not until 25 March, after exploring Musawwarat and 'l'Hardan' (Naqa), that he returned.[22] Once installed in a village house, his drawing was interrupted by a storm and then the robbery of two of his camels. Grabbing Finati's gun and barefoot, Linant furiously gave chase, intending murder but inflicting only minor injuries with the small-shot ammunition. Finati was immediately dispatched in hot pursuit of the culprit: the Ababde Sheikh 'Sahat Walet Nemmer'. Summary justice was meted out, an apology demanded, and Finati obtained a lavish dinner in the village by impersonating the Pasha's tax-officer.

Rumours of general disaffection and armed revolts did not deter Linant, who named the site, known only as the 'Valley of the Pyramids', after the province, 'Cabinna', as it lay between the equidistant villages of Begrawiya, Dangeil, and Es-Sur.[23] Although other travellers correctly thought it Meroe, the much grander remains at Musawwarat seemed to Linant a more likely candidate, with 'Cabinna' (although two days' march away) as its port.

He recognized the pyramids as tombs belonging to the extensive city ruins on the bank of the Nile where he made out the enclosure walls of a large temple retaining six ram-sphinxes and fragmentary stone monuments.[24] The sandstone for all the construction had come from the extensive quarries nearby.

The pyramids in the west group in the plain were reduced to heaps of debris, their chapels lost. On a small peak, a mile away, a semicircle of twenty-two pyramids and chapels with decorated interiors and pylons were better preserved, and small holes suggested missing emplacements atop the truncated summit platforms.[25] Each pyramid was objectively described but Linant was struck by the melancholic effect of their desolate situation.

Walking along the Nile on his last day at the site, 2 April, he saw smoke rising from the village and rushed back to discover a house on fire and his servants moving his belongings to safety. He instantly pulled down the burning house to stop the flames spreading through the straw roofs, later rebuffing the villagers' demands for compensation by declaring the fire (caused by the carelessness of his own cook) to be the work of Allah.

The entrances to the underground burial chambers lay some way in front of the chapels and eluded his discovery. The well-preserved 'Pyramid N 6' and several others were virtually razed to the ground only twelve years later by Giuseppe Ferlini during a successful treasure-hunt in which many exquisite items of gold jewellery were found and taken out of the country for sale.[26] A wave of public excitement at this discovery sadly exposed the remaining pyramids to rampant ransack and destruction. Linant recorded a pyramid with its capstone intact (pl. 95) but all the capstones subsequently fell, and even the form of the pyramids became unrecognizable. Fortunately, Linant copied reliefs and inscriptions, surveyed, drew exquisite views, and compiled full structural reports, plans, and descriptions of each pyramid and chapel summed up in analytical conclusions.[27] His work remained unsurpassed by that of subsequent travellers.

After sketching the ruined Meroitic temple at Wadi Banat (now destroyed to its foundations) and its reliefs, Linant reached Musawwarat es-Sufra in February 1822. The purpose of this vast and perplexing site, on an old route between Shendi and Naqa, still baffles scholars.[28] The warren of ruined structures within the enclosure, which include ramps and representations of elephants, was probably connected with the ceremonial function of the site, and has been interpreted in various ways: palace or temple complex, pilgrim centre, or even housing for elephants used in cults or for war.[29] Beyond the enclosure lay further temples, other buildings, and the ruins of reservoirs, but no ruins of any ancient town.[30]

It is hardly surprising that Linant took its impressive ruins to be those of Meroe; its enclosure as perhaps a fortified monastery, a palace, or college, believing the brick town outside lost by the effects of time or rain. He carried a memorandum from Bankes that Meroe was seventy miles from the river, and persuaded himself that, if this meant the distance to the port, rather than the river, then Musawwarat was Meroe. He staked out his claim as the first European to have visited the site (one month before Cailliaud who retaliated with a similar graffito):

'L'AN DE JÉSUS 1822
LOUIS LINANT A VISITÉ CES RUINES RENOMMÉES IL EST VENU MANDÉ PAR
L'ANGLETERRE ET IL A PÉNÉTRÉ JUSQU'AU ROYAUME DE SENNAR GRACE AUX
CONQUETES D'ISMAEL PACHA GÉNÉRAL DES ARMÉES DE SON GRACE MAHAMET ALI
VICE ROI D'EGYPTE.'[31]

Five days' work produced a remarkable record in sixteen drawings: architectural details, the un-Egyptian style and subjects of its reliefs (pl. 96), secondary inscriptions, plans of the Great Enclosure (pl. 97) and the South East Temple (Meroitic), and wonderful views, including the Great Temple (pl. 98). The discovery that the missing key to the plan of the great enclosure produced for Bankes is to be found on the copy which Linant kept, now allows us to position securely fragments, inscriptions, etc. mentioned in his journal.

The settlement at Naqa, with two *hafirs* (reservoirs) and two cemeteries, lies about eighteen miles from the Nile, further up the valley leading from Wadi ban Naqa. Close to a distinctive Graeco-Roman-style temple stands the best preserved temple of the indigenous Meroitic lion-headed god Apedemak (pls 100 and 102), dating to Natakamani and Amanitere (late first century BC to early first century AD).[32] These and other surviving religious buildings have been extensively studied but not, until recently, the town or cemeteries.[33]

Since 1995 the site has been re-investigated by the Egyptian Museum Berlin Naqa Project, beginning with a surface survey tracing the outlines of many buildings which had remained undisturbed below the covering sand since Richard Lepsius's 1845 visit.[34]

Passing and sketching the ruins of Wadi ban Naqa, Linant set out for Naqa on 27 February 1822, without Finati, who had dysentery. On the advice of his guide, his tent was concealed inside the temple and he anxiously kept the camels in a state of readiness against a sudden attack by the Shukriya Arabs, who then dominated Butana. He eventually sent off excess camels, baggage, and men, keeping only his guide and two fast camels, and working until midnight. He finished sixteen drawings, but a stone ram and some comments on the hieroglyphs were still left to record when he was finally chased out of the valley by armed Arabs on 4 March.

The ruins, which took the name of the nearby mountain, Gebel Hardan ('l'Hardan'), owed their profuse surrounding vegetation to the copious rains. The valley was teeming with wildlife: antelope, gazelles, wild donkeys, hares, and guinea-fowl. One night he heard the roar of a lion.

Linant distinguished the ruins of a large town of which only four structures remained, but the plentiful ruins were evidence of many other monuments, some up to two miles away. A fine description brings to life the scattered ruins, and the most delicate pencil lends his drawings an exceptional quality and a very high finish. The detail, unlike that of Cailliaud, is very faithful. On his plan Linant marked the position of a ram-sphinx at the rear of the Great Temple (pl. 101), and the remains of a construction of Roman-type brick on the temple ramp; neither of these is shown by Cailliaud or Lepsius. In 1998 the Berlin Naqa Project rediscovered this lost ram-sphinx, and, after counting the sphinxes in the existing ram-sphinx avenue, realized that Linant's ram-sphinx was the sole remainder from another, previously unknown, avenue. They also discovered Linant's intrusive brick tomb on the temple ramp.[35]

❧❧❧❧

Linant was as dilatory in bringing his portfolio to England as he had been in setting forth, and 1823 saw thirteen long and irate letters pass from Bankes to Salt. Linant, whose journey had ended on 24 July 1822, demanded payment of his debts and an advance, threatening to withhold the Greek papyrus.

Some moneys were advanced, but Linant was still in Cairo at the end of March 1823 with Bankes regretting his mere gentleman's agreement. Linant submissively ran through a gamut of excuses: the plague season, misunderstandings, drawings to be finished, missing the boat, a near-shipwreck, debts, another trip, and difficulties transporting the Maharraqa granite.

Linant 'talks of travelling like a gentleman through France and pretensions of that sort', thunders Bankes. 'They are quite out of the question' and he must come directly. 'Remind him that his coming to England was actually a part of his agreement with me, & he must very well remember that so soon as he had got to Meroe his next step was to be that of join- ing me here … What is Linant to be doing in the Upper Country that I am to be paying him a salary? … it is not enough to talk to me of finishing drawings for this could be done any- where else as well.' Whatever Linant has collected belongs to Bankes. Linant should have gone into the Upper Country at once, the journey to Mount Sinai was 'so far as my views are concerned so much time lost, & gave the young man dilatory habits'. The whole thing should have been accomplished in one year and not three. Why had Linant not heeded his extremely concise instructions for transporting the weight of the Maharraqa stones? And yet Bankes admitted to retaining feelings of kindness toward Linant and a 'sincere regard that an intimate observation of him for so long had originated'.[36]

Salt also found excuses for him: 'a too great love of dress as well as of the fair sex are his weak points [funds were required for the expenses of a baby] and are the natural faults of his age'. He intended coming to England 'dressed as a Turk … and I believe it to be his inten- tion to appear in that costume in England, which, as he will no doubt be a great lion, is not I think, objectionable … You must watch over him while in London.'[37]

Linant arrived at Soughton in November 1824, joining Finati whose presence was required for the deposition against Buckingham.[38] He duly (if belatedly) presented his plans and drawings, the skins of many rare and beautiful birds, his journals, and a treatise on the history and customs of Nubia: *General Notices upon the principal countries and peoples comprehended in the journey of A. Linant when sent by William John Bankes to seek for Meroe and to examine the course of the Nile*. Bankes was ravished by the results: 'The remains which he has seen, especially those of Meroe, are magnificent beyond expectation; there is a crowd of Pyramids [pl. 92].' Most remarkable was the figure of the Meroitic queen (pl. 93) whose immense protuberance of her hips and behind would have defied belief had not Lady Hester assured him she had wit- nessed at the baths the similar girth of a sister of the Abyssinian king.

The portfolio joined the pile of unpublished papers, to be overshadowed in 1823 by the acclaim which greeted Cailliaud's *Voyage à Méroé et au Fleuve Blanc*: four volumes with a hand- some atlas of plates. Cailliaud could never understand why Linant had chosen to work for an Englishman, albeit one for whom he appeared to have a high regard, rather than publish to the glory of France.

In 1826 Bankes joined the Association for Promoting the discovery of the Interior parts of Africa, and was immediately invited on to the committee, having introduced Linant to become their agent in recording Meroitic sites and exploring the White Nile in the Association's boat. Although Linant succeeded in disproving Bruce's assertion that the 'Dindere' and the 'Rahat' rivers flowed into the Nile at the same spot, the committee soon found themselves beset by problems already familiar to Bankes. Adverse weather and the state of the country were excuses for procrastination; some information was sent back but the expenses were 'considerable'. By 1829, with Linant having completed a journey to Petra with Laborde, no drawings or maps had been received 'although M Linant has repeatedly announced that he is on the point of transmitting them and on one occasion he reported that he had actually transmitted a part of them to England'. His agreement was abruptly rescinded and his salary curtailed. Linant's expenses having 'considerably reduced the funds of the Association', Bankes was not re-elected, and in 1830, with funds and membership low, the Association joined forces with the Geographical Society of London.

◈◈◈

Bankes was returned to represent Marlborough in Parliament from 1829 to 1832. He was a guest in September 1830 on the inaugural journey of the Liverpool & Manchester railway, in the party of the Duke of Wellington, the guest of honour, and was an eye-witness to the fatal accident. They had been instructed to quit the carriages while the train stopped to take on water. While they were 'straggling and lounging on the railway line' there was the sound of an engine on the parallel line. 'Mr Huskisson (instead of remaining quiet where he was, when no harm could have happened to him) endeavoured to scramble round it.' He slipped or was caught by the passing engine 'which in an instant crushed his left leg to pieces... The shrieks from the car were dreadful... & the spectacle bloody & horrid to the last degree.' Huskisson knew immediately he could not live, crying 'Let me die here! only bring my wife to me!' He was carried at the rate of 34 miles an hour to a parsonage at Eccles, surgical aid was brought 'but before nine he expired'. The party continued the journey but the Duke declined the public dinner.

Huskisson's death removed a man whose policies Ultra-Tories such as Bankes feared and despised. Peel was informed that, according to Bankes and Lord Salisbury, many of their friends who would have gone into total opposition immediately had Huskisson rejoined the government were now favourably disposed towards Wellington.[39]

The Reform Bill was printed in March 1831 and the diarist Greville was convinced that though the mood of the people made it inevitable, for now it would be thrown out and Parliament dissolved. There was noisy confusion in Parliament with anti-Reformers such as Bankes, who 'looked as if his face would burst with blood' announcing certain revolution as a result. On the second reading, according to Hobhouse, a Reformer, 'Bankes rose and made one of the most extraordinary exhibitions I had ever seen. He whined, clasped his hands, and put himself into attitudes, concluding one of his sentences thus: "The Lord deliver us out of their hands, I say!" To be sure he was in earnest, for the Bill annihilated the Corfe Castle dynasty.'[40] Bankes stood in the consequent elections of 1831: all electoral considerations were put aside for the issue of Reform, and Reformers were swept in 'no matter what the characters of the Candidates, if they are only for the bill. Calcraft and Wellesley, the former not respected, the other covered with disgrace, have beat Bankes and Tyrrell.' In the new House of Commons the bill was carried in 1832. 'Peel is now aware (as everybody else now is) of the enormous fault that was committed in not throwing it out at once, before the Press had time to operate, and rouse the country to the pitch of madness it did. On what trifles turn the destinies of nations! William Bankes told me last night that Peel owned this to him; said that he had earnestly desired to do so, but had been turned from his purpose by Granville Somerset!! And why? Because he (in the expectation of a dissolution) must have voted against him, he said, in order to save his popularity in his own county.'[41]

'After the enactment of Reform he [Bankes] was one of the three members elected (with opposition) for the county of Dorset.' Reselected in 1832, he was not in 1835; this note from Bankes's obituary in *The Gentleman's Magazine* remains silent as to the reason.

On 3 December 1833, Bankes awoke to find himself, not famous, but with an entire page of *The Times* newspaper devoted to a verbatim report of the case in the Court of the King's Bench, Westminster, against himself and one Thomas Flowers, a private in the Guards,

THE MEROE EXPEDITION AND THE OUTLAW

charged with having met together for unnatural purposes.[42] Bankes had pleaded not guilty. On 6 June, in the churchyard between Westminster Abbey and St Margaret's Church, a watchman had seen him talking to the soldier, after which both entered the public convenience where there was room only for one person. Why had Bankes not walked the 260 feet to his own house? Was their 'linen' dishevelled? Why was there a sovereign in Bankes's raincoat pocket? Why were they in there so long? Unfounded statements had circulated in the newspapers: a witness had been paid to leave for America; Henry Bankes had turned his back on his son at the bail hearing believing the charge true. (Henry had actually gone straight to the police station and advised his son to keep his undergarments as an examination of them would negate the foul charge.)

Bankes's explanation was that after dining with Lord Liverpool he was returning to vote in an important division on Portugal in the House of Commons when he was taken short. He had spoken to the soldier, mistaking him for a man he knew abroad. Since the age of twelve he had suffered from a urinary complaint, 'sometimes 24 hours without making water … then much longer in the act than the ordinary time' and reluctant to go to a place where he might be interrupted by others. Weighty witnesses vouched for his manly and honourable character. Among the vast number of noblemen and gentlemen paraded were Samuel Rogers, Dr Butler, the master of Harrow, Gally Knight, MP and writer on architecture, and the travellers Henry Beechey and David Baillie. His father touchingly stated: 'I have lived with him as with my best friend; we were like brothers.' His valet observed: 'His manners are very distant to his servants.' The Duke of Wellington testified they had been very intimate since 1812 when Bankes had passed much time at his Peninsula headquarters among his aides-de-camp and officers. Bankes had been with Sir Henry Wellesley at Madrid and went with him to Valencia to meet King Ferdinand. 'I should think him utterly incapable of such an offence as he is now charged with.'

Barely a week before the hearing and on the advice of his lawyers, Bankes had '*most earnestly*' begged the Duke to appear in court as a character witness. Following the verdict, Bankes's jubilant express communication to the Duke with the result was answered by a congratulatory letter. He had been acquitted without a stain on his character. The Earl of Bathurst wrote to Wellington: 'Bankes's business ended triumphantly. I was apprehensive, I confess, that prejudice and something of party ill-will would have made his acquittal (for conviction I think was not probable) coupled with something like a stain behind it.' Wellington himself confided to the Marquess of Salisbury: 'I consider Bankes as he is described by the verdict; and if I had a party of persons at my house with whom he had been on terms of intimacy I should ask him to meet them. If Bankes is wise however he will not expose himself to the world for some time. He might be formally or coldly received by some; which would make a lasting impression upon him. The example might be followed by others. A little patience will set everything right.'[43] Bankes's social life, if not unruffled, resumed its hectic pace. On one busy winter day in London in 1837 he met Joseph Bonaparte (receiving a letter of Napoleon's as a token of Joseph's esteem) then dined with the Duke of Wellington. Nevertheless he was not re-elected in 1835 and never again stood for Parliament.

⤎◉◉◉⤏

Following the death of his father in 1834, Bankes threw himself into the time-consuming, six-year reconstruction of Kingston Lacy; once more 'a prisoner to my workmen'. Charles

Barry put Bankes's ideas into practice, converting the house into an Inigo-Jones-style Roman palazzo, with stone cladding, a balustrade and cupola on the roof, and long balustraded terrace to the south garden; the house now entered through a low basement on the north side. Many of the interior rooms were replanned, and crowned by the most striking feature and his great pride: a magnificent Carrara marble staircase and loggia. Not only had Bankes, as one would expect, 'described what I wished to Mr Barry', but all the features of the house were researched carefully from earlier models. His own sketches also reveal an unrealized project for restoring the ruins of Corfe Castle as a residence in the Gothick style.

In 1840 a fine Rubens portrait of the Marchesa Brigitta Spinola, and its companion piece, the Marchesa Maria with her attendant dwarf, from the Grimaldi Palace at Genoa, joined his art collection. Bankes's collection of Egyptian antiquities was not pursued, nor displayed, with the same fervour as his Old Masters. There is no trace of anything in the Egyptian style in the remodelling of the house or its contents; the fashion for such things had passed, and Bankes favoured classical designs. His architectural concerns, however, never entirely eclipsed his interest in either Egypt or his inscriptions. During the 1820s and 1830s he was still kept informed of events and consulted for his copies, and was exchanging information with other travellers and scholars as well as former companions. On a more personal level, he lent money to Beechey in 1822 enabling him to travel to North Africa to survey the coast with his brother Frederick, was asked in 1827 to give his permission for a special edition of Irby and Mangles' letters to benefit the impoverished widow of Belzoni,[44] and supported Salt's attempts to get a decent price for his Egyptian antiquities from the British Museum.

In 1833 Bankes viewed Joseph Sams's Egyptian collections, and after learning 'that the curious ancient Mss on linen' were new to him, Sams begged 'to enclose a specimen in a box … to place with his other antiquities from ancient Egypt'. Sams, in turn, was 'highly interested with Mr. B's choice Papyrus' and requested 'a sight of his other Egyptian rarities'. He agreed with Bankes that ancient chisels were uncommon, but had two in his own collections which he would be delighted to show him.[45]

In 1841 William Hamilton forwarded a letter to Bankes from the archaeologist and scholar Jean Letronne[46] about the Greek inscriptions on the Philae obelisk. The eminent Egyptologist Karl Richard Lepsius, who had visited Kingston Lacy in 1839 to copy the inscriptions for publication and whom Bankes met again in Turin in 1841, was another correspondent, following Bankes's inquiry about paintings by Tintoretto and Veronese.

୬ଡ଼୬ଡ଼

The news of Bankes's re-arrest in 1841 was shocking. The circumstances were so damning that this time flight, and that of necessity a speedy one, appeared his only recourse. Bankes kept the indictment and charge amongst his papers and it reads in sad and sordid detail.[47] There were five counts of indecent behaviour including one of assault, graphically and repeatedly described as those of 'a person of a wicked lewd filthy and unnatural mind and disposition'. He had climbed over the railings of Green Park on the night of 29 August, where a police constable discovered him with a guardsman on a park bench. He had offered the constable money not to arrest him and then given a false name, 'John Harris', at the police station. Events moved swiftly. On 30 August he was bound over on certain sureties to appear at the next sessions on 20 September. By 11 September he was choosing trustees to whom he would pass over all rights to the estate: his brothers George and Edward, and Lord

Boscawen, his nephew, the son of the Earl of Falmouth and his sister Anne. Falmouth, whom Bankes considered to have been his greatest support and the source of sound advice during this time of crisis, died that same year. It was he who advised Bankes not to leave his affairs in the hands of a single person, and to retain as many rights as possible, particularly stressing that he should not promise never to return to England or never to marry.

A mysteriously unsigned letter to Bankes of 14 September suggests that 'it would be an advantage to you at the present moment to make some compensation to a Lady you were once attached to and whose unfortunate affection blighted her whole life. Your strange, and allow me to say culpable neglect of her for many years, has been a matter of surprise to me from my knowledge of your kind feeling sense of justice.' She is not named but the writer is perhaps alluding to Lady Buckinghamshire.

Bankes had reached Southampton by 18 September and was at the port of Le Havre in France a week later. A multitude of complications ensued. Events had taken place so swiftly that Bankes was unsure of the legal position of his flight, but his solicitors now confirmed that the Home Office were threatening to act in an unusual and vindictive manner in his case and it seemed the government might either demand that he be handed over to the British by the country in which he was residing or else have him declared an outlaw. Either they were being pressed on this matter by an unnamed enemy of Bankes at the Treasury, or they were courting popularity by making an example of him to show that they dealt out 'equal justice to the great and the little'. The government arbitrarily wished to pursue the matter as if they were the Public Prosecutor whereas normally in a case of 'misdemeanor' the accused would simply forfeit his bail. The 'Powers' (of Attorney?) for the estate were sent to him in France but he was advised, under the circumstances, not to contact the consul. He was also advised against revealing his address. All Bankes's correspondence after this date is addressed Poste Restante or to hotels.

His solicitor informed him that a question mark hung over the witnesses. A 'persevering foreigner' whom Bankes had seen in London had 'addressed another letter to your relative in which he insists that if the matter is left with him he will arrange it – to use his own expression – to the greatest and utmost satisfaction'. Once Bankes had made a final decision on whether to stand trial or not, he must advise his solicitor, who added: 'If there were to be a trial it might not be worth while to sift once more the grounds for his assertion as to the two witnesses although my decided impression on that point is that the whole is a mere fabrication.'

Italy, with its art and culture, its benign climate, and his command of the language, was an obvious choice for Bankes's exile. From there he would send back not merely 'accessories or afterthought ornaments' for the house but contribute to the 'integral parts ... of a fine work left incomplete'. Art would be his solace. Misquoting Cicero, he wrote to his brother in 1844: 'Who ever could say of the Arts with more truth than I can *Res secundas ornant, in adversis solatium et perfugium praebent*' (Art is the ornament of good times and a consolation in bad times).

It is hardly surprising that the arrangement by which he vested control in others yet maintained it himself did not run smoothly. A letter which includes the sentence 'I am not a man of complaints' of course prefaced a long diatribe against some action taken against his wishes in respect of the trusteeship by George. Falmouth had advised that the income from the estate should not be accumulated but spent on the house and estate, and Bankes claimed he did not wish to keep up a large establishment abroad. He had been sending weekly instructions to his steward but the latter's indisposition had caused problems. He wished every detail of the house to remain under his control. He had never trusted his father with works of art (several valuable prints had been practically destroyed by his mistreatment) and George was equally incapable: not only did he lack understanding but his taste, judgement, and competence in these matters were wanting, so that Bankes was now corresponding directly with the clerk of the works. The endless detail which was so hard to administer by correspondence was satisfying yet at the same time frustrating. George had failed to consult him and as a result there were oak door-knobs fitted to a room with *gilding* in it! Why had no architect supervised and corrected the 'dreadful absurdity & meanness' of the proportions of the doorways of the marble landing on the principal floor? The handles of the doors between the great rooms were incorrectly placed for an Italian door; 'a simple reference to me would have saved' this solecism. The letters from Italy show Bankes's almost total preoccupation with planning, designing, purchasing works of art, and carrying through various schemes for the house. His prodigious memory, once used for ancient inscriptions, was now tuned to the contents of the house. In 1844 he was able to produce for George, apparently from memory, virtually a complete inventory of the contents of the London house, Old Palace Yard, with valuations. He was negotiating to purchase the freehold of Old Palace Yard to save the tenure being in jeopardy in the case of the government seizing it as Charles Barry informed him ultimately they would do.

Even more worrying than this was the prospect of changes to the arrangements by which he had handed over control of the entire estate, and what further arrangements should be made in the case of the death of any of the parties. Various suggestions by George led to the usual intemperate response in which Bankes, at least twice (in 1844 and again in 1853), threatened to return to England, surrender to the authorities, *and* face a trial, *and* marry and produce an heir, rather than have his civil rights 'trampled' on by his brother. He would have to be imprisoned since he could not produce bail, but he would rather 'be in a Prison *for life*' than have his expressed wishes overturned. Histrionics and bluff? Perhaps, although by 1853, alarmed at the possible consequences of the premature death of his nephew, one of the trustees, he was making secret enquiries to see whether the sole witness to his 'misdemeanor', the police officer, was still actively serving in the force. His solicitor's reply advised that a conviction remained inevitable and his outlawry was unlikely to be reversed.

That he did return to the house on clandestine visits was not just a romantic family legend: according to the family biographer, Viola Bankes, he arrived in Studland Bay on his yacht, taking advantage of a loophole in the law which allowed outlaws to 'set foot on English soil only between the hours of sunrise and sunset on Sundays'. The fact that he visited several times in 1854 is based on detailed instructions given to a workman, Seymour, for marble niches for the saloon.[48]

The years of exile were spent in almost constant travel. The first winter abroad was spent in the south of France, then he was on the move through Italy during 1843–51. In 1851 he visited Vienna, Berlin, Cologne, and Heidelberg, returning to Venice at the end of October. From 1853 further travel around Italy again ends in Venice at the end of October. Calais on 15 July 1854 was perhaps preparatory to a clandestine visit to Dorset, the next entry being his return to Paris on the 31st. Notes were kept on the art and architecture of every city and town he passed through. His return to Venice on 15 November (?) 1854 is the last entry in his itinerary. These years were devoted to his obsessional acquisitions for the house; his correspondence is almost one long series of bills. What distinguished this endless purchasing from that of other collectors was the quite extraordinary input of his own creative spirit. Furniture was crafted to his designs, many pieces were specially commissioned, and he collaborated with the distinguished sculptor Baron Carlo Marochetti on the bronze sculptures of his ancestors. September 1853 saw him carry a live tortoise across Paris in a bag so that Marochetti could model sixteen of them to support sculpture.

His greatest attachment at home was his fondness for his widowed sister Anne, who had moved into Kingston Lacy. Planned alterations to the library ceiling were abandoned in case they spoiled her enjoyment of the room; he would derive more pleasure from being assured of her comfort. The prepared plans were preserved so that 'when we are both gone' their successors 'may do it if they will'.

Anne could be relied on for her taste, unlike George, who 'is but a poor judge in art, & has but an indifferent eye'. 'Good taste is, to my mind, little else but a refined good sense, & a nice perception of propriety.' Marochetti had suggested the keys held by his life-size bronze of the family Civil War heroine Dame Mary should be smaller, but Bankes overruled him: 'small keys in a woman's hand could denote nothing but a housekeeper'.

The last letter to Anne, on 29 March 1855, two weeks before his death, includes a cough recipe for his niece and speaks of future plans. 'I am so charmed with the success of my first bas-relief [of which he had been sent a photograph] that I am meditating another.' Anne is not to mention this to Marochetti since he is thinking of asking someone else to carry out the work. Anne wrote on the back of the letter: 'This was the last letter written to me by my very dear kind brother – taken ill April 2nd – he died on the 15th of that month at [ ] in the Morning quite conscious to the very last moment.'[49]

In 1825, as a member of the committee to raise a monument to Byron, Bankes agreed with Hobhouse that Byron's Memoirs should be destroyed and Tom Moore should not write a biography, saying 'Byron's best friends could always recur to his poetry and conceal his life'.[50] Bankes and his family evidently emulated this feeling for, like the story of his last years in Italy, the exact circumstances and place of Bankes's death remain shrouded in mystery. His body was returned to England for burial in the family vault at Wimborne Minster.

86 A view of the pyramids in the north group at Gebel Barkal, by Linant.

87 This drawing by Linant is the only view recorded of this lower group of pyramids at Gebel Barkal, now destroyed. Linant's men can be seen on the right, excavating with picks.

88 A scene at a Nubian village, by Linant.

[178]

89 A view of the ruins surrounding the holy mountain of Gebel Barkal, by Linant.

90 Linant's drawing of the double pyramid at Nuri.

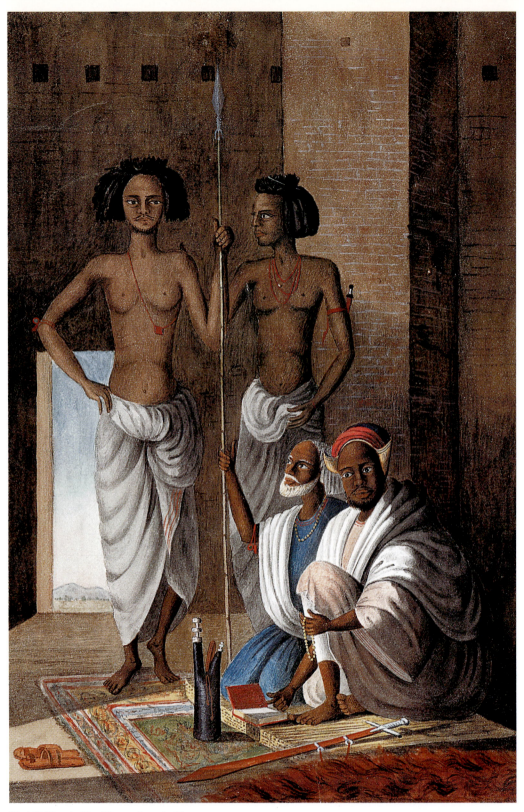

91 A Nubian sheikh with attendants, by Linant.

92 Linant's view of the north and south pyramid fields at Meroe.

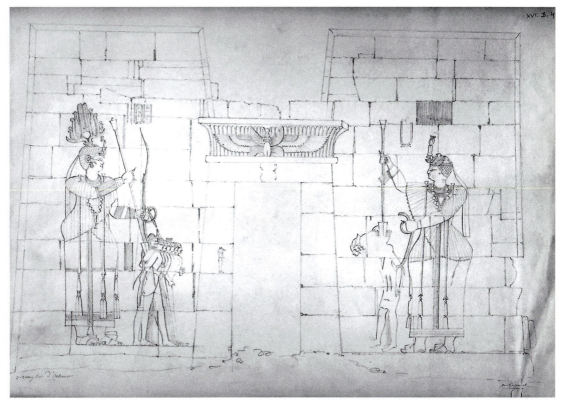

93 Reliefs on the pylon of the pyramid chapel of Queen Amanishakheto at Meroe. Drawing by Linant.

94 Nubian
women,
by Linant.

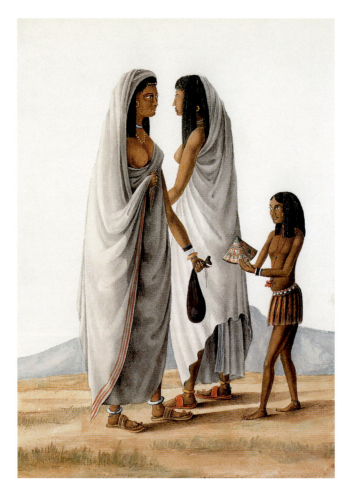

95 Linant's drawing of a pyramid at Meroe with its capstone still intact.

96 Relief-scenes on a column from the South East Temple at Musawwarat. Drawing by Linant.

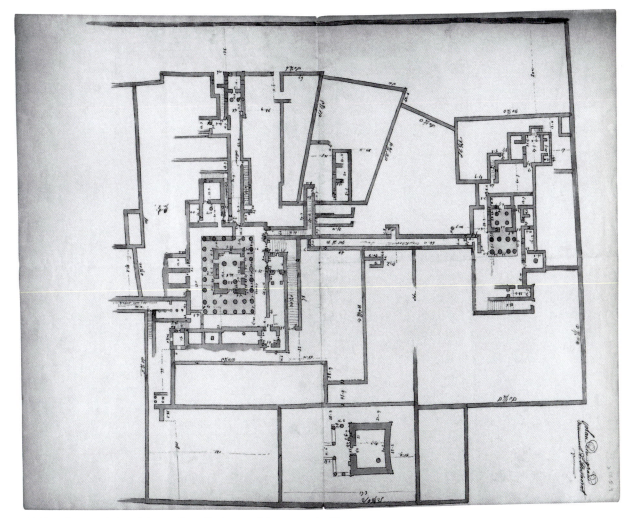

97 Part of a ground plan of the vast Great Enclosure at Musawwarat, by Linant.

98 Linant's view
of the Great Temple
at Musawwarat.

99 Nubian men,
by Linant.

100 A relief showing the Nubian lion-headed god, Apedemak, adored by the royal family on the Lion Temple at Naqa. Drawing by Linant.

101 Linant's view of the Great Temple of Amun at Naqa.

102 A view of the
Lion Temple and
Roman kiosk at Naqa,
by Linant.

103 Linant's painting
of the Pasha's pet
giraffe at Sennar.

104 William Bankes, by
Sir George Hayter, 1836.

105 The sarcophagus of
Amenemope in the
grounds of Kingston Lacy.

106 *The Judgement of Solomon*, by Sebastiano del Piombo, c.1505–10. Purchased by Bankes as a Giorgione.

107 A wall-painting fragment in Bankes's collection, showing an offering bearer with flaming braziers, from an unknown Theban tomb.

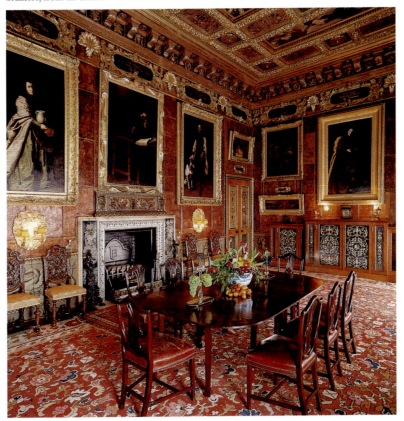

108 The Spanish Room designed by William Bankes at Kingston Lacy.

109 Antiquities, including a very rare ancient wooden manacle (second row from top, centre), displayed at Kingston Lacy.

110 RIGHT Lithographic stones for Bankes's inscriptions project, displayed below a stuffed crocodile at Kingston Lacy.

111 BELOW The king-list from the temple of Rameses II at Abydos. Drawn by Bankes and used as the frontispiece for Salt's book on hieroglyphs.

112 Bankes's designs for the ornamentation of his obelisk.

A Collection and a Legacy

Generations of the Bankes family succeeded each other to the house and estates with varying degrees of interest in its contents. William Bankes's drawings remained undisturbed, hidden away in their elegant custom-built cabinets, and his papers drifted into the flotsam of family history.

It was not until after the Second World War that the indefatigable Rosalind Moss, in characteristically energetic pursuit of early manuscript sources for the provenance of ancient Egyptian reliefs and objects, tracked down the Bankes manuscripts, and was permitted to remove them to the Griffith Institute in Oxford for study. She identified and numbered most of the subjects of the drawings of ancient sites for inclusion into the Porter and Moss *Topographical Bibliography*, a primary research tool for Egyptologists.

Bankes's collection of Egyptian objects, never part of the scheme for his house, was probably of little interest to his descendants. Perhaps few English families today would care to entertain a mummified head in their reception rooms, even one reputed to be that of a pharaoh. In any case, Bankes himself had never collected with any great zeal, preferring to copy inscriptions. In this he was not typical of his day.

Many contemporary travellers collected assiduously from a variety of motives. For some it was financial gain, for others a genuine interest in ancient Egypt and its civilization. What were once just the curiosities of antiquarians had become the subject of scientific inquiry, to be removed not only to private collections but to satisfy the burgeoning demands of European museums where they might be studied by specialists and viewed by the general public.

Bankes appears to have had an ambivalent attitude towards the collection of Egyptian antiquities. He insists that he never damaged intact monuments by actively breaking them up, and certainly the coveted head of 'Memnon' and the Philae obelisk were both already loose fragments. He did not cut out the Abydos king-list, although Finati hinted that it may simply have proved too difficult to move as it consisted of several stones.[1] He has been castigated for detaching and removing sections of stucco paintings from 'one of the most interesting and best preserved of the lesser tombs' in Thebes (as he also did from Sidon). He claimed to have removed the paintings for their antiquity and historical interest, not for their beauty.[2] Saulnier accused him of having planned with Salt to obtain saws, chisels, and other instruments to hack out the Dendera zodiac and send it back to England. Bankes expostulated that this story was 'WHOLLY UNFOUNDED' and, 'so far from its having ever entered my thoughts to cut down the circular planisphere at Dendera, I have always deprecated, in the strongest manner, such spoliations of existing and entire monuments, such as that temple is, (the only instance in which I ever deviated at all from this principle having been in cutting the paintings from a mutilated private tomb at Thebes, which I saw no chance or hope of preserving)'. He considered that the removal of the zodiac by 'these French pilferers' was absurd since neither the workmanship nor the material was at all fine and a drawing or plaster cast would have sufficed. Indeed 'experience proves to us, that the soft sandstone of Egypt will not bear our damp northern climate, which I am convinced is principally owing to the quantity of salt with with it is infected'.[3] (By this observation Bankes had unwittingly foreseen the future threat of environmental damage to monuments in Egypt presented by increasing irrigation and land use in modern times.)

His strong views on the subject of damage were already known, for Bartholomew Frere wrote to him in Cairo, 'I sympathise with you most sincerely in all your reflections upon the barbarity of the destruction which I hear from all parts is carrying on in Egypt.' Frere thought it would continue so long as 'our Maudlin Dilettante Ladies... will crowd to see a fragment because it comes from they do not perhaps know where; how few travellers there are whose vanity is proof against such allurements?'[4] One of Bankes's few publications concerned his Philae obelisk, but, if scholarship alone had been the reason for its removal, surely a copy of the text, such as Bankes made at Abydos, would have served.

On the occasion of the great head of 'Memnon' finally being presented to the British Museum in 1816, Burckhardt had entreated: 'Do let this be a stimulus to Yourself, not to bury your treasures at Your country house, where they can never generally be admired.' But even the inducement of the honour attaching to the gift of the 'tablets from Thebes' (the Deir el-Medina stelae) and other antiquities to the nation failed to move their owner. The prized Homer papyrus was one of the few objects to leave the house, sold to the British Museum by a descendant in 1879.[5]

The assorted antiquities did not fit into his new decorative scheme for Kingston Lacy, being viewed with a different aesthetic to that governing his connoisseur's eye for Western European art and architecture.[6] His own designs for Egyptianizing frames for the wall-paintings, and a bronze fleur-de-lis to top his obelisk, with decorative bronze Horus birds at the base (pl. 112), were never put into effect. Following generations relegated the collection to basement rooms and attics; it is currently arranged as a small museum and occupies the former billiard room.[7]

Among a number of small items are *shabti* figures (funerary figurines), amulets, scarabs, a pre-dynastic stone cosmetic palette shaped like a fish, and a very rare object: a wooden manacle carved in the form of a lion mauling the head of a Nubian prisoner (pl. 109). A careful drawing, restoring much original detail, gives the provenance 'Found near Radamone... at Temneh [Tuna el-Gebel?] behind Ashmunein'.[8] Little other documentation or provenance exists for the collection; most pieces were probably purchased from Theban dealers or obtained from colleagues rather than excavated personally. Apart from Roman busts of Mark Antony and Cleopatra, he seems not to have increased his collection by auction purchases on his return, despite the opportunities. His attitude to the display of his collection is exemplified by his request to Salt in 1823: 'Should you have no particular value yet for those pots and vessels of alabaster which I brought with me from Eileitheya & left for you in your library, I should be very glad of them & of anything that may be forthcoming of that description as I find them susceptible of a polish & therefore ornamental as well as curious – could a set of pots be found for me in alabaster with the four heads of the Baboon, Woman, Jackal & Hawk [canopic jars] they would be particularly acceptable.'[9]

The huge granite sarcophagus of Amenemope (pl. 105), discovered in Thebes by d'Athanasi in 1821, arrived as an unsolicited gift from Salt, and was placed in the garden, gradually disappearing into the undergrowth, while a greywacke statue of the little-known god Hetepbakef from the time of Rameses II was discovered face down in the fernery when the eccentric Ralph Bankes, the last family member to inhabit the house, died in 1981.[10] The whereabouts of two large black-granite Sekhmet statues from the temple of Mut, Karnak, taken after his failure to dislodge the 'Memnon', were unknown until 2000, when they were unexpectedly rediscovered at Chatsworth.[11] Surplus to the decorative scheme of Kingston Lacy, they had been languishing in storage with a Mr W. Adron, in the New Road, where in 1832 they attracted the attention of the sixth Duke of Devonshire. Bankes, showing his usual financial acumen, promptly sold them to him for £150 (justified as his costs), throwing in some free advice on restoration.[12] They are now displayed within the house at Chatsworth, having spent many years outside in the grounds.

Despite this lack of enthusiasm Kingston Lacy holds some real ancient treasures, in particular the fine stucco Theban wall-paintings (pl. 107),[13] and an important series of stelae from the village of the royal tomb-builders at Deir el Medina.[14] From Nubia comes a small group of simple grave-stelae inscribed in Greek and Coptic.

Because of Bankes's interest in inscriptions, his papyri, although then unreadable, were highly prized. Among several now in the British Museum, he and Salt obtained two halves of a rare and important Ramesside letter.[15] Its significance remained a mystery but this did not prevent him from pondering the status of the writer from the hand, noting that one papyrus was a discrete entity, and observing pertinently that one was a palimpsest (written over a rubbed-out original), implying that 'papyrus was either not very abundant or not very cheap'. An inscribed fragment of linen from the mummy wrapping of Djedher born of Ta was a gift from the collector Joseph Sams. Bankes scribbled on the envelope: 'These writings on linen are rarer than those on papyrus.'

Still missing is a potentially very important find, proudly described to Byron. 'By the bye, I have brought over one piece of antiquity which would, I think, hardly fail to interest your imagination: it is the embalmed head of a King of Egypt of the Theban dynasty (that is to say of the greatest king then reigning in the world). You will ask me how I know this? By the same rule, I answer, as one who should purloin a skull from a grave in poets' corner, might, without Dr Gall's aid, have a reasonable suspicion of it's being a Poet's.'[16] The kings' sepulchres were 'ascertained beyond dispute' and from one, 'full of painting & sculpture, out of a noble sarcophagus of red granite ... I removed the Head: It is sufficiently perfect to show that it is that of a young person, & not of a negro race. The hair has been shaved, & shows about one days growth. To prevent it's perishing (which it otherwise soon would in this climate) a Globe of glass is to be blown round it. A poor Globe in Comparison of that which it once governed! I wish you would send me some lines to engrave upon it.'[17]

The obelisk and other antiquities were shipped back from Alexandria in May 1821 with a box containing Linant's Sinai portfolio and journals.[18] By September the Egyptian objects had reached Bankes's London house. The Duke of Wellington, met at the theatre, 'insisted upon coming the next day – yesterday – to see my importations from Egypt, & brought an immense party with him, who seemed to be very much surprised & amused … It is amazing what an interest the Duke has taken in my obelisk, he has a great wish to take charge of it himself completely, & to carry it down all the way by land, in some of the artillery contrivances … I saw it yesterday morning [at Deptford docks] … The state of preservation of it is really wonderful, & I am still of the opinion that there is no piece of Egyptian antiquity that can at all compete with it in this country … I believe that I never can consent to remove so fine a monument out of sight of the House … Two of my Egyptian pictures [Theban tomb paintings] are now safe in their wainscot frames, the great one comes out surprisingly, & will I hope be also in its frame tomorrow.'[19] At the docks he was able to admire the famous alabaster sarcophagus of Sety i[20] and other antiquities which had just arrived in a frigate belonging to the Pasha.

An obelisk was acceptable as an antiquity which encompassed both cultures through its incorporation into the art and architecture of ancient Rome.[21] With an architect's care for proportion, Bankes had experimented with a thirty-eight-foot fir trunk (four foot going underground) to judge the most effective distance to place the obelisk from the house. The Duke of Wellington ceremoniously laid the foundation stone in April 1827, but the obelisk was not finally placed on its pedestal at Kingston Lacy until the beginning of October 1830.[22] While the obelisk undoubtedly constituted an unusual and grand addition to the garden statuary, and the social cachet of securing such a magnificent ornament to his house must have been irresistible, its main attraction for Bankes was undoubtedly its potential as a second Rosetta Stone.

The basket of drawings, so admired by Barry in Egypt, was to rise to a portfolio of over fifteen hundred unsigned and undated drawings for Egypt and Nubia alone, supported by hundreds of Bankes's notes, loose scraps and bound notebooks, plus countless additional drawings, and manuscripts. Many are rough working sketches and diagrams rather than finished watercolours. The team of draughtsmen and artists he had assembled successfully supplied the skills which he himself lacked, particularly in copying hieroglyphs. While his numerous fine copies of Greek inscriptions reflect his familiarity with the language and script, he failed to develop any ease in copying hieroglyphic reliefs and inscriptions, being sometimes careless as to the direction of the hieroglyphs and inclined to represent the script in a rudimentary form.

Each member of the party had his speciality. Ricci was not an artist but an expert and experienced copyist reproducing reliefs and hieroglyphs. The breathtaking views (and probably the assured copies of Salt's work) are from Beechey, who also collaborated with Bankes on most of the architectural plans. Linant was competent in all spheres, leaving Bankes to concentrate on his passions: architectural details and unusual inscriptions. Both Salt and Sack appear to have taken their own work away.

For Bankes, his inscriptions were paramount. Through a study of these texts, the imminent breakthrough in the decipherment of hieroglyphics would at last reveal the primary sources for the history of ancient Egypt, hitherto known only from the accounts of the later classical writers. The accuracy of the epigraphy (the copying of relief scenes and texts) was therefore perceived as essential. His draughtsmen laboured to copy texts in a script of which they had no understanding. This very ignorance carried the advantage that no preconceived assumptions affected what they saw and recorded. They strained to replicate only what they saw before them, even though experience gradually taught them to recognize the formulaic and repetitive nature of many of the texts.

Bankes's portfolio was perhaps the first serious attempt to make a comprehensive and accurate survey of ancient sites since the appearance of the massive *Description de l'Égypte*, considered the first publication to place the study of ancient Egypt on a scientific basis.[23] This work, scrupulously checked by Bankes against the evidence of his own eyes, was found severely wanting. The *Description* plates of Qau el-Kebir were wearily noted to be 'as usual, highly inaccurate'.[24] The traveller John Fuller, who met Bankes in Cairo in 1819, agreed, finding the *Description* 'in many parts inaccurate to a degree scarcely to be credited by those who have not had an opportunity of comparing it with the originals on the spot'.[25]

Leaving aside Bankes's personal antipathy to those contemporaries who published their travel journals, most of these were useless for study purposes unless the plates were large-scale. Most illustrations were too small to show details, views were often taken from similarly picturesque angles so that parts of the structure remained unknown, and reliefs and views might be engraved ignorantly by other hands after the original drawings.

Bankes's team's careful technique (his own annotations show that most drawings were double-checked) ensured results of a high standard, comparable to the best modern methods of epigraphy. They scrupulously preserved the style of the original subject matter, unlike many of the European gentlemen-travellers who distorted the style of scenes they sketched to fit the Western European tradition familiar to them. The sketch might then be redrawn, possibly even 'improved', by a professional draughtsmen and engraved by a third person, neither of whom had seen the original.[26] A (literally) classic example of this process is the Westernizing corruption of the harpist figure from a royal tomb relief illustrating James Bruce's work *Travels to Discover the Source of the Nile* (1790). The same tendencies were true for depictions of Egyptian architecture, where it might be adjusted and altered to fit classical proportions and designs, giving the false impression that Egyptian art was the immediate ancestor of classical art.[27] Bankes's failure to publish had the advantage that the drawings, which were made on the spot, were never worked up by others or 'improved'.

Henry Beechey warned Bankes of this problem in relation to the proposed publication of Linant's work, which would give 'general satisfaction, particularly if Murray pays attention to the plates and the engraver does not give some fanciful effect destructive of the character of the drawings'.[28] John Fuller complained of engravings in the *Description*, made by the inferior hands of road and bridge engineers, 'which bear scarcely any resemblance to the objects they profess to represent'. Ancient buildings were too often shown as they were supposed to have been rather than as they were, and the artists were altogether 'too fond of restorations'.

Remaining in Bankes's hands, the portfolio carries his name, and the contributions of each individual member of the party became confused. In most cases their styles are not hard to distinguish and most of the drawings can now be properly attributed.

⁂

Having joined Bankes's second voyage at the age of just nineteen, Linant de Bellefonds (1799–1883) next accomplished arduous journeys to Siwa Oasis and to Sinai in 1820. The resulting drawings were to be sent back to Bankes, but Linant's own copies illustrated the *Voyage à l'Oasis de Syouah*, published by Edmé Jomard, one of Napoleon's savants, in 1823.

Linant kept copies of almost all his drawings and journals, which are now held in the Bibliothèque du Louvre, Paris.

After his work for Bankes and his commissions from the African Association ended, Linant continued to travel and explore, visiting Petra in 1828 with Léon de Laborde, then the Atbai gold-mining area between the Nile and the Red Sea for Mohammed Ali, into whose service he passed in 1831. He specialized in irrigation projects, was involved in the planning of the Suez Canal, and investigated the fertile area of the Fayoum lake. In 1847, together with Bourdaloue, he directed topographical studies of the isthmus of Suez.

Linant was to enjoy an illustrious career in the service of Mohammed Ali and his successors. With increasing expertise in engineering and geography, he was appointed Minister of Public Works in 1869. Created Pasha in 1873, he had long before established himself in Cairo in splendid Oriental style. He published many maps, also *Mémoirs sur les principaux travaux d'utilité publique exécutés en Égypte depuis la plus haute antiquité jusqu'à nos jours: Accompagnés d'un Atlas renfermant neuf planches grand in-folio imprimées en couleur* (1872–73) and *Mémoire sur le Lac de Moeris, présenté et lu à la Société Égyptienne le 5 juillet 1842. Carte* (1843).[29] Linant never published the work he did for Bankes.

Many other travellers were to visit him in Cairo, receiving hospitality, advice, and assistance. Bankes received a gossipy glimpse of Linant's lifestyle in 1831, from John Barker, who had replaced Salt as consul-general. 'Linant is going on as usual – the best dressed man in Cairo, having Slaves, Dromedaries, & Horses with no *apparent* adequate means. He has however lately obtained a certain quantity of sheep & camels for his daughter, whom he has married to a rich Arab Sheikh. You know he pretends to be a creditor of the African Association, and refuses to give up their time-piece &c till his demands are satisfied!'[30]

Henry Salt (1780–1827) died prematurely in Cairo, perhaps best remembered today for the major collections he amassed and his long dispute with the British Museum over their purchase: a bitter wrangle in which he was championed by Bankes, whose father was a Trustee of the Museum. Many of Salt's extensive collection of notes and drawings from Egypt did not survive.[31] There are no original drawings by Salt in the portfolio, but the fine copies made of his work have preserved a record which would otherwise be lost.

He was already collecting and drawing hieroglyphic inscriptions before Bankes's arrival, and maintained an excellent classical and modern library in Cairo on Egyptian matters. With so many interests in common, Bankes and Salt enjoyed what appears to be genuine friendship and mutual collaboration, inevitably overlaid with some patronage on Bankes's part. Salt effectively acted as an agent for Bankes after the latter's departure: directing the artists and organizing the necessary financial arrangements, forwarding letters and the latest news, and arranging for items to be shipped back to England. In return, Bankes promoted Salt's interests in his negotiations with the British Museum.[32]

Although failing to record the tombs of Beni Hasan as requested by Bankes after his departure in 1819, Alessandro Ricci joined Linant on expeditions to Siwa Oasis and Sinai in 1820, and he too delivered the resulting drawings to Bankes, while keeping his own copies. The following year he accompanied Baron von Minutoli and his wife into Upper Egypt.

Abandoning Linant on the journey to Meroe in 1821 was to make Ricci's fortune. He became Ibrahim Pasha's physician, and the generous financial reward for saving Ibrahim's life from dysentery enabled Ricci to return to Italy in 1822.

He set up his large collection of antiquities in a museum in his house in Florence and in 1824 he was offering for sale his drawing portfolio and his journals, both much admired by Champollion on his visit in 1825. Ricci returned to Egypt in 1828–29 with the Franco-Tuscan expedition of Champollion and Rosellini, in the multiple role of experienced adviser and guide, doctor, and artist.

Failing to be awarded the post of Tuscan consul in Egypt in 1830 (it was considered he was not up to the job), he was employed by Rosellini in 1831 to recruit subscribers in Germany and England for the publication of the Franco-Tuscan expedition. He took with him five hundred pieces of his collection, three hundred of which were purchased by the state of Dresden.[33]

By 1832 Ricci was gravely ill in Florence and on his behalf the rest of his collection was sold to the Grand Duke of Tuscany in return for a lump sum and a life pension. His collection and about one hundred of his drawings remain in the Museo Egizio, Florence.[34] He deposited the journal of his travels and other drawings with Champollion Figeac (Jean-François' elder brother) in Paris in 1836, but they were never returned and were subsequently lost. Rediscovered in Paris in 1928, they passed to his biographer Sammarco, only to disappear again on the verge of publication, after the latter's death in 1948. The brief travel diary which has now been discovered, forgotten, among Bankes's papers is little compensation for the loss of what, judging from the style of his letters, would have been a lively and fascinating story.

Ricci died in Florence in 1834 of the debilitating illness from which he suffered in his last years, said to have originated in a scorpion sting received in Thebes; however, his symptoms of paralysis and derangement are not medically attributable to this event and appear to be those of syphilis.[35]

He is shown standing majestically in Angelelli's formal group-portrait of the Franco-Tuscan expedition, which contrasts with the informal sketch of him, ruffled hair and bespectacled, in the Renéaume Collection.[36] He may be ranked among the finest early epigraphers, even surpassing his contemporary fame as one of the few men to have returned home after making his fortune in Egypt.

Henry William Beechey (c.1789–1862) accompanied Bankes back to Europe in 1819 and they remained in contact. Bankes provided a gift of £100 enabling Beechey to join an expedition with his brother Frederick in 1822 to explore and record the ancient sites of Cyrenaica; although the project ended abruptly with the withdrawal of British Foreign Office support. The endless rain of the North African coast left Beechey nostalgic for the days of their travel together in Egypt. He 'fairly wished himself once in some of our old berths above the cataracts where the ground was as good a bed as anyone could desire and the sky as fine a canopy as the highest stars could make it'.[37] The record of their journey includes plates from Beechey's drawings.[38] Frederick, appointed by the Admiralty for the survey, drew the maps, while Henry, appointed personally by Earl Bathurst, reported on the antiquities.

In 1825 Beechey became a Fellow of the Society of Antiquaries, and continued with his painting: a portrait of Mrs Worthington in 1838, and seascapes which were exhibited at the Royal Academy in 1829 and the British Institute in 1838. In 1835 he published an erudite three-hundred page memoir on Sir Joshua Reynolds.

Beechey never seems to have established himself in a successful career as either artist or explorer and suffered financial problems. In 1851, at the advanced age of sixty-one, he emigrated to New Zealand with his second wife and family to become a farmer. In a final stroke of misfortune he is said to have 'acquired nearly the whole of the land now covered by Christchurch, but disposed of it before it became valuable'. He died at Lyttleton near Christchurch, of pulmonary congestion, on 4 August 1862, aged seventy-three.[39]

But where would the travellers have been without the services of their dragoman Giovanni Finati (born 1787, died after 1831), referred to by all as 'Mahomet'? While the others wielded their pens and brushes, he was ever ready with his gun; when not called upon to defend them, frequently shooting both dinner and any interesting species for their collections. Without the evidence of Finati's narrative, we would know far less about Bankes's journeys, and, without Finati's practical protection, perhaps the portfolio might never have existed.[40]

Bankes left Finati in 1819 with the task of retrieving the pedestal of the Philae obelisk, paying all his expenses. After this he was to receive half a dollar a day until he landed the pedestal at Rosetta, when his engagement with Bankes would cease. Bankes had promised him a watch from England but prudently instructed Salt that, should Finati prove unduly extravagant with his expenses, the watch should not be handed over. The same arrangement applied to some necklaces bought from Belzoni, which were to be reserved as a reward for a successful operation. Finati was also be to reimbursed for any antiquity purchases.[41]

Finati's aversion to the long sea voyage, necessitated by his presence in England in 1824 to testify in the libel trial, was mitigated by his being shown around Liverpool, and invited to a splendid ball 'where my rich Turkish dress seemed to attract general attention'. He stayed with Bankes in Wales at Soughton Hall, despite it being in the midst of rebuilding work, and was joined there by Linant, who was 'still wearing his Eastern habit and with his Abyssinian lady'. Finati then moved to London, where his own narrative ends.

Finati left London for Egypt as dragoman to Lord Prudhoe on 19 November 1826. After their tour Prudhoe left him at Alexandria on 5 June 1829. Three days earlier Finati sent Bankes a copy of an inscription he had found on a piece of black granite in the village of Akhmim,[42] with the request that he be sent a copy of his book at cost, and also his portrait, which had been painted so that an engraving might be made for the frontispiece.[43] He hoped for a continuation of Bankes's kind patronage and that, his service to Lord Prudhoe ended, John Barker would accede to Bankes's request to find him employment in the consulate. This was done, and he was placed under Barker's protection: 'His situation will be, to take charge of passengers and goods to & from India – when the steam navigation is established on the Red Sea. The first packet is expected to arrive … from Bombay … in November next month. Mahomet's situation promises to be very satisfactory – he has been recommended by Mr Barker to keep a Lodging House for the English at Alexandria.'[44]

In 1831 Barker asked Bankes to supply 'a few more copies of his *Life* at the prime book-seller's cost (for which I will be responsible) as he can dispose of them, to some little profit, to travellers passing through Alexandria'.

❧⟲☺⟳❧

As for the legacy of William Bankes, if Kingston Lacy remains his greatest monument, its obelisk stands witness to the rediscovered treasures of his portfolio, reflecting his own words: 'of all the parts of the world which I have visited, Egypt and Nubia are those which interested me, beyond all comparison, the most, and have made the deepest impression upon my mind'.

CHRONOLOGY

Italics give the names of rulers mentioned in the text.
All dates before 690 BC are approximate.

PREDYNASTIC 5500–3100 BC

EARLY DYNASTIC PERIOD 3100–2686
FIRST DYNASTY 3100–2890
SECOND DYNASTY 2890–2686

OLD KINGDOM 2686–2181
THIRD DYNASTY 2686–2613
FOURTH DYNASTY 2613–2494
FIFTH DYNASTY 2494–2345
SIXTH DYNASTY 2345–2181

FIRST INTERMEDIATE PERIOD 2181–2055
SEVENTH AND EIGHTH DYNASTIES 2181–2125
NINTH AND TENTH DYNASTIES
(HERAKLEOPOLITAN) 2160–2025
ELEVENTH DYNASTY (THEBES ONLY) 2125–2055

MIDDLE KINGDOM 2055–1650
ELEVENTH DYNASTY (ALL EGYPT) 2055–1985
TWELFTH DYNASTY 1985–1795
Senusret I 1965–1920
Senusret III 1874–1855
THIRTEENTH DYNASTY 1795–AFTER 1650
FOURTEENTH DYNASTY 1750–1650

SECOND INTERMEDIATE PERIOD 1650–1550
FIFTEENTH DYNASTY (HYKSOS) 1650–1550
SIXTEENTH DYNASTY 1650–1550
SEVENTEENTH DYNASTY 1650–1550

NEW KINGDOM 1550–1069
EIGHTEENTH DYNASTY 1550–1295
Thutmose III 1479–1425
Hatshepsut 1473–1458
Amenhotep II 1427–1400
Thutmose IV 1400–1390
Amenhotep IV/Akhenaten 1352–1336
Ay 1327–1323
Horemheb 1323–1295
NINETEENTH DYNASTY 1295–1186
Sety I 1294–1279
Rameses II 1279–1213
Merenptah 1213–1203
Sety II 1200–1194
TWENTIETH DYNASTY 1186–1069
Rameses III 1184–1153

THIRD INTERMEDIATE PERIOD 1069–747
TWENTY-FIRST DYNASTY (TANITE) 1069–945
TWENTY-SECOND DYNASTY
(BUBASTITE/LIBYAN) 945–715
TWENTY-THIRD DYNASTY (TANITE/LIBYAN) 818–715
TWENTY-FOURTH DYNASTY 727–715

LATE PERIOD 747–332
TWENTY-FIFTH DYNASTY (KUSHITE) 747–656
Taharqo 690–664
TWENTY-SIXTH DYNASTY (SAITE) 664–525
Psamtek I 664–610
TWENTY-SEVENTH DYNASTY
(FIRST PERSIAN PERIOD) 525–404
TWENTY-EIGHTH DYNASTY 404–399
TWENTY-NINTH DYNASTY 399–380
THIRTIETH DYNASTY 380–343
SECOND PERSIAN PERIOD 343–332

PTOLEMAIC PERIOD 332–30
MACEDONIAN DYNASTY 332–305
PTOLEMAIC DYNASTY*
Ptolemy I Soter I 305–285
Ptolemy II Philadelphus 285–246
Ptolemy III Euergetes I 246–221
Ptolemy IV Philopator 221–205
Ptolemy V Epiphanes 205–180
Ptolemy VI Philometor 180–145
Ptolemy VII Neos Philopator 145
Ptolemy VIII Euergetes II 170–116
Ptolemy IX Soter II 116–107
Ptolemy X Alexander I 107–88
Ptolemy IX Soter II (restored) 88–80
Ptolemy XI Alexander II 80
Ptolemy XII Neos Dionysos (Auletes) 80–51
Cleopatra VII Philopator 51–30
Ptolemy XIII 51–47
Ptolemy XIV 47–44
Ptolemy XV Caesarion 44–30

ROMAN PERIOD 30 BC–AD 395
Augustus 30 BC–AD 14
Tiberius AD 14–37
Trajan 98–117
Hadrian 117–138
Antoninus Pius 138–161
Commodus 180–192
Diocletian 284–305

*All the rulers of the Ptolemaic Dynasty are listed
because Bankes identified the Ptolemies only by name.

GLOSSARY

abacus/abaci Bearing slab placed on top of a capital to support the architrave.

architrave Horizontal stone beam connecting pillars, columns, and door frames, and supporting a ceiling.

bark [barque] The sacred boat of the gods.

Bey Turkish honorary title meaning 'Sir' or 'Prince'. A governor of a province in the Turkish dominions.

cangia Typical sailboat used on the Nile.

capital Crowning feature of a column.

Casheff Turkish administrative office. A sub-governor responsible to a Bey for administering a province and collecting taxes.

cella see sanctuary.

Defterdar Title used in the Ottoman empire for a lieutenant-colonel, or officer of finance.

dollars see piastres.

dowel Wooden or bronze peg fitted into corresponding sockets.

dragoman Interpreter and guide.

dromos Avenue leading to a temple.

drum Cylindrical block of a column shaft.

enceinte wall Enclosure wall of a temple.

entablature Upper part of an order (one of the classical types of column styles), consisting of architrave, frieze and cornice.

ex-voto Offering made in accordance with a vow, or to express devotion.

firman Permit or licence granted by the Pasha to a consul or his agents, which was used to allocate the areas in which they were allowed to excavate the monuments and remove antiquities.

Franks The term used for Europeans in Egypt.

hypostyle Many-columned hall.

Janissary Soldier in the Ottoman army.

kiosk Small open-sided pavilion or chapel.

lintel Horizontal beam bridging the opening of a doorway or window.

Mamelukes Originally, the name given to the white slaves conscripted into the army by the Ottoman sultan. In time they became a military caste and took control of Egypt, ruling from the thirteenth to the sixteenth century. Defeated in the Battle of Abouqir during Napoleon's Egyptian campaign, they were eventually eliminated by the Pasha Mohammed Ali.

mammisi Small chapel or 'birth-house' celebrating the divine birth.

mash Large transport boat used on the Nile.

mud-brick Unbaked brick.

naos Stone shrine at the heart of a temple, containing the cult statue of the god.

paras see piastres.

Pasha Turkish honorary title meaning 'Lord', given to high military officials and governors of provinces. The title is senior to Bey. Travellers frequently referred to Mohammed Ali simply as 'the Pasha'.

peripteral temple Temple surrounded by a single row of columns.

peristyle Colonnade enclosing an open space or building.

piastres Although Spanish dollars circulated in Egypt during Bankes's time, the legal tender was the piastre, which was divided into 40 paras. A piastre was worth 12 soldi. While calculating the modern values is difficult and approximate, a piastre would have been roughly equivalent to £1.90 in today's money. A soldo would have been worth about 16p, and a Spanish dollar worth about 10 piastres or £19.00 today.

platebands In classical buildings, a flat rectangular moulding or fascia, the projection of which is less than its breadth. Bankes used this term frequently in connection with the structure of ceilings, but his usage is often unclear since he was applying classical architectural terms to Egyptian architecture.

portal Gateway.

Porte The Ottoman court in Constantinople, seat of the imperial government, so-called after the gate of the sultan's palace where justice was administered.

portico Column or pillar arrangement at the entrance to a building.

pronaos Vestibule of a temple, often columned, preceding a hypostyle hall.

propyleum Entrance gateway to an enclosure, usually temple precincts.

propylon Free-standing version of a pylon.

pylon Ceremonial gateway in front of a temple, consisting of twin towers with battered walls.

Ramesseum Name given to the mortuary temple of Rameses II at Thebes, known to the Greeks as the Memnonium.

rock-cut Cut into the natural rock face.

sanctuary Bankes used this term for the private abode of the god at the rear of the temple containing the naos.

scarab Common type of amulet made in the shape of the sacred scarab beetle.

sekos Term used by Bankes for the innermost chamber of a temple.

shabti Funerary figurine placed in tombs to spare the tomb owner from menial corvée labour in the afterlife.

Sheikh A term generally used by the travellers in its broadest sense, indicating the village chiefs who were independent of the central authority.

soffit Underside of a part of a building, or any structural component.

speos Cave or grotto.

stela/stelae Upright inscribed stone slab.

uraeus/uraei The cobra goddess, Wadjyt, whose image protrudes from the brow of the king's crown or headdress and represents kingship.

votive Dedicated or offered in fulfilment of a vow, or to express devotion.

Note: Bankes used a classical architectural vocabulary to interpret Egyptian temples, therefore some definitions for architectural terms may differ slightly from the classical interpretation.

ABBREVIATIONS AND SOURCES

Bankes Albums Two leather-bound manuscript volumes containing Bankes's travel notes from Egypt 1818–19, presented to the British Museum in 1923 by G. Nugent Bankes.

CEDAE Centre d'Études et de Documentation sur l'ancienne Égypte.

D/BKL Deposited/Bankes Kingston Lacy. The Bankes papers are divided between Kingston Lacy, Dorset and Dorset Record Office, Dorchester. Dorset Record Office has classified the papers under D/BKL and subdivisions have been established for the cataloguing. William Bankes's personal correspondence is catalogued under the heading: D/BKL HJ 1. Other papers relating to William Bankes are in the course of arrangement. D/BKL HH refers to the personal and family papers of William Bankes's father, Henry Bankes. At the time of writing, these were not yet numbered. Bankes's Egyptian drawings and some miscellaneous Egyptian papers are on temporary loan to the Department of Ancient Egypt and Sudan, the British Museum.

HH *see* D/BKL.

HJ *see* D/BKL.

JEA *Journal of Egyptian Archaeology*.

John Murray archive Archives held by John Murray (Publishers) Ltd, London.

KMT *KMT, A Modern Journal of Ancient Egypt*.

RCK *The Royal Cemeteries of Kush*.

This book is based on the author's doctoral thesis submitted to the University of London in September 1998: *William John Bankes' Collection of Drawings and Manuscripts Relating to Ancient Nubia*, 2 vols (unpublished).

NOTES

PROLOGUE

1 Letter to Hobhouse, Ravenna, 4 August 1819. Marchand 1973, vol. 6, 200.

2 *The Gentleman's Magazine and Historical Review*, August 1855, 205.

3 Cholmondeley 1950, 255–6.

4 Later Sir Charles Barry.

5 See Bankes 1986, 171; Dawson and Uphill 1972; and Fiechter 1994, 268 (*bibliographie*) where it is given as '*Travels in Egypt and Nubia, Syria and Asia Minor during the years 1817 and 1818*. Londres, 1823'.

CHAPTER 1

1 D/BKL 8c/76.

2 Westminster School lists him in 1795, 1797 and 1801.

3 See Mitchell 1994 for the history of the house and family, and William's collections.

4 Grieg 1924, vol. IV, 111.

5 Grieg 1924, vol. IV, 112. When his wife died in November 1823, *The Times* reported that William's father was 'in such a dangerous state' that the knowledge of the funeral was kept from him.

6 Letter to Byron, 16 March (?)1806. John Murray archive.

7 The house, referred to generally here as Kingston Lacy, was, until Bankes's rebuilding, known as Kingston Hall.

8 Leitch 1855, 443.

9 *Heber Letters*, 255 (26 June 1818), quoted in Thorne 1986, 134.

10 Two small modern obelisks were placed in the Upper Park; one remains. Mitchell 1994, Introduction.

11 Bankes 1986, 133. This sum by 1821 would have been roughly equivalent to £350,000 today.

12 Hobhouse, a classical scholar with political and literary ambitions, was to be Byron's companion on his travels in the East.

13 He was a brilliant and openly homosexual aesthete and collector who espoused radical politics.

14 Marchand 1973, vol. 7, 230.

15 Letter to Edward Noel Long, 23 February 1807. Marchand 1973, vol. 1, 110.

16 Ilchester 1923, 170.

17 Letter to Byron, 3 March 1807. John Murray archive.

18 *Hours of Idleness: A Fragment* (1803).

19 Letter to Bankes, 6 March 1807. Marchand 1973, vol. 1.

20 Quoted in Mitchell 1994, 24.

21 Letter to Bankes, March 1809. Marchand 1973, vol. 1, 198.

22 Marchand 1973, vol. 7, 230.

23 Letter to Byron, 24 September 1812. John Murray archive.

24 Letter to Byron, 20 April 1812. John Murray archive.

25 Letter to Byron, 2 January 1822. John Murray archive.

26 Quoted in Bankes 1986, 128.

27 Letter to Scrope Berdmore Davies, 2 September 1811. Marchand 1973, vol. 11, 159.

28 Letter to Hobhouse, 30 August 1811. Marchand 1973, vol. 2, 84.

29 Letter to James Wedderburn Webster, 31 August 1811. Marchand 1973, vol. 2, 87.

30 Bourne 1979, 11; 153, n 1.

31 Clark and Hughes 1890, 1 February 1823.

32 Letter to Byron, 2 January 1822. John Murray archive.

33 Letter to Bankes, 28 September 1812. Marchand 1973, vol. 2, 214–15.

34 Thorne 1986.

35 Thorne 1986, 133.

36 Thorne 1986, 133.

37 Marchand 1973, vol. 2, 214–15.

38 Uncatalogued, D/BKL Box 8c/91.

39 Bankes did not actually introduce this payment, but spent a vast sum on it.

40 Teignmouth 1878, 300–3.

41 Printed canvass letter. John Murray archive.

42 Clark and Hughes 1890.

43 Quoted in Bankes 1986, 133.

44 According to Bankes 1986 who mentions Douglas. Marchand 1971, 120, adds the name of Foster.

45 Quoted in Bankes 1986, 134.

46 Bankes 1986, 134.

47 Marchand 1973, vol. 3, 103.

48 Letter to Byron, 9 November 1812. John Murray archive.

49 Letter to Byron, 21 December 1812. John Murray archive.

50 Troas is the mountainous north-west corner of Asia Minor, dominated by the Ida Massif and washed on three sides by the sea. It was believed that all this area was once under Trojan rule.

51 Marchand, 1973, vol. 2, (26 December 1812), 261.

52 Letter to Byron, 16 March 1813. John Murray archive.

53 Letter to Byron, 16 March 1813. John Murray archive.

54 *Quarterly Review*, vol. 25, 125.

55 Sir Brindsley Ford: personal communication.

56 Curto and Donatelli 1985, 165, Letter 130.

57 Searight 1980.

58 Quoted in Bankes 1986, 138.

59 Bankes 1986, 139.

60 Quennell 1937, 155.

61 Letter to George Bankes, quoted in Bankes 1986, 178.

62 HJ 1/25.

CHAPTER 2

1 Unless otherwise specified, all Bankes's descriptions quoted in this chapter are taken from an uncatalogued twenty-five page journal. D/BKL.

2 Baron Dominique Vivant Denon (1747–1825) accompanied Bonaparte's expedition as a scholar-artist, recording the monuments and collecting antiquities. On his return to France he was appointed Director-General of Museums in 1804, and was instrumental in building up the Louvre collections.

3 The antiquary and diplomat William Richard Hamilton (1777–1859) had been sent to Egypt by Lord Elgin in 1801 and was present when the Rosetta Stone was ceded to the British forces.

4 Halls 1834, vol. I, 500.

5 Fuller 1829; Forbin 1819a and b. Count Auguste de Forbin (1777–1841) followed Denon as Director-General of Museums and visited Egypt twice, acquiring antiquities for the Louvre.

6 A former strong-man and showman of the British stage, the Paduan Giovanni Battista Belzoni (1778–1823) was to explore and excavate on behalf of both Henry Salt and himself, developing the ability to remove huge antiquities. Among other discoveries he entered the second pyramid at Giza, opened the temple of Abu Simbel, and located the tomb of Sety I at Thebes. His account of his time in Egypt was published in English.

The French mineralogist Frédéric Cailliaud (1787–1869) explored Egypt and Nubia, collected antiquities, and drew many previously unknown Nubian monuments. He published accounts of all his expeditions, unlike Linant de Bellefonds (1799–1883), much of whose early work, commissioned by Bankes, remained at Kingston Lacy unpublished.

7 HJ 1/34.

8 Missett's arms and legs were paralysed. Buckingham 1855, 130–58.

9 Probably Sir Robert Wilson, *The History of the British Expedition to Egypt*, 1802.

10 Travellers referred to the monasteries as 'convents'.

11 Burckhardt to E. D. Clarke, Cairo, 28 June 1816. Otter 1824, 621.

12 Burckhardt 1822.

13 For early travellers to Nubia see Dewachter 1971b; Christophe 1965; Schiff Giorgini 1965a.

14 For the discovery of Meroe see Ahmed 1997, 1; Török 1997, xxi, 1. For Bruce see Hill 1967; Bruce 1813; Bredin 2000.

15 For the history of archaeological research in the Sudan see Hakem 1978; Ahmed 1997.

16 HJ 1/24 and 1/25.

17 The Journal of Mrs Arbuthnot for 1 August 1821, quoted in Bankes 1986, 160.

18 William Turner (1792–1867) was a diplomat at the British Embassy in Constantinople who published his travel journals (Turner 1820). Belzoni 1822, vol. II, 33, also mentions that Bankes 'arrived in this country and proceeded almost immediately to Sinai'.

19 Peter Lee, British consul at Alexandria and a member of the firm headed by Samuel Briggs, British merchant and banker of Alexandria. Turner 1820, 325.

20 Turner 1820, 484.

21 Turner 1820, 364.

22 Turner 1820, 357.

23 Finati 1830, 73–4.

24 Turner 1820, 607.

25 Turner 1820, 393.

26 Turner 1820, footnote, 443-4.

27 D/BKL uncatalogued notes on Sinai.

28 I am indebted to Norman N. Lewis for suggesting that Bankes may have returned four of the books he had removed. John Hyde's letter to him dated 7 October 1819 (HJ 1/103) mentions that 'The four Books you intrusted to my care I saw placed upon a shelf in the Library.' Hyde visited Sinai 4 September – 5 October 1819. 'When Burckhardt himself visited the monastery almost a year later he had some difficulty in persuading the monks to let him take books because, as he put it, "the monks had been scolded by their superiors" in Cairo for allowing Bankes to have some. Nevertheless, Burckhardt was able to "carry off by stealth", though with the permission of the Prior, the two Aldine volumes.' Burckhardt 1822, 551, as quoted in Lewis and Macdonald, forthcoming.

29 The drawings from Serabit are not by Bankes as suggested in James 1997, 69–70.

CHAPTER 3

1 HH. In addition to the two colossi of Memnon there was a colossal granite head of Rameses II, from the Ramesseum, known as the head of Memnon, or the younger Memnon. It was later removed by Belzoni and presented to the British Museum by Salt and Burckhardt (EA 19).

2 Finati 1830, 73.

3 Finati 1830, 72. Giovanni Finati, born in Ferrara in 1787, deserted the French army in 1809 and later enlisted under Mohammed Ali in Alexandria. He led a colourful and adventurous life, taking part in the capture of Mecca and Medina and the Wahabi and Arabian campaigns before serving as a dragoman for European travellers.

4 Unless otherwise specified, all the fragmentary journal material quoted for this journey is taken from uncatalogued D/BKL box, 'Egypt'.

5 'August' must be an error since his own footnotes to Finati 1830 give their departure date as 16 September 1815

and their return as 16 December 1815, and Bankes wrote from Cairo on 3 September 1815 before his departure for Nubia.

6 Bankes also travelled with a copy of Denon 1803.

7 The pink granite obelisk, later removed to Kingston Lacy, was inscribed with the names of Ptolemy IX, his sister Cleopatra, and his wife, also named Cleopatra, and was one of a pair placed before the temple of Isis, Philae. Its pedestal records tax exemptions awarded by the same ruler to the priesthood of the temple. Habachi 1977, 106–8. Iversen 1972, 62ff.

8 This confirms the journal date as 1815.

9 Qasr Ibrim and Abu Simbel are both described in another journal fragment, X.F.33.

10 Bankes's footnote, Finati 1830, 86.

11 Near Ashmunein.

CHAPTER 4

1 'Syria' was the term used by Bankes and his contemporaries to denote the Holy Land and adjoining regions. For information on Bankes in Syria I am deeply indebted to Norman N. Lewis, who supplied me so generously with the fruits of his own research.

2 Finati 1830, 110.

3 Bowsher 1997, 244.

4 Finati 1830, 132.

5 Finati 1830, 152.

6 Bowsher 1997, 240.

7 Seetzen 1810.

8 Bowsher 1997, 230. I am indebted to this article for my understanding of Bankes's work in the Decapolis.

9 Itineraries dealing with land-routes and giving distances along roads were common in the Roman Empire but few have survived. The chief of those known is the *Itinerarium Antoninianum*, which may be a third-century collection of routes used for troop movements (Hammond and Scullard 1970, 558).

10 With Bankes's Syria papers, Dorset Record Office.

11 Bowsher 1997, 234.

12 This was the same Bruce who had ridiculed Bankes when they were both Cambridge students. Lady Hester's scathing references to 'Bankes, whom she disliked very much', including one to his meanness, are quoted by B. B.

Barker in his biography of his father John Barker. Barker 1876, 267, 270–1.

13 Letter to Michael Bruce, 5 March 1816, quoted in Bruce 1951, 379.

14 *The Dictionary of National Biography* (London, 1898).

15 See Lewis 1997. Bankes's frescos, now exhibited anonymously in the billiard room at Kingston Lacy, are the portraits Fig. 3, p. 146, and Fig. 5, p. 147.

16 For details of Bankes's work in the Hauran see Lewis *et al.* 1996.

17 Lewis *et al.* 1996, 161–4.

18 Lewis *et al.* 1996, 70.

19 HJ 1/57.

20 Unnumbered HH letter from Bankes to his father, postmarked 22 September 1821.

21 HJ 1/59

22 D/BKL uncatalogued letter, Tripoli 17 June 1816.

23 Our sources are: places mentioned in the portfolio, letters of introduction, Finati 1830, Irby and Mangles 1823, 183.

24 Leake 1830, Preface.

25 D/BKL draft letter, 'Greece' folders XIV–XIX.

26 *Encyclopaedia Britannica* (15th edition 1991), vol. 9, 150.

27 HJ 1/56.

28 HJ 1/61.

29 HJ 1/54.

30 This has been pieced together from a bill, HJ 1/71, for expenses for a ball at the house of a man named as Consul in HJ 1/84.

31 Unidentified, but possibly Amorgos.

32 These later descriptions are from *Murray's Hand-Book, Greece* (London, 1876), 753–4.

33 Leake 1826, and letter from Leake HJ 1/365.

34 Letter from Bankes in Cyprus to unnamed recipient (perhaps Burckhardt, who died that day in Cairo), 15 October 1817, HJ 1/75.

CHAPTER 5

1 Halls 1834, vol I, 410, for the sanitized version. The unexpurgated manuscript is in the *Correspondence of Visct. Valentia with Salt, Pearce and others, relative to Abyssinia and Egypt 1804–1826*, British Library Mss Annesley. Add. Mss 19347, fol. 144.

2 Throughout, Luxor refers to the area around the temple known as the temple of Luxor, and is not used as the modern term for Thebes. Forbin 1819a, 50.

3 Finati 1830, 218–21.

4 Irby and Mangles 1823, 232–33.

5 *The Ruins of Palmyra*, London, 1753.

6 Irby and Mangles 1823, 336.

7 Burckhardt 1822, iv.

8 D/BKL Syria papers: II.F.1.

9 Henry Maundrell's celebrated narrative, *A Journey from Aleppo to Jerusalem at Easter AD. 1697*, was first published in 1703 and continuously reprinted.

10 In addition to two other servants, Legh took James Curtin with him

11 Irby and Mangles 1823, 406.

12 Irby and Mangles 1823, 418.

13 XXI.F.10.

14 John William Burgon, 1845.

15 See Lewis and Macdonald (forthcoming).

16 This adventure is corroborated by Bankes's sketch plans of the mosques: D/BKL Syria papers: I.A.26 and 27.

17 Marcellus 1839, vol. II, 29–31. Mrs Belzoni, in her *Trifling Account*, at the end of Belzoni 1822, 462.

18 MacMichael 1819, 184, quoted in Lewis and Macdonald (forthcoming).

19 Letter from Naples, 24 January 1820, HJ 1/125.

20 Letter from Naples, 1 May 1820, HJ 1/130.

21 Buckingham 1825, 633.

22 HJ 1/130.

23 L. de Laborde, *Voyage de l'Arabie Pétrée* (Paris, 1830), 30–31, quoted in Lewis *et al.* 1996, 59, n 4.

24 Lewis *et al.* 1996, 60, n16.

25 There is evidence of a plan to publish the Egyptian and Nubian inscriptions separately under the title *Inscriptiones Africanae*. (See unpublished list of miscellaneous manuscripts kept with the Bankes Egyptian drawings.)

26 M. Sartre quoted (in translation) in Lewis *et al.* 1996, from which all my conclusions on Bankes's Syrian epigraphy are taken.

CHAPTER 6

1 Irby and Mangles 1823, 293, 232.

2 Alessandro Ricci (died 1834), son of a Florentine stone-mason, was born in Siena, where he studied medicine at the University. He arrived in Egypt around 1817. By the time he worked for Bankes in 1818–19 he was an experienced epigrapher, having spent almost a year working in Thebes. He was forced to return early from the Berenice expedition through illness.

3 Baron Albert Sack, aged over seventy, a noted naturalist and former chamberlain to the king of Prussia, had travelled from Rome to the warmer climes of Egypt as he was in poor health. He brought with him as his companion, F. C. Gau. The two fell out almost immediately, and Gau, finding himself alone and friendless in Egypt, decided to take up his sketchbook and travel into Nubia (Gau 1822). Sack collected specimens of fauna on the 1818–19 journey, having previously spent nearly three years travelling and collecting in Dutch Guiana (Sack 1810).

4 Linant de Bellefonds had arrived in Egypt with the party of Count de Forbin in December 1817 after travelling through Athens, Constantinople, Ephesus, Acre, and Jerusalem. He was born in Lorient, France, on 23 November 1799; his father, a naval captain, was the great-grandson of the Marquis de Bellefonds, Maréchal de France. Linant was destined for a career at sea, and his education included mathematics and drawing. A year after passing his examinations in 1814, he boarded *Le Huron*, then charting the coast of Newfoundland and Canada. He was later midshipman on a ship of the squadron which left Toulon on 12 August 1817, carrying Forbin and Huyot to Greece and the Near East. Their artist Prévost's nephew and assistant, Cochereau, had died during the voyage, and Huyot their draughtsman had been injured, so Linant took their place. He was left in Cairo with Prévost to draw a panorama of the city while Forbin went into Upper Egypt. It was Forbin who introduced him to the service of Mohammed Ali, where he spent six months working as an architect and overseeing the cutting of a new canal.

5 Letter from Lord Prudhoe, 16 January 1830, HJ 1/360.

6 Bankes's letter to his father, HH, and Young's letter affixed to Bankes Album, II, 3.

7 Letter to Hamilton, 4 May 1819. Halls 1834, II, 119.

8 Finati 1830, 343.

9 Letter to Bankes, Calais, 21 October 1822, Leitch 1855, 234.

10 Budge 1951, 3.

11 Letter, 9 January 1823, HJ 1/195.

12 Letter to Gell, 13 September 1823, Leitch 1855, 371.

13 Letter to Chev. San Quintino, 24 November 1827, Leitch 1855, 453.

14 Letter to Young, 16 December 1822, Leitch 1855, 247–9.

15 Salt 1825, 7ff.

16 Bankes 1821.

17 Unnumbered HH letter from Bankes to his father, postmarked 22 September 1821, states that 'the oval containing what Dr Young declares to be the name of Ptolemy is that which occurs on the obelisk, & that which I myself found elsewhere to signify Cleopatra is immediately below, which seems to leave no doubt at all that it has a direct connection with the Greek inscription on the Pedestal'.

18 A leg injury had forced Huyot to separate from his travelling companion Forbin. Huyot left Cairo on 26 November 1818 with Edouard de Montulé, whom he had met in Alexandria. They passed Thebes on 9 December 1818 and arrived at Aswan on 14 December. On 19 December de Montulé returned north, leaving Huyot at Aswan (Montulé 1821, 14–33). The fact that Huyot joined Bankes was not previously known: see Leclant 1961, 36; Dewachter 1971b.

19 HH.

20 Sesostris was the name used erroneously by the Greek authors for a legendary figure, perhaps based on Rameses II, or a conflation of other great pharaohs. Unnumbered HH letter from Bankes to his father, (undated) 1818.

21 Letter to Hudson Gurney, early 1816, Wood 1954, 215.

22 Letter to Young, 1826, Leitch 1855, 392.

23 Halls 1834, vol. II, 139.

24 HH.

25 Finati 1830, 299.

26 Probably Tell el-Timai (Thmuis). San el-Hagar is now recognized as being ancient Tanis.

27 Probably Tell el-Timai (Thmuis).

28 Behbeit el-Hagar, the site of one of the most important temples of Isis in Egypt, noted for its delicacy of relief.

29 Halls 1834, vol. I, 488.

30 HJ 1/180.

31 Finati 1830, 300.

32 Fuller 1829, 144.

33 Bankes's letter of 20 April 1816 to Buckingham, Buckingham 1825, 627.

34 Salt's letter to Mrs Morgan, Cairo, 22 May 1819. Halls 1834, vol. II, 122.

35 Salt's letter to Mrs H-N., Cairo, 22 May 1819. Halls 1834, vol. II, 133–4.

36 Probably most of these are missing from Finati's narrative in order to minimize the impression that the Nile was full of travellers at this time.

37 Belzoni 1822, vol. II, 105–6; Halls 1834, vol. II, 135.

38 Bankes was the first to record this tomb at 'Radimore' (Deir el-Bersha) with its famous painted wall, now mainly destroyed, showing the transport of a colossal statue of the tomb-owner. 'Mr Bankes and Mr Beechey are the only travellers who have visited this tomb since we discovered it: the former has accurate drawings of all its contents.' Irby and Mangles 1822, 165.

39 They were unlike the unfortunate traveller de Montulé. 'Not knowing that it was necessary to be provided with everything in order to travel in Egypt, we had forgotten the article of candles; so that we were in the midst of the most profound darkness in the cabin' (Montulé 1821, 6).

40 Dates up to 26 February 1819 from Ricci's diary, written in Italian, previously unidentified in Dorset Record Office.

41 Linant de Bellefonds Mss 267, Bibliothèque du Louvre, Paris.

42 John Hyde Mss 42102-8.

43 This antagonism ended in violence against Belzoni; see Belzoni 1822, vol. II, 107; Fiechter 1994.

44 Osman was a British soldier and adventurer who had converted to Islam and was in the service of Belzoni. See Bierbrier 1995, 315.

45 Ricci also kept fifteen drawings, constituting an important record of the temples; see Usick 1998.

46 Finati 1830, 307.

47 See Belzoni 1822, vol. II, 109–124.

48 Finati 1830, 309. The tone of Belzoni's letters is often quite unpleasant, combining obsequiousness with underlying aggression, believing that Bankes despised him for not being a learned gentleman. Bankes did write slightingly of him in 1823: 'Belzoni is on some wild project in Africa and writes puffing letters home which are published in the newspapers, his aim seems to be Timbuctoo.' HJ 1/227, letter to Salt.

49 'Je vous apprend avec peine que l'obelisque est déjà sur Cange et que demain il aura quitté l'Ile.' Curto and Donatelli 1985, 116, letter 90 (but incorrectly transcribed there as from 'Guyot').

50 Finati 1830, 310.

CHAPTER 7

1 HJ 1/185, 22 November 1822.

2 Vercoutter 1992, 82.

3 Linant de Bellefonds 1872–73, 420.

4 C. Barry, Mss diary of travels in the Drawings Collection, Royal Institute of British Architects, London, quoted in Clayton 1984, 45.

5 Also referred to by scholars as Azekheramun, or Azagraman.

6 Bankes Album, II, 18.

7 Cailliaud ignored the Nubian monuments because they had been thoroughly recorded by the distinguished architects Gau and Huyot, and by Linant for Bankes, whom Cailliaud called 'the English traveller-Savant from whom we await the most precious researches on Egypt and Nubia' (translated from Cailliaud 1826, vol I, 304).

8 Lepsius 1849.

9 Ducamp 1852.

10 Roeder 1911.

11 No mention of the portfolio is to be found in Roeder 1911, Almagro 1971, Priego and Martin Flores 1992, or Daumas 1960.

12 Daumas 1960.

13 Weigall 1907, 61–4.

14 Weigall 1907, 64–7.

15 Säve-Söderbergh 1987, 140–1.

16 The following description of Kalabsha and its temple is taken from Weigall 1907, 68–73.

17 See Monneret de Villard 1941 for a study of the settlement.

18 Museo Egizio di Firenze, inv. 1789, Cat. Schiaparelli 1503; Bankes drawing in Bankes Album, I, 11; see Curto et al. 1965, 82.

19 Light 1818, 64, 55, and Preface, xv.

20 Säve-Söderbergh 1987, 127.

21 This 'testimony to the final triumph of Christianity … officially in year

543 AD' was, in actuality, probably a slow process over perhaps a century 'and the role of Silko is not clear'. Säve-Söderbergh 1987, 40.

22 Bankes Album, I, 5.

23 Bankes Album, II, 35.

24 Quoted in Gauthier 1911, xxviii.

25 Bankes Album, I, 5. The error still appears in Baedeker's guidebook of 1908.

26 Gauthier 1911, Introduction, ix.

27 Bankes Album, I, 35.

28 The identification of the name of Ptolemy x is not certain; see VII.A.14.

29 H. de Meulenaere, *Ptolémée IX Soter II à Kalabcha*, in *Chronique d'Égypte*, no. 71 (1961), 103; Meulenaere et Dewachter 1964–70, Fascicule II, 3; and Gauthier 1911.

30 Stock and Siegler 1965.

31 Daumas 1970, 1.

32 Meulenaere and Dewachter 1964–70.

33 Säve-Söderbergh 1987, 132.

34 Bankes Album, I, 5.

35 These are the forecourt, vestibule and sanctuary of Porter and Moss 1951.

36 Roeder 1938.

37 Ricke *et al.* 1967.

38 Greener 1962, 130–7.

39 Greener 1962, 130–7.

40 The following information has been obtained from Weigall 1907, 78–80, Blackman 1911, and the three volumes of the Centre d'Études et de Documentation sur l'ancienne Égypte publication of Dendur Temple: El-Achirie 1972, Aly *et al.* 1979, and Ibrahim and Leblanc 1975, which are also the sources against which the drawings have been compared.

41 Weigall 1907, 78.

42 Blackman 1911, 82, quoting from Griffith, *Zeitschrift für Aegyptische Sprache und Alterthumskunde*, 1863 etc. 46, 132.

43 Bankes Album II, 52.

44 Weigall 1907, 80.

45 Bankes Album II, 52.

46 Weigall 1907, 80.

47 Maspero 1911, 87.

48 Weigall 1907, 81–83.

49 Weigall 1907, 81. Jaquet (*sic*) and El-Achirie 1978, Preface, III.

50 He is probably referring to the Christian monastery (Weigall 1907, 83)

and to the ruins of an ancient town at the village of Kirsh, opposite Gerf Husein (Weigall 1907, 85).

51 See Bankes drawing VIII.B.8 and 13 (verso).

52 The following information is found in Weigall 1907, 85–89, unless otherwise specified.

53 Emery 1931, 70.

54 Emery and Kirwan 1935, 55.

55 Weigall 1907, 92.

CHAPTER 8

1 Halls 1834, vol. II, 119.

2 Bankes's description of the temple of Wadi es-Sebua, quoted here, is taken from Bankes Album, II, 78–82.

3 Cailliaud 1826, vol. III, 266.

4 Rifaud 1830b, 266.

5 Gauthier 1912.

6 C. Barry, Mss diary of travels in the Drawings Collection, Royal Institute of British Architects, London, quoted in Clayton 1984.

7 See El-Achiery (*sic*) *et al.* 1967, Barguet and Dewachter 1967, Barguet *et al.* 1967, Aly *et al.* 1967, Cerny 1967, and Gauthier 1913.

8 Dewachter 1971a, 149, suggests 1821, but they were passing along the opposite bank and did not visit the temple.

9 See Blackman 1913.

10 El-Achirie and Jacquet 1980.

11 Desroches-Noblecourt *et al.* 1968.

12 Finati 1830, 82.

13 This information is taken from Caminos 1968, Introduction.

14 Dewachter 1971b, 94, suggests Huyot's visiting Ibrim on this date, 21 January 1819. This can now be confirmed since he is with Bankes' party.

15 Caminos 1968.

16 Finati 1830, 313–15.

17 Finati 1830, 314, Bankes's footnote.

18 John Hyde Mss 42102, 82.

19 See letter to Huyot, Curto and Donatelli 1985, 94. Lachaise, author of *Costumes de l'empire Turc, etc.* (Paris, 1821) studied architecture under Huyot, who was Professeur d'histoire at the École des Beaux-Arts in Paris. Lachaise travelled out with Forbin's party and accompanied Huyot to Asia Minor, Constantinople, Greece, and Egypt.

20 Finati 1830, 315–16.

21 Bankes Album, II, 111.

22 Bankes Album, II, 112.

23 John Hyde Mss 42102, 83.

24 Griffith 1921, 3.

25 Griffith 1921, vol. VIII, nos 3–4, 84, and plan of grotto, pl. I.

26 Karkowski 1981, 2.

27 See Karkowski 1981, pl. 1 position 2. I am grateful to a personal communication from Wlodzimierz Godlewski for this information, when he was kind enough to look over the Faras drawings.

28 Karkowski 1981, 3.

29 Michalowski 1966.

30 For a general description and history of the fortress of Buhen see Emery *et al.* 1979, chapter 1.

31 Smith 1976, 217 (citing Caminos 1974, vol. I, 82–86).

32 Finati 1830, 317.

33 Finati 1830, 318.

34 Randall-Maciver and Woolley 1911.

35 Caminos 1974.

36 Caminos 1974, II, 105.

37 Emery *et al.* 1979, Preface.

38 Caminos 1974, I, 12.

39 Randall-Maciver and Woolley 1911, Text, 94.

40 Macadam 1946, 60; Smith 1976, 50.

41 Bush 1986.

42 Halls 1834, vol. II, 112.

43 John Hyde Mss 42102, 92.

44 Finati 1830, 320.

CHAPTER 9

1 Finati 1830, 322.

2 Dunham and Janssen 1960.

3 Finati 1830, 322–23.

4 Dunham and Janssen 1960 published the excavation reports of George Reisner, who worked at the site in 1927–28. For the rescue see Hinkel 1966, Hinkel 1977 (English version: Hinkel 1978). Also, R. Caminos, *Semna-Kumma*, 2 vols, Thirty-eighth Memoir, Archaeological Survey of Egypt (ed. T. G. H. James), Egypt Exploration Society (London, 1998).

5 D'Athanasi 1836, 43.

6 D'Athanasi 1836, 44.

7 John Hyde Mss 42102, 123.

8 D'Athanasi 1836, 45.

9 D'Athanasi 1836, 45.

10 John Hyde Mss 42102, 126. At the end of this journey in Thebes, 5 July 1819, there still remained '4 bottles of Brandy d'Anisette, 2 bottles of Rum, 6 bottles of Hermitage and 5 bottles of Claret' (John Hyde Mss 42103, 40).

11 Finati 1830, 328–32.

12 John Hyde Mss 42102, 126–7.

13 Finati 1830, 333.

14 John Hyde Mss 42102, 127–8.

15 John Hyde Mss 42102, 131–2.

16 Finati 1830, 334–35.

17 Finati 1830, 336–38.

18 John Hyde Mss 42102, 138, and Finati 1830, 339.

19 John Hyde Mss 42102, 140.

20 Finati 1830, 340.

21 See Vila 1977, 37.

22 Quoted from a note received from L. P. Kirwan on the temple at Amara in *JEA* vol. 22 (1936), *Notes and News*, 101.

23 Fuller had met Jowett, an agent of the Missionary and Bible Societies, at Alexandria in January 1819 and they travelled together to Cairo. They joined Pearce, a wild-looking individual who had just returned from a fourteen-year stay in Abyssinia, at Salt's house in his absence.

24 Fuller 1829, 194.

25 Fuller 1829, 211.

26 When the Romans defeated the Meroitic attack in 25–24 BC the Dodekaschoinos came under Roman control and the treaty of Samos established a permanent frontier at Maharraqa. See Taylor 1991, 48.

27 Possibly Qurta.

28 Finati 1830, 341.

29 Finati 1830, 341–2.

30 John Hyde Mss 42102, 194.

31 John Hyde Mss 42102, 215.

32 HJ 1/124, 20 January 1820.

33 Adkins and Adkins 2000, 255.

34 Finati 1830, 343.

35 Fuller 1829, 230.

36 John Hyde Mss 42102, 216.

37 John Hyde Mss 42102, 217.

38 John Hyde Mss 42103, 39.

39 Bankes noted a temperature of 115° which was 'hot enough … to break a glass vessel used by the Dr. as a mortar for grinding his medicines' (D/BKL uncatalogued).

40 The tomb of Rameses III. Hyde's journal lists and describes seventeen tombs then open. John Hyde Mss 42102, 219–20.

41 D'Athanasi 1836, 49.

42 From Belzoni's description this would appear to be Dimai (Soknopaiou Nesos), north of the lake, rather than the site with the classical name of Bacchias which lies to the north-east of the lake. He describes finding the 'Greek town' which 'cannot be any other than the city of Bacchus' (Belzoni 1822, vol. II, 158). The letter to Bankes begins by his being 'not a little mortified' to find Bankes denying that Belzoni has found the Temple of Jupiter Ammon: 'I see that such discoveries are preserved for Travelars of high knowledge and Capacity.' He also refers to the 'unpleasant affair of Carnak', presumably the attack made on him at Thebes (Belzoni 1822, vol. II, 124ff.) which he considered to have been prompted by the enemy camp following his successful removal of the disputed Philae obelisk.

43 Unless otherwise specified, all the details of this period in Cairo, quoted here, are taken from Fuller 1829, 235–49.

44 John Hyde Mss 42103, 47.

45 A copy of Pearce's will, made in Alexandria on 31 July 1820, is found in his own publication: Pearce 1831, 348. He leaves his papers to Salt, and among other bequests: 'In case of skins or horns, which belong to me, arrive in safety from Abyssinia, I leave entirely to William John Bankes Esq.'

46 Finati 1830, 344.

CHAPTER 10

1 Browne had been murdered, Mungo Park killed, and Burckhardt died of dysentery. Letter to Bankes, Venice, 20 November 1819. Marchand 1973, vol. 6.

2 Tita (Giovanni Battista Falcieri), Byron's steadfast servant from a family of gondoliers, entered Byron's service in Venice and remained with him until his death. The monkey was probably part of Byron's menagerie.

3 Letter to Bankes, Ravenna, 19 February 1820. Marchand 1973, vol. 7.

4 'According to Moore, Bankes had told Byron that a Mr. Saunders, whom he met in Venice, had said that "Don Juan was all Grub-street". Bankes told Moore that Byron was so affected by this disparagement that he could not bring himself to write another line of the poem for some time.' Quoted in n. 2, Marchand 1973, vol. 7, letter from Byron to Bankes, Ravenna, 19 February 1820.

5 Letter to Bankes, Ravenna, 19 February 1820. Marchand 1973, vol. 7.

6 Walter Scott's novels had been published anonymously.

7 Letter to Bankes, Ravenna, 26 February 1820. Marchand 1973, vol. 7.

8 Letter to Bankes, Ravenna, 26 February 1820. Marchand 1973, vol. 7.

9 Letter to John Murray, October 1820. Marchand 1973, vol. 7.

10 Mitchell 1994, 27.

11 Letter to Byron, 2 January 1822. John Murray archive.

12 D/BKL, undated letter postmarked 16 October 1821.

13 Letter, 10 October 1821, from Salt, Alexandria, to Bankes, mentioning the news of Bankes's arrival on the continent and his plans to visit Meroe, HJ 1/159. Also a letter from Linant; 'Vous m'avez fait espère dans votre dernière lettre que peut être bientôt vous seriez en Egypt …' HJ 1/147.

14 Bamford and the Duke of Wellington 1950, vol. I, 1 August 1821, 113.

15 Lane Poole 1888, vol. I, 292–3.

16 HJ 1/120.

17 D/BKL uncatalogued copy letter, Tripoli, 17 June 1816.

18 HJ I/125.

19 Mitchell 1994, 25.

20 Finati 1830, 148–9, footnote.

21 It was common for his colleagues to register in print how eagerly they anticipated Bankes's superior publication.

22 26 November 1824, HJ 1/248.

23 HJ 1/145. Young refers to the importance of his access to Bankes's copies in Young 1823, 30.

24 HJ 1/253.

25 I am grateful to Virginia Murray, Archivist at John Murray, for her help in accessing the account books.

26 HJ 1/180.

27 SD 414, Searight collection, Victoria and Albert Museum, London.

28 Bamford and the Duke of Wellington 1950, vol. I, 3 September 1821.

29 HJ 1/173.

30 Anne Glover, illegitimate daughter of Sir Arthur Pigot, Attorney General in Grenville's 1806–07 Ministry of All the Talents (named from the supposed brilliance of its members), married in 1819 (from Keppel St) George Robert Hobart, 5th Earl of Buckinghamshire (died 1849). In 1854 she married David Wilson of Brook Street, living on until 1878 (Bamford and the Duke of Wellington 1950, vol. I, 170–1, n 3; and Debrett's Peerage Ltd).

31 The Journal of Mrs Arbuthnot, quoted in Bankes 1986, 162.

32 Recollections of the Table-talk of Samuel Rogers, London 1856, 288.

33 Teignmouth 1878, vol. I, 300–1.

34 Letter from Aleppo, 20 June 1825, HJ 1/251.

35 Williams Wynn 1864, 81–91; HJ 1/150, 1/156.

36 Ilchester 1923, 106, 170.

37 Bamford and the Duke of Wellington 1950, vol. II, 57.

38 Bamford and the Duke of Wellington 1950, vol. II, 232–3.

39 Letter to Murray, 12 November 1822.

40 Maxwell 1913, vol. 1, 37, quoted in Bourne 1982, 242.

41 Clark and Hughes 1890, 276–7.

42 All the information on this election is taken from J. Ridley, Lord Palmerston (London 1970), 84–7.

43 Broughton 1909–11, vol. 3, 314.

44 The Gentleman's Magazine, 1824, 1825.

45 HJ 1/143. Undated but watermarked 1821.

46 According to Lady Holland, as quoted in Bankes 1986, 158. Also Ilchester 1923, 165.

47 Letter to Murray, 3 December 1826. John Murray archive.

48 Undated letter to Murray, 1831. John Murray archive.

49 All the details of this trial are taken from Buckingham 1826.

50 Buckingham 1845.

51 See Bowsher 1997, 227–45.

CHAPTER 11

1 Letter from Salt to Hamilton, 10 October 1821, HJ 1/160.

2 Finati 1830, 355–6. For a detailed description of the military operations of Ismail's campaign see Crawford 1951, chapters XXVIII–XXXII. The accounts of Cailliaud, Linant, and English were used in compiling this history.

3 See Crawford 1951.

4 According to English 1823 (Preface, vii) the reason for the military action was the interruption to the 'inland commerce' as 'The chiefs of Shageia had formed themselves into a singular aristocracy of brigands' and there were civil wars distracting Sennar. Four thousand troops were sent.

5 Finati 1830, 359–61. Cailliaud also complained of the difficulties in obtaining provisions, their meagre diet and reliance on game, and the army's practice of setting fire to the grain-fields.

6 Shinnie 1958, 77.

7 This view does seem to be supported by other incidents in Ricci's life, although nuances of social position are more difficult to understand today. As Salt wrote to Pearce, when inviting him to Egypt, 'You must not expect to be a gentleman; but I can insure you a comfortable maintenance with little work, such as looking after my garden or collecting antiques.' Halls 1834, vol. II, 106.

8 HJ 1/187, 14 December 1822.

9 HJ 1/183, 22 September 1822.

10 I am indebted to Timothy Kendall for pointing out which drawings contained lost information. Photographs of some drawings are reproduced in RCK, III.

11 See Kendall 1991, 302; Reisner 1917–20; Dunham 1970; and Kendall 1994, 139–45, (site plan: 142).

12 Shinnie 1958, 44; Dunham 1950.

13 Finati 1830, 378–9, and XV.C.5.

14 Shinnie 1958, 52.

15 The travellers called the temple the 'Typhonium', mistaking the grotesque features of the ancient Egyptian god Bes (whose image is carved on the columns), with those of the malevolent Greek god Typhon, whom the Greeks actually equated with the Egyptian god of chaos, Seth. The temples at this site are now known by numbers.

16 This is likely to be the Italian traveller and geologist G. B. Brocchi, who journeyed to Nubia and the Sudan and died at Khartoum on 23 September 1826, just eleven days after Linant wrote his journal entry. His diaries were published posthumously: Brocchi 1841.

17 Macadam 1946.

18 Personal communication from Timothy Kendall.

19 Shinnie 1958, 97, note 1, suggests 'Sereiwa'.

20 Although there was a mutual exchange of drawings between Cailliaud and Linant to make up deficiencies in their individual portfolios.

21 Finati 1830, 355. The site was actually discovered in 1772 by James Bruce who correctly identified it with the 'ancient City of Meroe'; Bruce 1813, vol. IV, 295. A history of those who recorded and excavated the site is given in Török 1997, vol. I, 1.

22 Shinnie 1958, 75, 143–51.

23 Today the name of Begrawiya is also used for Meroe, and RCK uses it to designate the pyramids, e.g. Beg. N. 1. (Begrawiya North 1). Porter and Moss 1951 use the same numbering system for the pyramids, which follows that made by Reisner. Linant gave his own numbers to those of the pyramids he found most interesting.

24 For the excavation of Meroe city see Török 1997.

25 See Hinkel 1986, 99–105. He discovered an ancient incised architectural design for a truncated pyramid, actual capstones, and evidence for the presence of vertical wooden poles through the axis of the pyramids.

26 Ferlini 1837.

27 Linant's drawings appear in Chapman and Dunham 1952.

28 See Budge 1907, 146–51, and Hoskins 1835, 100.

29 Welsby 1996, 143–6.

30 Papers on the work taking place at Musawwarat, and also at Meroe and Naqa, were given at the Eighth International Conference for Meroitic Studies, London, September 1996. I am grateful for the kind help of Pawel Wolf, Friedrich Hinkel, and Janice Yellin who looked through the drawings and gave me much useful information. For reports on previous excavations see Hintze 1962b 170–202; Hintze 1962a; Hintze 1963, 217–26; Hintze 1967–68, 283–98.

31 Louis Linant visited these famous ruins. He came at England's command and penetrated as far as the kingdom of Sennar thanks to the conquests of

Ismael Pasha, general of the armies
of his grace Mohammed Ali, king
of Egypt. See Whitehead 1926, 66,
as quoted in Shinnie 1958, 115.

32 Welsby 1996, 119–20.

33 See Welsby 1996, 150–1. For the
excavated grave see Hintze 1959,
171–96.

34 Frey and Knudstad 1996, 138;
Kroeper 1996; Kroeper 1996a and
1996b; Hinkel 1996.

35 Personal communication from
Dietrich Wildung.

36 HJ 1/227.

37 HJ 1/200.

38 After leaving England, Linant
was in Malta by 18 August 1825
(HJ 1/351).

39 Moore 1976, 218.

40 Broughton 1909–11, vol. 3,
119–20; vol. 4, 103–11.

41 Fulford 1963, 75, 85.

42 All the information about the trial
is taken from *The Times* newspaper
of 3 December 1833.

43 Bathurst to Wellington, 5
December 1833. Wellington to
Salisbury, 10 December 1833. Quoted
in Brooke and Gandy 1975, vol. I,
376–8.

44 HJ 1/332.

45 Letter from J. Sams, 10 April 1833.
HJ 1/384.

46 HJ 1/620.

47 All the details of this case are
taken from the indictment and charge.
Queen v. Bankes, HJ 1/627.

48 Mitchell 1994, 32, 57.

49 D/BKL box, 8c/89.

50 Broughton 1909–11, vol. 3, 92–3,
124–5.

CHAPTER 12

1 Finati 1830, 343. Made up of half-a-
dozen separate pieces, it was later
removed by the French consul-general
J. F. Mimaut and purchased by the
British Museum (EA 117).

2 Finati 1830, 343.

3 His reproof was published in the
Quarterly Review, vol. 28, October 1822.

4 HJ 1/77; envelope marked received
31 January 1818.

5 Papyrus CXIV, *Catalogue of Ancient
Manuscripts in the British Museum* (Part I,
Greek) (London, 1881), 6.

6 For the criteria of eighteenth-century
collectors of Egyptian objects see
Quirke 1997.

7 See James 1993–94, 20–32, the main
source for the information on Bankes's
collection.

8 See Ritner letter, *KMT*, vol. 5, no. 1
(Spring 1994).

9 HJ 1/227.

10 See Assmann 1991, 267ff.,
and HJ 1/169 for the sarcophagus.
For Hetepbakef see T. G. H. James.
'A Ramesside divine statue at Kingston
Lacy' in C. Eyre *et al.* (eds) *The Unbroken
Reed. Studies in the Culture and Heritage of
Ancient Egypt in Honour of A. F. Shore*
(London, 1994).

11 Finati 1830, 96; Forbin 1819a,
92.The provenance of the Chatsworth
statues was discovered by Charles
Noble, LVO, Deputy Keeper of
Collections, Chatsworth, who kindly
provided me with the details of the
Chatsworth acquisition.

12 Devonshire Mss, Chatsworth. 6th
Duke's group nos: 2463, and 2478.

13 See Manniche 1987, 101, and
Davies 1958, pls 2, 5, 6.

14 If Burckhardt is referring to the
Deir el-Medina stele in HJ 1/57, this
means that the site was open from as
early as 1815. For the stelae see Cerny
1958.

15 See Quirke 1996. As Quirke points
out, the inclusion of the Rameside
letters – unattractive, cursive,
pictureless fragments which we now
know to be important documents for
Pharaonic political history – is much
to Bankes's credit.

16 Franz Joseph Gall (1758–1828)
was the founder of phrenology.

17 Letter to Byron, 2 January 1822.
John Murray archive.

18 Salt's letter of 10 October 1821,
HJ 1/159.

19 Unnumbered HH letter from
Bankes, Old Palace Yard, to his father.
No date, but postmark 22 September
1821. The frames were probably
wooden panel-work lining the walls
of the room.

20 This was rejected by the British
Museum as too expensive and
subsequently purchased by Sir John
Soane.

21 See Iversen 1972, 62.

22 Letter to John Murray from Bankes,
9 October 1830, John Murray archive.

23 Bankes ordered his own volumes of
the *Description* from Paris in July 1818.
Individual volumes appeared between
1809 and 1828.

24 Finati 1830, 100.

25 Fuller 1829, 230.

26 Conner 1983, 9.

27 Conner 1983, 9.

28 HJ 1/171.

29 Bierbrier 1995, 256–7. See Borrer
1849.

30 Letter from Barker, 2 May 1821,
from Alexandria, HJ 1/374.

31 See Bierbrier 1995; Halls 1834;
James 1997, chapter two.

32 See his two biographies: Halls
1834; Manley and Rée 2001.

33 Elsner 1993, 8.

34 See Usick 1998.

35 I am most grateful to Professor
David Warrell for this information.

36 Renéaume 1988, 41–9; also
Dewachter 1988b, 50–4. For the group
portrait see Dewachter 1988a, 50;
Rosellini 1982, 39 and Cat. No. 44.

37 HJ 1/186, 26 November 1822 (?).

38 Beechey and Beechey 1828.

39 I am most grateful to Peta Rée for
the details of Beechey's later life.

40 For the graffiti he left see
Dewachter 1971a, 147–51.

41 HJ 1/80.

42 According to Prudhoe this was the
dedication of a colossal temple in the
Roman era. Letter of 16 January 1830
to Bankes, HJ 1/360.

43 This was never used. HJ 1/350.

44 Letter from Lord Prudhoe, written
from London (?) after leaving Egypt,
HJ 1/360.

BIBLIOGRAPHY

Adams, W. Y. 1961. Archaeological survey of Sudanese Nubia, *Kush, Journal of the Sudan Antiquities Service*, vol. IX, 7–10, Introduction. Khartoum.

Adkins, L. and R. 2000. *The Keys of Egypt: The Race to Read the Hieroglyphs*. London.

Ahmed, Salah Mohammed 1997. More than a century of archaeological research in the Sudan, in *Sudan, Ancient Kingdoms of the Nile*. Paris and New York.

Almagro, M. 1971. *El Templo de Debod*. Madrid.

Aly, M., F. Abdel-Hamid, and M. Dewachter 1967. *Le Temple d'Amada*, Cahier IV, Dessins. Tables de Concordance. Centre de Documentation et d'Études [*sic*] sur l'ancienne Égypte. Cairo.

Aly, M., F.-A. Hamid, and Ch. Leblanc 1979. *Le Temple de Dandour*, II, Dessins, Centre d'Études et de Documentation sur l'ancienne Égypte. Cairo.

Anderson, R. and I. Fawzy 1987. *Egypt in 1800*. London.

Assmann, J. 1991. *Das Grab des Amenemope (TT 41)*. 2 vols. Mainz.

d'Athanasi, Giovanni 1836. *A Brief Account of the Researches and Discoveries in Upper Egypt made under the direction of Henry Salt Esq*. London.

Atil, E., C. Newton, and S. Searight, 1995. *Voyages and Visions / Nineteenth-century European Images of the Middle East from the Victoria and Albert Museum*. Washington.

Atkins, S. 1824. *Fruits of Enterprize Exhibited in the Travels of Belzoni in Egypt and Nubia; Interspersed with the Observations of a Mother to her Children* (fourth edition). London.

Baines, J. and J. Malek 1996. *Atlas of Ancient Egypt*. Oxford.

Bamford, F. and the Duke of Wellington (eds) 1950. *The Journal of Mrs Arbuthnot*, 2 vols. London.

Bankes, V. 1986. *A Dorset Heritage* (second edition). London.

Bankes, W. J. 1821. *Geometrical Elevation of an Obelisk from the Island of Philoe*. London.

Barguet, P., A. Abdel-Hamid Youssef, and M. Dewachter 1967. *Le Temple d'Amada*, Cahier III, Textes, Centre de Documentation et d'Études [*sic*] sur l'ancienne Égypte. Cairo.

Barguet, P. and M. Dewachter 1967. *Le Temple d'Amada*, Cahier II, Description Archéologique, Centre de Documentation et d'Études [*sic*] sur l'ancienne Égypte. Cairo.

Barker, B. B. 1876. *Syria and Egypt under the Last Five Sultans*. London.

Beckerath, J. von 1984. *Handbuch der Ägyptischen Königsnamen*. Berlin.

Beechey, F. W. and H. 1828. *Proceedings of the Expedition to explore the Northern Coast of Africa, from Tripoly Eastward; in MDCCCXXI and MDCCCXXII, etc*. London.

Beechey, H. W. 1835. *The Literary Works of Sir Joshua Reynolds … to which is prefixed a memoir of the author* etc. (2 vols.). London.

Belzoni, G. 1822. *Narrative of the Operations and Recent Discoveries within the Pyramids, Temples, Tombs and Excavations, in Egypt and Nubia; and of a Journey to the Red Sea, in Search of the ancient Berenice; and another to the Oasis of Jupiter Ammon* (third edition, 2 vols.). London.

Bierbrier, M. L. 1983. The Salt watercolours, *Göttinger Miszellen*, 61, 9–12.

Bierbrier, M. L. (ed.) 1995. *Who Was Who in Egyptology* (third revised edition). London.

Blackman, A. M. 1911. *The Temple of Dendûr*, Les Temples immergés de la Nubie. Cairo.

Blackman, A. M. 1913. *The Temple of Derr*, Les Temples immergés de la Nubie. Cairo.

Borrer, D. 1849. *A Journey from Naples to Jerusalem etc., with a translation of M. Linant de Bellefonds' Mémoire sur le lac Moeris*.

Bosticco, S. 1959. *Le stele egiziane dall'antico al nuovo regno, Museo Archeologico di Firenze*, vol. I, Florence.

Bourne, K. (ed.) 1979. *Palmerston, Henry John Temple, Viscount: The letters of the third Viscount Palmerston to Laurence and Elizabeth Sullivan, 1804–1863*. London.

Bourne, K. 1982. *Palmerston - The Early Years 1784–1841*. London.

Bowsher, J. M. C. 1997. An early nineteenth century account of Jerash and the Decapolis: the records of William John Bankes, *Levant*, vol. XXIX.

Bredin, M. 2000. *The Pale Abyssinian*. London.

British Museum (preface by E. A. W. Budge) 1913. *Hieroglyphic Texts from Egyptian Stelae &c. in the British Museum*, vol. IV. London.

Brocchi, G. B. 1841. *Giornale delle osservazioni fatte ne viaggi in Egitto, nella Siria e nella Nubia*. Bassano.

Brooke, J. and J. Gandy (eds) 1975. *The Prime Minister's Papers, Wellington*, vol. I. London.

Broughton, Lord 1909–11. *Recollections of a Long Life*, 6 vols. London.

Bruce, I. (ed.) 1951. *The Nun of Lebanon: The Love Affair of Lady Hester Stanhope and Michael Bruce*. London.

Bruce, J. 1813. *Travels to Discover the Source of the Nile in the Years 1768–73* (7 vols.). London–Edinburgh.

Buckingham, J. S. 1825. *Travels among the Arab Tribes inhabiting the Countries East of Syria and Palestine … etc. with an Appendix containing a refutation of certain unfounded calumnies industriously circulated against the author of this work, by Mr. Lewis Burckhardt, Mr. William John Bankes, and the Quarterly Review*. London.

Buckingham, J. S. 1826. *Verbatim Report of the Action for Libel in the Case of Buckingham versus Bankes, etc*. London.

Buckingham, J. S. 1845. *Slander of Punch! An Address to the British Public etc.* (pamphlet). London.

Buckingham, J. S. 1855. *Autobiography of James Silk Buckingham* (2 vols.). London.

Budge, E. A. W. 1907. *The Egyptian Sudan, its History and Monuments* (2 vols.). London.

Budge, E. A. W. 1951. *The Rosetta Stone*, London.

Burckhardt, J. L. 1822. *Travels in Nubia*. London.

Burnett, T. A. J. 1981. *The Rise and Fall of a Regency Dandy: The Life and Times of Scrope Berdmore Davies*. London.

Bush, M. 1986. The Yam jam and Florence stele 2540, in *Wepwawet; Papers in Egyptology*, UCL (London), Summer 1986.

Cailliaud, F. 1823. *Voyage à Méroé et au Fleuve Blanc, au-delà du Fazoql, à Syouah et dans cinq autres oasis fait dans les années 1819, 1820, 1821, 1822* (4 vols.). Paris.

Caminos, R. A. 1968. *The Shrines and Rock-Inscriptions of Ibrim*. London.

Caminos, R. A. 1974. *The New-Kingdom Temples of Buhen*, Egypt Exploration Society, Thirty-third and Thirty-fourth Memoirs. London.

Capart, J. and M. Werbrouk 1926. *Thebes*. London.

Cerny, J. 1958. *Egyptian Stelae in the Bankes Collection*. Oxford.

Cerny, J. 1967, *Le Temple d'Amada*, Cahier V, Les Inscriptions Historiques. Centre d'Études et de Documentation sur l'ancienne Égypte. Cairo.

Champollion, J. F. 1835. *Monuments de l'Égypte et de la Nubie*. Paris.

Champollion, J. F. 1844. *Monuments de l'Égypte et de la Nubie: Notices Descriptives conformes aux manuscrits autographes rédigés sur les lieux par Champollion le Jeune* (vols. I and II). Paris.

Champollion, J. F. 1989. *L'Égypte de Jean-François Champollion*. C. Ziegler, Preface; D. Harlé, index, commentaires, légendes. Suresnes.

Chapman, S. and D. Dunham 1952. *Decorated Chapels of the Meroitic Pyramids at Meroë and Barkal*. The Royal Cemeteries of Kush, vol. III. Boston.

Chauvet, M. 1989. *Frédéric Cailliaud. Les aventures d'un naturaliste en Egypte et au Soudan, 1815–1822*. Saint-Sébastien.

Cholmondeley, R. H. 1950. *The Heber Letters, 1783–1832*. London.

Christophe, L. A. 1965. *Abou-Simbel et l'épopée de sa découverte*. Brussels.

Clark J. W. and M. Hughes 1890. *The Life and Letters of the Reverend Adam Sedgwick*, 2 vols. Cambridge.

Clayton, P. 1984. *The Rediscovery of Ancient Egypt*. London.

Conner, P. (ed.) 1983. *The Inspiration of Egypt*, Brighton.

Cooper, E. J. 1824–7. *Views in Egypt and Nubia, or Egyptian Scenery*. London.

Crawford, O. G. S. 1951. *The Fung Kingdom of Sennar*. Gloucester.

Curto, S. 1970. *Il tempio di Ellesija*, Quaderno n. 6 del Museo Egizio di Torino. Turin.

Curto, S. and L. Donatelli (eds) 1985. *Bernadino Drovetti: Epistolario (1800–1851)*. Milan.

Curto, S., G. Geraci, V. Maragioglio, and C. Rinaldi 1973. *Dehmit*. Rome.

Curto, S., V. Maragioglio, C. Rinaldi, and L. Bongrani 1965. *Kalabsha*, Orientis Antiqui Collectio, V. Rome.

Dafa'alla, S. B. Art and industry, the achievements of Meroe, *Expedition: The University Museum Magazine of Archaeology and Anthropology, University of Pennsylvania*, vol. 35, no 2.

Daumas, F. 1958. Les mammisis des temples égyptiens, *Annales de l'Université de Lyon*. Paris.

Daumas, F. 1960. *Debod: Textes hiéroglyphiques et description archéologique*, Centre d'Études et de Documentation sur l'ancienne Égypte. Cairo.

Daumas, F. 1970. *La Ouabet de Kalabcha*, Centre d'Études et de Documentation sur l'ancienne Égypte. Cairo.

Davies, N. M. 1958. *Egyptian Tomb Paintings, from originals mainly of the Eighteenth dynasty in the British Museum and the Bankes collection*. London.

Dawson, W. R. and E. P. Uphill 1972. *Who Was Who in Egyptology*, second revised edition. London.

Denon, V. 1803. *Travels in Upper and Lower Egypt*, etc. (2 vols.). London.

Desroches-Noblecourt, Ch., E. Edel and S. Donadoni 1971. *Grand Temple d'Abou Simbel: La bataille de Qadech*. Centre de Documentation et d'Études [*sic*] sur l'ancienne Égypte. Cairo.

Desroches-Noblecourt, Ch., Gamal Moukhtar and S. Donadoni, avec la collaboration de H. El Achiery et M. Dewachter 1968. *Le Speos d'El-Lessiya*, Cahier I and II. Centre de Documentation et d'Études [*sic*] sur l'ancienne Égypte. Cairo.

Desroches-Noblecourt, Ch. and G. Gerster 1968. *The World Saves Abu Simbel*. Vienna and Berlin.

Desroches-Noblecourt, Chr. and Ch. Kuentz 1968. *Le Petit Temple d'Abou Simbel*, Centre de Documentation et d'Études [*sic*] sur l'ancienne Égypte (2 vols.). Cairo.

Dewachter, M. 1971a. Graffiti des voyageurs du XIXe siècle relevés dans le temple d'Amada en Basse-Nubie, *Bulletin de l'Institut Français d'Archéologie Orientale*, vol. 69, 131–69. Cairo.

Dewachter, M. 1971b. Nubie – Notes diverses, *Bulletin de l'Institut Français d'Archéologie Orientale*, vol. 70, 83–117. Cairo.

Dewachter, M. 1988a. L'expédition franco-toscane en Égypte, Clés et notes pour le tableau commémoratif d'Angelelli, *Cahiers du Musée Champollion*, vol.1. Figeac.

Dewachter, M. 1988b. Nouveaux documents relatifs à l'expédition franco-toscane en Égypte et en Nubie (1828–29), *Bulletin de la Société Française d'Égyptologie*, vol. 111, April 31–73.

Donadoni, S., H. El-Achirie and Ch. Leblanc 1975 *Grand Temple d'Abou Simbel: Les Salles du Tresor Sud*, I and II, Centre d'Études et de Documentation sur l'ancienne Égypte. Cairo.

Ducamp, M. 1852. *Égypte, Nubie, Palestine et Syrie 1849–1851*. Paris.

Dunham, D. 1947. Four Kushite colossi in the Sudan. *JEA*, vol. 33, 63–5.

Dunham, D. 1950. *El Kurru*, The Royal Cemeteries of Kush, vol. I. Cambridge, Mass.

Dunham, D. 1952. *Royal Tombs at Meroë and Barkal*, The Royal Cemeteries of Kush, vol. IV. Boston.

Dunham, D. (ed.) 1963. *The West and South Cemeteries at Meroë*, The Royal Cemeteries of Kush, vol. V. Boston.

Dunham, D. 1970. *The Barkal Temples*. Boston.

Dunham, D. and J. M. A. Janssen 1960. *Semna-Kumma*, Second Cataract Forts, vol. I. Boston.

Edwards, I. E. S. 1982. The Bankes Papyri I and II, *JEA*, vol. 68, 126–33.

El-Achirie, H. 1972. *Le Temple de Dandour*, I, Architecture. Centre d'Études et de Documentation sur l'ancienne Égypte. Cairo.

El-Achirie, H. and J. Jacquet 1980. *Le Temple de Derr*, I, Architecture. Centre d'Études et de Documentation sur l'ancienne Égypte, Cairo.

El-Achirie, H. and J. Jacquet 1984. *Le Grand Temple d'Abou-Simbel*, I, Architecture, Centre d'Études et de Documentation sur l'ancienne Égypte. Cairo.

El-Achiery, H., P. Barguet, and M. Dewachter 1967. *Le Temple d'Amada*, Cahier I, Architecture. Centre de Documentation et d'Études [*sic*] sur l'ancienne Égypte. Cairo.

Elsner, G. 1993. *Ägyptische Altertümer der Skulpturensammlung, Ausstellung im Albertinum zu Dresden*, 30 July 1993–24 July 1994. Dresden.

El-Tanbouli, M. A. L., Ch. Kuentz, and A. A. Sadek 1975. *Garf Hussein*, III, La grande Salle. Centre d'Études et de Documentation sur l'ancienne Égypte. Cairo.

El-Tanbouli, M. A. L., H. de Meulenaere, and A. A. Sadek 1978. *Gerf Hussein*, IV, La grande Salle. Centre d'Études et de Documentation sur l'ancienne Égypte. Cairo.

El-Tanbouli, M. A. L., and A. F. Sadek 1974. *Garf Hussein*, II, La Cour et l'entrée du Speos. Centre d'Études et de Documentation sur l'ancienne Égypte. Cairo.

Emery, W. B. 1931. Preliminary Report of the work of the Archaeological Survey of Nubia, 1930–31, *Annales du Service des Antiquités de l'Égypte*, vol. XXXI. Cairo.

Emery, W. B. and L. P. Kirwan 1935. *The Excavations and Survey between Wadi-es-Sebua and Adindan, 1929–31*, vols. 1–2. Cairo.

Emery, W. B., H. S. Smith, and A. Millard 1979. *The Fortress of Buhen: The Archaeological Report*, Egypt Exploration Society, Forty-ninth Excavation Memoir. London.

English, G. B. 1823. *Narrative of the Expedition to Dongola and Sennaar under the command of His Excellence Ismael Pasha … etc*. Boston.

Fagan, B. M. 1975. *The Rape of the Nile: Tomb Robbers, Tourists, and Archaeologists in Egypt*. New York.

Ferlini, G. 1837. *Cenno sugli scavi operati nella Nubia e Catalogo degli oggeti ritrovati*. Bologna.

Fiechter, J. J. 1994. *La moisson des dieux*. Paris.

Finati, G. 1830. *Narrative of the Life and Adventures of Giovanni Finati*, edited by W. J. Bankes, 2 vols., vol. II. London.

Forbin, Count de 1819a. *Travels in Egypt, being a continuation of the Travels in the Holy Land, in 1817–18*. London.

Forbin, Count, 1819b. *Travels in Greece, Turkey, and the Holy Land, in 1817–18* (second edition). London.

Forbin, M. le Cte de 1819c. *Voyage dans le Levant en 1817 et 1818*. Paris.

Frey, R. and J. Knudstad 1996. Lepsius reconsidered: a new architectural survey of Naga, in *Eighth International Conference for Meroitic Studies, Pre-prints of the main papers and abstracts*, compiled by I. Welsby Sjöström. London.

Fulford, R. (ed.) 1963. *The Greville Memoirs*. London.

Fuller, John. 1829. *Narrative of a Tour Through Some Parts of the Turkish Empire*. London.

Gardiner, A. 1961. *Egypt of the Pharaohs*. London. (Reprinted 1966.)

Gardiner, A. 1964. *Egyptian Grammar* (third edition). London.

Gau, F. C. 1822. *Antiquités de la Nubie*. Stuttgart and Paris.

Gauthier, H. 1911. *Le Temple de Kalabchah*, I and II, Les Temples immergés de la Nubie. Cairo.

Gauthier, H. 1912. *Le Temple de Ouadi es-Sebouâ*, I and II, Les Temples immergés de la Nubie. Cairo.

Gauthier, H. 1913. *Le Temple d'Amada*, Les Temples immergés de la Nubie. Cairo.

Gauthier, H. 1916. *Le Livre des Rois d'Égypte*. L'Institut Français d'Archéologie Orientale, Tome 20. Cairo.

Greener, L. 1962. *High Dam over Nubia*. London.

Greig, J. (ed.) 1924. *The Farington Diary* (James Farington RA). London.

Griffith, F. L. 1911. *Meroitic Inscriptions*, Part I (published in the same volume as J. W. Crowfoot, *The Island of Meroe*) Archaeological Survey of Egypt, Nineteenth Memoir. London.

Griffith, F. L. 1912. *Meroitic Inscriptions*, Part II, Archaeological Survey of Egypt, Twentieth Memoir. London.

Griffith, F. L. 1921. Oxford Excavations in Nubia, *Annals of Archaeology and Anthropology* (issued by the Institute of Archaeology, University of Liverpool), vol. VIII. Liverpool.

Griffith, F. L. 1929. Scenes from a destroyed temple at Napata, *JEA*, vol. XV, 26–8.

Habachi, L. 1977. *The Obelisks of Egypt*. New York.

Habachi, L. 1981. Sixteen studies on Lower Nubia, Supplement to *Annales du Service des Antiquités d'Égypte*, Cahiers № 23. Cairo.

Hakem, Ahmed M. Ali 1978. A history of archaeological work in Nubia and the Sudan, in *Africa in Antiquity: The Arts of Ancient Nubia and the Sudan*, I, The Essays, Chapter 3. The Brooklyn Museum, New York.

Halls, J. J. 1834. *The Life and Correspondence of Henry Salt, Esq. F.R.S. &c. His Britannic Majesty's late Consul General in Egypt* (second edition(s), 2 vols.). London.

Hamilton, W. 1809. *Remarks on Several Parts of Turkey*, Part One, *Aegyptiaca or some account of the ancient and modern state of Egypt, as obtained in the years 1801, 1802*. London.

Hammond, N. G. L. and H. H. Scullard (eds) 1970. *The Oxford Classical Dictionary* (second edition). Oxford.

Hill, R. 1967. *A Biographical Dictionary of the Sudan* (second edition). London.

Hinkel, F. W. 1966. *Tempel ziehen um.* Leipzig.

Hinkel, F. W. 1977. *Auszug aus Nubien.* Berlin.

Hinkel, F. W. 1978. *Exodus from Nubia,* Berlin.

Hinkel, F. W. 1986. Reconstruction work at the Royal Cemetery at Meroe, in M. Krause (ed.) *Nubische Studien: Tagungsakten der 5. Internationalen Konferenz der International Society for Nubian Studies,* 99–108. Mainz am Rhein.

Hinkel, F. 1996. The Lion Temple at Naqa – results of investigations in 1996, in *Eighth International Conference for Meroitic Studies, Pre-prints of the main papers and abstracts, compiled by I. Welsby Sjöström.* London.

Hintze, F. 1959. Preliminary Report on the Butanan expedition 1958, *Kush,* vol. VII, 171–96. Khartoum.

Hintze, F. 1962a. *Die Inschriften des Löwentempels von Musawwarat es Sufra.* Berlin.

Hintze, F. 1962b. Preliminary Report on the excavations at Musawwarat es Sufra 1960–61, *Kush,* vol. X. Khartoum.

Hintze, F. 1963. Musawwarat es Sufra: preliminary report on the excavations of the Institute of Egyptology, Humboldt University, Berlin, 1961–62 (Third Season), *Kush,* vol. XI. Khartoum.

Hintze, F. 1967–8. Musawwarat es Sufra: report on the excavations of the Institute of Egyptology, Humbolt University, Berlin 1963–1966 (Fourth–Sixth Seasons), *Kush,* vol. XV. Khartoum.

Hintze, F. 1971. *Musawwarat es Sufra, Der Löwentempel,* Band I, 2. Tafelband. Berlin.

Hintze, F., K.-H. Priese, S. Wenig, C. Onsch, G. Buschendorf-Otto and U. Hintze 1993. *Musawwarat es Sufra, Der Löwentempel,* Band I, 1. (2 vols.). Text and plates. Berlin.

Hoskins, G. A. 1835. *Travels in Ethiopia, above the Second Cataract of the Nile; exhibiting the state of that country, and its various inhabitants, under the dominion of Mohammed Ali; and illustrating the Antiquities, Arts, and History of the ancient Kingdom of Meroe.* London.

Hyde, John of Manchester. Journals and Notebooks. British Library Add. Mss, ref. 42102–8.

Ibrahim, F. and Ch. Leblanc 1975. *Le Temple de Dandour,* III, Planches photographiques et Indices, Centre d'Études et de Documentation sur l'ancienne Égypte. Cairo.

Ilchester, Lord 1923. *The Journal of the Hon. Henry Edward Fox.* London.

Irby, C. L. and J. Mangles, 1823. *Travels in Egypt and Nubia, Syria and Asia Minor; during the years 1817 and 1818.* London.

Iversen, E. 1972. *Obelisks in Exile, II: The Obelisks of Istanbul and England.* Copenhagen.

Jacquet, J. and H. El-Achirie, 1978. *Gerf Hussein,* I, Architecture. Centre d'Études et de Documentation sur l'ancienne Égypte. Cairo.

James, T. G. H. 1993–34. Egyptian Antiquities at Kingston Lacy, Dorset, *KMT,* vol. 4, no. 4, Winter. San Francisco.

James, T. G. H. 1997. *Egypt Revealed: Artist-Travellers in an Antique Land.* London.

J[olliffe], T. R. 1820. *Letters from Palestine;* to the second edition of which was added, *Letters from Egypt.* London.

Karkowski, J. 1981, *Faras V: The Pharaonic inscriptions from Faras.* Warsaw.

Kendall, T. 1990. *The Gebel Barkal Temples 1989–90: A Progress Report of the Work of the Museum of Fine Arts, Boston, Sudan Mission* (Geneva: Seventh International Conference for Nubian Studies, 3–8 September 1990: privately distributed).

Kendall, T. 1991. The Napatan palace at Gebel Barkal: a first look at B I200, in *Egypt and Africa: Nubia from Prehistory to Islam,* ed. W. V. Davies. 302–13. London.

Kendall, T. 1994. A new map of the Gebel Barkal temples, in *Études Nubiennes, Conférence de Genève, Actes du*

VII*ᵉ Congrès international d'études nubiennes, 3–8 Septembre 1990.* Geneva.

Kozloff, A. P. and Bryan, B. 1992. *Egypt's Dazzling Sun: Amenhotep III and his World.* Cleveland.

Kroeper, K. 1996a. The Egyptian Museum Berlin – Naqa Project 1995–1996, in *Eighth International Conference for Meroitic Studies, Pre-prints of the main papers and abstracts, compiled by I. Welsby Sjöström.* London.

Kroeper, K. 1996b. The rediscovery of the Kushite site at Naqa, 1822 to 1996, *The Sudan Archaeological Research Society Newsletter,* no. 10, June 1996, 18–23. London.

Laborde, L. de, and L. M. A. Linant de Bellefonds 1994 (Preface and notes by Ch. Augé and P. Linant de Bellefonds). *Pétra Retrouvée, Voyage de l'Arabie Pétrée, 1828.* Paris.

Lacovara, P. 1991. The stone vase deposit at Kerma, in *Egypt and Africa,* ed. W. V. Davies, 118–28. London.

Lane Poole, S. 1888. *The Life of Stratford Canning, Viscount Stratford de Redcliffe* (2 vols.). London.

Leake, W. M. (ed.) 1826. *An Edict of Diocletian.* London.

Leake, W. M. 1830. *Travels in the Morea* (3 vols.). London.

Leclant, J. 1961. Le Voyage de Jean-Nicolas Huyot en Égypte (1818–1819) et les manuscrits de Nestor L'Hôte, *Bulletin de la Société Française d'Égypte,* vol. 32.

Leclant, J. 1964. Un cent cinquantenaire: J. L. Burckhart et la découverte des temples d'Abou-Simbel (1813), *Cahiers d'Histoire Mondiale,* vol. 8, no. 3, 585–95. Neuchatel.

Legh, T. 1816. *Narrative of a Journey in Egypt and the Country beyond the Cataracts.* London.

Leitch, J. (ed.) 1855. *Miscellaneous Works of the late Thomas Young, M.D., F.R.S., &c.* London.

Lepsius, R. 1849. *Denkmäler aus Aegypten, Aethiopien und dem Sinai* (12 vols. plates, 5 vols. text). Berlin (reduced photographic reprint, 3 vols, Geneva, 1972).

Lepsius, R. 1913. *Denkmäler aus Aegypten und Aethiopien, Ergänzungsband.* Leipzig.

Lewis, N. N. 1997. 'I. La Découverte du tombeau. W. J. Bankes à Sidon en 1816', from A. Barbet, P.-L. Gatier, and N. N. Lewis, 'Un tombeau peint inscrit de Sidon', *Syria*, vol. LXXIV. Beirut.

Lewis, N. N. and M. Macdonald (forthcoming). W. J. Bankes and the identification of the Nabatean script, *Syria*. Beirut.

Lewis, N., A. Sartre Fauriat, and M. Sartre 1996. William John Bankes: Travaux en Syrie d'un voyageur oublié, *Syria*, vol. LXXIII, 1–4.

Light, H. 1818. *Travels in Egypt, Nubia, Holy Land, Mount Libanon [sic], and Cyprus, in the Year 1814*. London.

Linant de Bellefonds, L. M. A. 1872–3. *Mémoires sur les principaux travaux d'utilité publique exécutés en Égypte depuis la plus haute antiquité jusquà nos jours; Accompagnés d'un Atlas refermant neuf planches grand in-folio imprimées en couleur*. Paris.

Macadam, M. F. Laming 1946. Gleanings from the Bankes MSS, *JEA*, vol. 32, 57–64. London.

MacMichael, W. 1819. *Journey from Moscow to Constantinople in the Years 1817, 1818*. London.

Manley, D. and P. Rée 2001. *Henry Salt: Artist, Traveller, Diplomat, Egyptologist*. London.

Manniche, L. 1987. *City of the Dead*. London.

Marcellus, Le Vicomte de, 1839. *Souvenirs de l'Orient*. Paris.

Marchand, L. A. 1971. *Byron, a Portrait*. London.

Marchand, L. A. (ed.) 1973 *Byron's Letters and Journals*, 11 vols. London.

Maspero, G. 1909. *Rapports relatifs à la consolidation des temples*, Temples immergés de la Nubie, Tome Premier, seconde livraison. Cairo.

Maspero, G. 1911. *Rapports relatifs à la consolidation des temples*, Temples immergés de la Nubie. Tome Second, Cairo.

Maxwell, Sir H. 1913. *The Life and Letters of George William Clarendon* (2 vols.). London.

Mays, S. 1959. *The Great Belzoni*. London.

Maystre, C. 1967–8. Excavations at Tabo, Argo Island, 1965–1968:

preliminary report, *Kush*, vol. XV, 193–9. Khartoum.

Mazuel, J. 1937. L'Oeuvre géographique de Linant de Bellefonds: étude de géographie historique, *Société Royale de la Géographie d'Egypte*.

Meulenaere, H. de 1961. Ptolémée IX Soter II à Kalabcha, *Chronique d'Égypte*, vol. 71.

Meulenaere, H. de and M. Dewachter 1964–70. *La Chapelle Ptolémaïque de Kalabcha*, Centre d'Études et de Documentation sur l'ancienne Égypte. Cairo.

Michalowski, K. 1966. *Faras, Centre artistique de la Nubie Chretienne*. Leiden.

Mitchell, A. (ed.) 1994. *Kingston Lacy*. The National Trust. London.

Monneret de Villard, 1941. *La Nubia Romana*. Rome.

Montulé, E. de 1821. *Travels in Egypt during 1818 and 1819*. London.

Moore, D. C. 1976. *The Politics of Deference*. New York.

Murray, M. c.1930. *Egyptian Temples*. London.

Norden, F. L. 1757. *Voyage d'Égypte et de Nubie*. Copenhagen.

O'Connor, D. 1978. Nubia before the New Kingdom, in *Africa in Antiquity: The Arts of Ancient Nubia and the Sudan*, I, The Essays, Chapter 4. The Brooklyn Museum, New York.

Otter, W. 1824. *The Life and Remains … of E. D. Clarke*. London.

Pearce, N. 1831. *The Life and Adventures of Nathaniel Pearce, written by himself …* J. J. Halls, 2 vols. London.

Porter, B. and R. Moss, 1951. *Topographical Bibliography of Ancient Egyptian Hieroglyphic Texts, Reliefs, and Paintings*, vol. VII. Oxford.

Priego, C. and A. Martin Flores 1992. *Templo de Debod*. Madrid.

Priese, K.-H. 1978. The kingdom of Kush: the Napatan Period, in *Africa in Antiquity: The Arts of Ancient Nubia and the Sudan*, I, The Essays, Chapter 6. The Brooklyn Museum, New York.

Quennell, P. (ed.) 1937. *The Private Letters of Princess Lieven to Prince Metternich 1820–1826*. London.

Quirke, S. 1996. The Bankes

Papyri, *British Museum Magazine*, no. 24, Spring. Recent Acquisitions, 16.

Quirke, S. 1997. Modern mummies and ancient scarabs, the Egyptian collection of Sir William Hamilton, *Journal of the History of Collections*, vol. 9, no. 2, 253–62.

Randall-Maciver, D. and C. L. Woolley 1909. *Areika*, University of Pennsylvania: Eckley B. Coxe Junior Expedition to Nubia, vol. I. Oxford.

Randall-Maciver, D. and C. Leonard Woolley 1911. *Buhen*. Eckley B. Coxe Junior Expedition to Nubia, vol. VII. Philadelphia.

Reisner, G. A. 1917–20. The Barkal temples in 1916, parts I–III, *JEA*, vol. 4 (1917), 213–27; *JEA*, vol. 5 (1918), 99–112; *JEA*, vol. 6 (1920), 247–64.

Reisner, G. A. 1960. The Egyptian forts from Halfa to Semna, *Kush*, vol. VIII, 11–24. Khartoum.

Renéaume, G. 1988. Remarques à propos du tableau de Guiseppe Angelelli consacré à l'éxpédition franco-toscane, *Cahiers du Musée Champollion*, no. 1, Figeac: 41–9.

Richardson, R. 1822. *Travels along the Mediterranean, and parts adjacent; in company with The Earl of Belmore, during the Years 1816–17–18: etc.* London.

Ricke, H., G. R Hughes and E. F. Wente 1967. *The Beit el-Wali Temple of Ramesses II*, Chicago.

Rifaud, J. 1830a. *Voyages en Egypte, en Nubie et lieux circonvoisins, depuis 1805 jusqu'en 1827*. Paris.

Rifaud, J. 1830b. *Tableau de l'Égypte, de la Nubie et des lieux circonvoisins*. Paris.

Roeder, G. 1911. *Debod bis bab Kalabsche*, Les Temples immergés de la Nubie (2 vols.). Cairo.

Roeder, G. 1930. *Der Tempel von Dakke*, Les Temples immergés de la Nubie (2 vols.). Cairo.

Roeder, G. 1938. *Der Felsentempel von Bet el Wali*, Les Temples immergés de la Nubie. Cairo.

Rosellini, I. 1832–44. *I Monumenti dell'Egitto e delle Nubia* (9 vols.). Pisa.

Rosellini, I. 1982. *Il Nilo sui Lungarni, Ippolito Rosellini, egittologo dell'Ottocento*. Pisa.

Rowse, A. L. 1975. Byron's friend Bankes: a portrait, *Encounter*, March.

Sack, Albert von, Baron 1810. *A Narrative of a Voyage to Surinam; of a residence there during 1805, 1806, and 1807, and of the author's return to Europe by way of North America* (2 parts). London.

Salt, H. 1825. *Essay on Dr. Young's and M. Champollion's Phonetic System of Hieroglyphics; with some additional discoveries etc.* London.

Säve-Söderbergh, T. 1987. *Temples and Tombs of Ancient Nubia*. London.

Schiff Giorgini, M. 1965a. *Soleb, I, 1813–1963*. Florence.

Schiff Giorgini, M. 1965b. Première campagne de fouilles à Sedeinga 1963–1964, *Kush*, vol. XIII. Khartoum.

Schneider, H. D. 1979. *Taffeh: Rond de wederopbouw van een Nubische tempel*. The Hague.

Searight, R. 1980. *A Middle Eastern Journey*, exhibition catalogue. Edinburgh.

Seetzen, U. J. 1810. *A Brief Account of the Countries adjoining the Lake of Tiberias, the Jordan and the Dead Sea*. London.

Sethe, K. 1906. *Urkunden der 18. Dynastie. Urkunden des Ägyptischen Altertums*, ed. G. Steindorff, vol. IV. Abteilung, Band I and II. Leipzig.

Sethe, K. 1924. *Aegyptische Lesestücke zum Gebrauch im akademischen Unterricht*. Leipzig.

Shinnie, M. (ed.) 1958. *Linant de Bellefonds. Journal d'un Voyage à Méroé dans les années 1821 et 1822*. Sudan Antiquities Service Occasional Papers (SASOP), no. 4. Khartoum.

Shinnie, P. L. 1967. *Meroë: A Civilisation of the Sudan*. London.

Shinnie, P. L. 1996. *Ancient Nubia*. London and New York.

Smith, H. S. 1976. *The Fortress of Buhen: The Inscriptions*, Egypt Exploration Society, Forty-eighth Excavation Memoir. London.

Sonnini de Mononcour, C. N. S. 1799. *Voyage dans la Haute et Basse Egypte, fait par l'ordre de l'ancien gouvernement (de 1777 à 1780), et contenant des observations de tous genres, etc.* (3 vols.); fol. Atlas. English translation 1800. London.

Stock, H. and K. G. Siegler 1965. *Kalabsha*. Wiesbaden.

Taylor, J. H. 1991. *Egypt and Nubia*. London.

Teignmouth, Lord, 1878. *Reminiscences of Many Years* (2 vols.). Edinburgh.

Thorne, R. G. (ed.) 1986. *The History of Parliament: The House of Commons 1790–1820*, vol. III, Members A–F. London.

Tillet, S. 1984. *Egypt Itself*. London.

Török, L. 1997. *Meroe City, an Ancient African Capital*. London.

Turner, W. 1820. *Journal of a Tour in the Levant* (3 vols.), vol. II. London.

Usick, P. 1996. Excavating the Bankes manuscripts and drawings, *The Sudan Archaeological Research Society Newsletter*, no.10, June, 31–6. London.

Usick, P. 1998. The Egyptian drawings of Alessandro Ricci in Florence, *Göttinger Miszellen*, vol. 162, 73–92.

Usick, P. 1999. The first excavation of Wadi Halfa (Buhen), in *Studies on Ancient Egypt in Honour of H. S. Smith*, Leahy, A. and J. Tait (eds). The Egypt Exploration Society. London.

Usick, P. 1999. Not the travel journal of Alessandro Ricci, in *Studies in Egyptian Antiquities, A Tribute to T. G. H. James*, ed. by W. V. Davies. British Museum Occasional Paper, no. 123, 115–21. London.

Vercoutter, J. 1958. Excavations at Sai 1955–7, a preliminary report, *Kush*, vol. VI. Khartoum.

Vercoutter, J. 1962. Un palais des 'Candaces' contemporain d'Auguste (Fouilles à Wad-ban-Naga 1958–1960), *Syria*, vol. XXXIX. Paris.

Vercoutter, J. 1963. Journal du voyage en Basse Nubie de Linant de Bellefonds, *Bulletin de la Société Française d'Égyptologie*, vol. 37–38 (Dec.), 39.

Vercoutter, J. 1964. Journal du voyage en Basse Nubie de Linant de Bellefonds, *Bulletin de la Société Française d'Égyptologie*, vol. 41 (Nov.), 23–32.

Vercoutter, J. 1992. *The Search for Ancient Egypt*. London.

Vidal Bey, 1882–85. Linant-Pacha de Bellefonds – Sa vie et ses oeuvres, *Bulletin Société Khédivale Géographique*, Série II, Cairo, 238–40. [This appears to be the same work cited by Mazuel as 'Vidal Bey: Linant, sa vie et ses oeuvres. *Bulletin de la Société Royale de Géographie*, Tome II. 1882'.]

Vila, A. 1977. *La Prospection archéologique de la vallée du Nil, au sud de la cataracte de Dal (Nubie Soudanaise)*. Paris.

Waddington, G. and B. Hanbury 1822. *Journal of a Visit to Some Parts of Ethiopia*. London.

Weigall, A. 1907. *Report on the Antiquities of Lower Nubia, 1906–1907*. Oxford.

Welsby, D. 1996. *The Kingdom of Kush*. London.

Wenig, S. 1978. *Africa in Antiquity: The Arts of Ancient Nubia and the Sudan, II, The Catalogue*. The Brooklyn Museum, New York.

Whitehead, G. O. 1926. Nagaa and Masawwarat, *Sudan Notes and Records*, vol. IX, no. 2, 59–68.

Wilkinson, G. 1843. *Modern Egypt and Thebes*. London.

Williams Wynn, F. 1864. *Diaries of a Lady of Quality from 1797 to 1844*, edited, with notes, by A. Hayward. London.

Wood, A. 1954 (later completed by F. Oldham). *Thomas Young, Natural Philosopher, 1773–1829*. Cambridge.

Young, T. 1823. *An Account of some Recent Discoveries in Hieroglyphical Literature, and Egyptian Antiquities, etc.* London.

Zach, M. 1988. 'Addendum: Die Besucherinschriften von Beg N10', *Beiträge zur Sudanforschung*, vol. 3. Vienna.

Illustration Acknowledgements

All the illustrations listed NT/BKL are reproduced by kind permission of The National Trust/The Bankes of Kingston Lacy & Corfe Castle Archives, Dorset Record Office. At the time of writing, these images are on temporary loan to the British Museum, London (with the exception of the Syrian drawings, numbered 72–4 and 76–7), but will be returned to Dorset Record Office, Dorchester, and deposited with the rest of the Bankes archive in perpetuity. The numbers in brackets following NT/BKL illustrations are the catalogue numbers given by Dr Rosalind Moss for use in the *Topographical Bibliography of Ancient Egyptian Hieroglyphic Texts, Reliefs, and Paintings*, by B. Porter and R. Moss, published in 1951.

1 National Trust Photographic Library/Derrick E. Witty
2 National Trust Photographic Library/Christopher Hurst
3 National Trust Photographic Library/Derrick E. Witty
4 By courtesy of the National Portrait Gallery, London
5 By kind permission of Pollinger Limited and the Earl of Lytton
6 National Trust Photographic Library/Richard Pink
7 NT/BKL (XX.D.3)
8 British Museum, London (EA 19)
9 NT/BKL (VII.A.19)
10 NT/BKL (VII.A.31)
11 NT/BKL (XI.A.97)
12 NT/BKL (XI.B.34)
13 NT/BKL (I.D.7)
14 NT/BKL (II.A.1)
15 NT/BKL (II.A.2)
16 NT/BKL (II.A.17)
17 NT/BKL (IV.C.6)
18 NT/BKL (IV.C.7)
19 NT/BKL (V.A.14)
20 Illustration from Atkins, S. 1824. *Fruits of Enterprize Exhibited in the Travels of Belzoni in Egypt and Nubia; Interspersed with the Observations of a Mother to her Children* (fourth edition). London
21 NT/BKL (VI.A.6)
22 NT/BKL (VI.A.10)
23 NT/BKL (VI.A.28)
24 NT/BKL (VI.A.31)
25 NT/BKL (VI.B.16)
26 NT/BKL (VI.B.24)
27 NT/BKL (VI.B.28)
28 NT/BKL (VI.C.9)
29 NT/BKL (VI.C.22)
30 NT/BKL (VII.A.11)
31 NT/BKL (VII.A.23)
32 NT/BKL (VII.A.41)
33 NT/BKL (VIII.A.23)
34 NT/BKL (VIII.B.33)
35 NT/BKL (VIII.B.41)
36 NT/BKL (VIII.C.17)
37 NT/BKL (VIII.C.19)

38 NT/BKL (VIII.C.39)
39 NT/BKL (VIII.D.2)
40 NT/BKL (VIII.E.3)
41 NT/BKL (VIII.E.11)
42 NT/BKL (IX.A.30)
43 NT/BKL (IX.A.17)
44 NT/BKL (IX.B.13)
45 NT/BKL (X.B.2)
46 NT/BKL (X.D.25)
47 NT/BKL (X.F.30)
48 NT/BKL (X.F.15)
49 NT/BKL (X.F.12)
50 NT/BKL (XI.A.3)
51 NT/BKL (XI.A.4)
52 NT/BKL (XI.A.5)
53 NT/BKL (XI.A.7)
54 NT/BKL (XI.A.6)
55 NT/BKL (XI.A.15)
56 NT/BKL (XI.A.28)
57 NT/BKL (XI.A.92)
58 NT/BKL (XI.A.95)
59 Photo Patricia Usick
60 NT/BKL (XI.A.100)
61 NT/BKL (XI.A.106)
62 NT/BKL (XI.A.108)
63 NT/BKL (XI.B.33)
64 NT/BKL (XII.A.20)
65 NT/BKL (XII.C.4)
66 NT/BKL (XII.C.6)
67 NT/BKL (XII.C.7)
68 NT/BKL (XIII.A.17)
69 V&A Picture Library
70 By kind permission of Charles L. A. Irby
71 By kind permission of Charles L. A. Irby
72 NT/BKL (V.D.2) Syrian
73 NT/BKL (VI.A.3) Syrian
74 NT/BKL (III.A.6b) Syrian
75 Royal Geographical Society, London
76 NT/BKL (IV.A.7) Syrian
77 NT/BKL (IV.A.3) Syrian
78 By kind permission of Pascale Linant de Bellefonds
79 Renéaume Collection. By kind permission of Guy Renéaume
80 NT/BKL (XIV.C.4)

81 NT/BKL (XIV.F.2)
82 NT/BKL (unnumbered)
83 NT/BKL (XV.A.10)
84 NT/BKL (XV.C.3)
85 NT/BKL (XV.C.2)
86 NT/BKL (XV.C.6)
87 NT/BKL (XV.C.5)
88 NT/BKL (XXI.G.11)
89 NT/BKL (XV.C.10)
90 NT/BKL (XVI.A.2)
91 NT/BKL (unnumbered)
92 NT/BKL (XVI.B.21)
93 NT/BKL (XVI.B.4)
94 NT/BKL (unnumbered)
95 NT/BKL (XVI.B.16)
96 NT/BKL (XVII.B.6)
97 NT/BKL (XVII.B.9)
98 NT/BKL (XVII.B.16)
99 NT/BKL (unnumbered)
100 NT/BKL (XVII.C.6)
101 NT/BKL (XVII.C.15)
102 NT/BKL (XVII.C.17)
103 NT/BKL (unnumbered)
104 National Trust Photographic Library/Angelo Hornak
105 Photo Patricia Usick. By kind permission of the National Trust
106 National Trust Photographic Library/Derrick E. Witty
107 Photo Harry James. By kind permission of the National Trust
108 National Trust Photographic Library/James Mortimer
109 Photo Harry James. By kind permission of the National Trust
110 Photo Harry James. By kind permission of the National Trust
111 Illustration from Salt, H. 1825. *Essay on Dr. Young's and M. Champollion's Phonetic System of Hieroglyphics; with some additional discoveries etc.* London
112 NT/BKL (XXI.F.37)

MAPS

p. 7 Map to Illustrate the Travels of Giovanni Finati in Asia and Africa: from Finati, G. 1830. *Narrative of the Life and Adventures of Giovanni Finati*, edited by W. J. Bankes, 2 vols. London
p. 8 Map to Illustrate the Travels of William John Bankes in Greece and Asia Minor: by Claire Thorne and Audrey Hutchison

INDEX